Carceral Utopia

Carceral Utopia

A Global History of Model Prisons

Grégory Salle

polity

First published in 2026 by Polity Press Ltd.

Polity Press Ltd.
65 Bridge Street
Cambridge CB2 1UR, UK

Polity Press Ltd.
111 River Street
Hoboken, NJ 07030, USA

ISBN-13: 978-1-5095-7146-8
ISBN-13: 978-1-5095-7147-5 (pb)

A catalogue record for this book is available from the British Library.

Library of Congress Control Number: 2026933689

Typeset in 11.5 on 14pt Adobe Garamond
by Cheshire Typesetting Ltd, Cuddington, Cheshire
Printed and bound in Great Britain by Ashford Colour Ltd

For further information on Polity, visit our website:
politybooks.com

Contents

Acknowledgements

It is customary to warn readers that although a book bears the name of an individual author, it is actually a collective endeavour. But non-academic readers often underestimate just how seriously this statement should be taken.

This book was made possible by financial support from the University of Lille, the Maison européenne des sciences de l'homme et de la société (MESHS), and my research unit, the Centre lillois d'études et de recherches sociologiques et économiques (Clersé). Thanks to this support, I was able to benefit from the invaluable work of Matthew Cunningham, who meticulously read and edited the manuscript, not at the end, but as it was being written – a task that was far from easy. I could not overstate the extent of his contributions, especially at a time when the work of translators is threatened by the widespread deployment of 'artificial intelligence'. Not only did he correct countless linguistic errors and stylistic irregularities (my red-marked copies were a lesson in humility!), but he also drew my attention to structural issues and logical gaps in my reasoning. In fact, his name could almost appear on the cover, for the final text is as much his as it is mine.

Two anonymous reviewers provided constructive and insightful feedback not once but twice: first on the synopsis and later on the first version of the full manuscript. Their comments pushed me to strengthen the book's relevance and coherence. I regret that I was unable to integrate all of their astute and inspiring suggestions, but their commitment deserves to be hailed, as this largely invisible work receives little recognition in the academic field. I am also indebted to the work of Justin Dyer, who considerably refined the whole manuscript during the crucial copy-editing phase.

This book is a fully revised and expanded version of a work originally published in France by Éditions Amsterdam in 2016 under the title *L'utopie carcérale. Petite histoire des prisons modèles.* I am grateful to Nicolas Vieillescazes and John Thompson for facilitating the process on both sides, as well as to Lindsey Wimpenny for her editorial supervision at Polity. I also extend my thanks to Gwenola Ricordeau, Joël Charbit, and Michel Daccache for their reviews of the French version; some of their comments stuck in my mind and I tried to take them into account.

Discussion within the editorial board of the international French-language journal *Déviance et société* continues to stimulate my thinking on issues I had somewhat neglected in recent years, as I shifted to other topics. A special nod to André Kuhn, who incidentally taught me that the façade of the former Neuchâtel Prison – mentioned in an August 1873 *New York Times* article on 'Model Prisons' as an offspring of the progressive 'Irish system' of classification – has been incorporated into a modern building that is none other than today's Faculty of Science at the University of Neuchâtel.

Introduction: A history within the history

The 'most horrific facility in the federal system', a 'solution unworthy of a civilized nation'. This is how the former model prison in Lewisburg, Pennsylvania, was described by a journalist in 2013. He was drawing on a study by geographer Karen Morin, who traced this prison's transformation from a progressive institution dedicated to rehabilitation into a special unit enforcing strict confinement. When this facility opened in rural Pennsylvania in 1932 (a time when it was commonly believed that the country air possessed therapeutic virtues), it was hailed as the 'quintessential modern prison' in terms of its penal philosophy and physical structure. Despite being steeped in monastic traditions with its spaces for meditation and study, it was architecturally innovative compared with conventional prisons, and was often likened to a university campus. Lewisburg embodied the rise of a correctional doctrine aimed at reforming souls and bodies, rather than merely inflicting vindictive or retributive punishment. Emphasis was placed on activities: inmates were expected to play sports, publish a prison newspaper, participate in theatrical performances, and engage in farming. As the latest in prison technology, Lewisburg was emulated from coast to coast, except in the southern states.[1]

Even if its actual daily operation never lived up to the noble ideal, the transformation it underwent around the 1970s was nonetheless dramatic, as it shifted to a security-based approach. By the turn of the twenty-first century, Lewisburg's original purpose had been completely reversed. In 2008, it became a federal 'special management unit' for unruly prisoners. Its inmates are now almost permanently confined to tiny cells they have to share, not due to overcrowding, but for deliberate punitive purposes. As the latest manifestation of the 'supermax' (as American high-security prisons are famously nicknamed), Lewisburg represents a new punitive phase in the context of mass incarceration. This typically late-modern paradigm differs from pre-modern elimination (public lethal torture) and modern disciplinary power (corrective confinement), focusing instead on institutionalizing fear, terror, cruelty, and ultimately death. In short, a 'socio-spatial nightmare'.[2]

Despite some unique features, this case illustrates a general trend. It might be an extreme example, but it is a telling one. Within the broad history of prisons, there is a smaller story: that of so-called 'model prisons'. Prisons that have promised to fix the failures of their predecessors and fulfil the righteous aims proclaimed by their champions – aims that inevitably go unattained, until a new project arises and revives the myth. As it turns out, despite its history of setbacks and stinging refutations, the prison utopia has not quite said its last word, even if it has been reduced to a recycled or degraded version of the 'fine' penitentiary ideal of yesteryear. Against all odds, 'model prisons' are still being built worldwide today. In Europe, the most famous example is certainly the Austrian prison called the Justice Centre Leoben: completed in 2004, its conspicuous 'modernity' has inspired much commentary, both supportive and hostile. It has spawned imitations, including Germany's Heidering prison, south of Berlin, which opened in 2013; designed by the same architect as Leoben, it, too, boasts a grand design fostering transparency, brightness, autonomy, and so on, setting a new standard for twenty-first-century prisons. In Japan, the Shimane

Asahi Rehabilitation Centre – a high-tech, low-security prison emphasizing restorative justice and therapeutic measures, completed in 2008 – was promoted by local authorities as a 'model prison for the next fifty years'. Entire building programmes are even designed to succeed where earlier initiatives have fallen short. For instance, in a 2013 report outlining a 'radical plan to reform the prison estate', a well-known conservative British think tank proposed building ten to twelve new 'hub prisons' based on 'cutting-edge architecture'.[3]

It is strange to witness the regeneration of the prison institution under the guise of normalcy after the dramatic cultural and political shift of the 1960s and 1970s, which seemed to have dealt a fatal blow to prisons after a long series of challenges. While that era is remembered for the radical, exhaustive critique of prisons by the far left, especially in European countries, another aspect is equally important to note. At that time, the prison system – including new, 'modern' prisons – was massively discredited, even among moderate political factions. Among broad segments of the Western public, this institution was viewed as inherently ineffective, unfair, and harmful. And it was reasonable to believe that this judgement would be final. As Loïc Wacquant pointed out in 2009, 'only thirty years ago the most eminent specialists of the penal question were unanimous in predicting its waning, if not its disappearance'; whether they were mainstream or critical, they agreed on the idea 'that it was an institution in inevitable decline, destined to be replaced in the medium run by more diffuse, discrete, and diversified instruments of social control'. This led to the development of sentences and measures that, rightly or wrongly, were labelled 'alternatives to detention' or 'diversionary programmes'. And yet, incarceration rates remain high in Western countries today, though the trends have varied widely over the past two to three decades from one country (and continent) to another.[4]

While this resurgence is inseparable from the neoliberal punitive turn, the persistent quest for 'model prisons' has also played a notable symbolic role, particularly in countries where prisons are expected to fulfil roles beyond mere punishment or confinement, such as rehabilitation and social reintegration. This enduring belief has come to justify renewed investment in the prison system in recent decades. More broadly, it has served to repeatedly revive the prison project. There is a persistent idea that certain prisons will somehow be able to redeem a failing system, and this fuels a stubborn belief in the possibility of a 'good' prison that is beneficial, if not healthy, one that will finally live up to its claims, as soon as the right architectural design and operational rules are found. So-called 'models' that are emerging nowadays seem to be driven by the hope that *this time* they will actually work, as if no real effort had been made before, with genuine commitment, imagination, and, of course, resources.

As this book will show, history suggests we have every reason to be sceptical. Countering the prevailing amnesia on the subject, it examines various cases that will remind us that this scenario has played out many times before, all over the world. At the same time, a historical inquiry must exhume the original – albeit equivocal – meaning of the expression 'model prisons', and remind us of the aims it initially expressed, in order to recount its development over two centuries. This detour through the past is necessary to grasp what is at stake in the present, with the clarifying benefit of hindsight. In so doing, I hope to shed some light on what these supposedly model prisons reveal, but also what they hide. Pursuing the notion of model prisons as a common theme running through the history of imprisonment, I will argue that this concealment contributes to an incomplete framing and distorted understanding of the prison issue as a whole. The notion of model prisons not only serves to re-legitimate a failing system, but also obscures the very foundation of its persistence as a 'successful failure': what Michel Foucault termed the 'differential management of illegalisms'.[5]

Did you say 'model'?

At first glance, it is tempting to dismiss the expression 'model prisons' as nothing but a contradiction in terms, well intentioned though it may be. If one refrains from doing so, the expression presents a problem of definition from the outset, as evidenced by the plethora of ways in which it is employed today. Not only is there no official definition of what a model prison is or is supposed to be, but the term also has no perfectly stable or clear meaning. Dictionaries, in turn, give related but distinct meanings for the word 'model'. It means something that serves or should serve as an object of imitation or emulation for making or reproducing something; an object whose image is replicated; something that represents a class or category in a concrete or restricted form; the simplified representation of a process or system; a structural design; even a set of plans for a building. From a general point of view, the expression 'model prison' can refer to all of these meanings and their synonyms (archetype, exemplar, matrix, pattern, standard, template, and so on). It designates a prison that is intended to be reproduced or to serve as an inspiration, but also, more broadly, a particular type of prison forming a consistent and distinctive whole distinguished by certain characteristics, or the material representative of a category (prisons based on radial architecture, for example). As we shall see later, the expression initially also contained the idea of a miniature representation/incarnation (as in a scale model) of an ideal society – hence its utopian meaning.[6]

In recent times, the media has haphazardly applied the label to numerous prisons worldwide (even if only once in some cases), including Bologna (Italy), Comayagua (Honduras), El-Jadida (Morocco), Potosi (Missouri, USA), Sabaneta (Venezuela), Saray (Turkey), Shotts (Scotland), Tipitapa (Nicaragua), Waterloo (Canada), and Wymott (England), and even the Guantanamo Bay detention camp (Cuba). The fact that the list of penitentiaries sporadically and selectively labelled 'model prisons' could go on almost indefinitely offers a clear indication of the extent of the problem. Justifications for using the (somewhat polysemous) adjective 'model' vary widely, and some are only superficial. For political purposes, it is often generously applied to institutions that hardly deserve it. Clearly, a prison cannot qualify as a 'model' solely on the basis of its having been described as such in newspaper articles or occasional references by authorities. Only prisons that have received widespread and consistent recognition as exemplary institutions should be considered for our study.[7]

Ten typical uses in the media (1970s–2020s)

'Brazil is to spend $16.6 million to reform the country's prison system, which has been severely criticized, even by government officials. Fifteen "model prisons" will be built in the next three years. [. . .] The new "model prisons" will be for 300 prisoners and near urban centers. They are planned to be self-supporting, with prisoners engaged in both farming and industrial occupations.' ('Brazil to build "model prisons"', *The New York Times*, 22 July 1973.)

'An Assembly panel that has been highly critical of the state's prison system says the Eastern New York Correctional Facility in Napanoch is a clean, "model" prison where the inmates have few complaints.' ('Assembly panel cites prison in Ulster County as a "model"', *The New York Times*, 21 November 1983.)

'What would happen if prisoners were given more responsibility? [. . .] Impossible? On the contrary, this is how Grendon operates. The category B prison near Aylesbury in Buckinghamshire is the only prison in Britain committed to therapeutic-based treatment. [. . .] Yet is it a prototype, or a fig leaf?' ('Model prison', *The Guardian*, 4 September 1992.)

'Once hailed as a model prison, Maghaberry has become a powder keg since the Good Friday agreement was signed.' (Jamie Wilson, 'Unwanted guest at model jail', *The Guardian*, 24 August 2000.)

'The authorities claim the Abovian camp is a model prison and that its 70 inmates have some of the best conditions in the former Soviet Union. Human rights activists agree that things are a lot better than they used to be, but say much more needs to be done for conditions to meet international standards.' (Karine Ter-Saakian, 'Doing time in Armenia's "model" prison', *The Guardian*, 13 March 2004.)

'If it weren't for the watchtowers and razor-wire, you might easily mistake Jordan's model prison for a recreational centre.' (Ruth Sherlock, 'Inside Abu Qatada's luxurious prison in Jordan', *The Telegraph*, 19 May 2012.)

'The model prison experiment in Misrata deserves a mention, as one among many. Here, in a city that is famous for its martyrs and generally averse to any form of pardon, the governor Fathi Abdessalam Dard is happy to explain to visitors his plans for rehabilitating former enemies through Islam. A splendidly bearded adherent of Wahhabi Salafism, he shows visitors all round the prison – which currently has 728 inmates, mainly former members of Gaddafi's forces. Almost all have beards and shaven heads. They are full of praise for the governor, who cracks jokes with them and is always ready to listen to any complaints about the physical conditions.' (Patrick Haimzadeh, 'Libya's unquiet election', *Le Monde diplomatique*, English edition, July 2012.)

'At least four inmates were killed and several wounded after an attempted mass escape at a prison in San Cristobal, officials said Friday. [. . .] The prison holds about 2,000 inmates who have been convicted of various crimes, primarily drug trafficking. It is one of the nation's new model prisons that promote education and better living conditions. A riot earlier this year in another model prison left two people dead and several wounded.' ('Dominican Republic: Inmates riot at model prison and try a mass escape', *Reuters/The New York Times*, 24 October 2014.)

'During its peak, Carandiru was South America's largest prison, holding over 8,000 prisoners. It opened in 1920 in response to the demands of the 1890 criminal code, and was considered to be a model prison at the time. The São Paulo prison is, unfortunately, best remembered for the 1992 Carandiru massacre.' (Julian Kimble, 'The 50 craziest prisons and jails in the world', *Complex*, 14 August 2015.)

'The cost of the project Model Prison in sector H-16 has been escalated by a whopping 365 percent than the original cost while the construction of the project also delayed for another two years, it has been learnt. [. . .] The project aims at construction of Model Prison/Jail in Sector H-16, Islamabad with a capacity for 2,000 inmates with future provision for 2,000 additional inmates.' (Tahir Niaz, 'Cost of Model Prisons Islamabad goes up by 365pc', *The Nation (Pakistan)*, 3 November 2022.)

This being the case, other ambivalent aspects need to be taken into account. First, the term is used to describe both prisons with an overtly security-oriented mission and others that theoretically prioritize principles like rehabilitation or respect for human rights. As we will see, this contradiction is not entirely new, having existed since the term was first used in the early nineteenth century. Second, in some cases, 'model prison' has become a near-official label (as we will see in chapters exploring regions from Spain to India via China), whereas some prisons have acquired this title unofficially, by reputation alone. Third, while there are prisons that have deserved the title 'model' because they have actually served as examples or references for other projects that have emulated them, the term has been used elsewhere to describe a one-of-a-kind experience, like a prison that served as a 'showcase' for the prison authorities, or, conversely, one that remained little known. Some places of confinement commonly labelled as 'models' are no ordinary prisons, such as Scheveningen (Netherlands), also known as the United Nations Detention Unit, linked to the International Criminal Court.[8]

We therefore have to walk a fine line. On the one hand, we need to establish a preliminary delimitation that outlines the scope of our investigation in a sound, manageable way. On the other hand, we must keep in mind the semantic flexibility that gives the term 'model prison' its influence and intrigue. In other words, we have to be nominalists, determining the scope of the expression 'model prison', but not rigidly pinning it down. Rather than rushing to provide a fixed definition, I will instead acknowledge and question multiple interpretations, examining designation criteria and shifts in connotation. Significantly, the phrase 'model prison' is increasingly used in contemporary discourse to describe fresh, well-maintained 'up-to-date' facilities, often simply because they boast of modern amenities and do not suffer from overcrowding. Sometimes it is even used to describe mere high-security institutions stripped of any correctional ambition. To understand this evolution, it is important to go back to the origins of the term. It would be too simple to assert that the expression was always merely an empty signifier. From its inception, the notion of 'model prison' was imbued with substantive, if contested, meanings within specific contexts.

The expression was coined in the early 1820s, at a time when prison philanthropy was developing in France after the foundation of the Société royale pour l'amélioration des prisons in 1819. Initially, it was mainly used to characterize the 'La Roquette' prisons in Paris. Before long, however, it was being used to refer to other establishments, many of them also in Paris, notably the Saint-Lazare Prison. The set phrase 'model prisons' swiftly spread in the following decades, not without differences in application and reception, as the idea of importing foreign penal models was not universally welcomed. Either way, the expression had soon become so popular that, as early as 1829, architect Victor Baltard (1805–74) was already criticizing what he called the 'theory of model prisons'.[9]

Early uses of the set phrase 'model prisons' (France, England, Ireland, USA)

'Finally, gentlemen, work has begun on a project that will one day, when our resources and influence have increased, enable us to found *a model prison* that will be able to demonstrate the results of success in compelling prisoners to change their ways and educate themselves during the unhappy years of their sentence, and to leave prison enlightened and improved.' (Charles Coquerel, Société de la morale chrétienne, *Journal de la Société de la morale chrétienne*, 5, 1825.)

'The Grand Jury are now disposed to present for the half of any sum necessary to erect a first-rate prison, to be paid by instalments, under the Act of Parliament, provided a grant of the other half can be obtained from Government, on the grounds of the inability of the city to meet the expense, and that in some degree a national benefit would arise from it, by providing a model prison for Ireland, exclusive of which, the city complain that they have to provide for the accommodation and support of many criminals from the neighbouring counties, whose resort for plunder is in the capital, though they are not resident in it.' (House of Commons, 'Papers relating to accommodation at Newgate Prison in Dublin', 23, 1826.)

'Two new prisons have been built, one on Rue de Clichy, intended for those imprisoned for debt, and the other on Rue de la Roquette, generally known as the Model Prison. [. . .] This prison, which was built with a view to having a model prison, is far from deserving to be held up as such, from the point of view of salubriousness. [. . .] Through these perverse, misplaced constructions, Saint-Lazare, which could be held up as a model prison, has lost its salubriousness. . .' (Jean-Gabriel-Victor de Moléon, *Rapports généraux sur la salubrité publique*, 1828.)

'To help you understand my idea, let me briefly explain the system that Bentham presented to our constituent assembly, which the prisons committee recommended in the programme for the model prison in Paris, and which Geneva has largely adopted.' (Jean-Baptiste Bayle-Mouillard, 'Observations sur la prison de Clermont-Ferrand', Académie des sciences, belles-lettres et arts de Clermont-Ferrand, *Annales scientifiques, littéraires et industrielles de l'Auvergne*, 3, 1830.)

'Those who see in Paris a model prison, destined for four hundred prisoners, and costing 4,000,000 of francs, conclude with apparent reason, that it would require 320,000,000 of francs, to lodge, upon the same plan, 32,000 criminals; i.e. 10,000 francs for each. But we must remember, that this enormous expense has been occasioned by the deplorable extravagance with which the construction of that prison was attended.' (Gustave de Beaumont and Alexis de Toqueville, *On the Penitentiary System in the United States, and Its Application in France. . .*, 1833.)

'. . . it would be extremely desirable that there should be one or more Central Prisons [. . .]. These should be situated either in the metropolis or its immediate vicinity, and would serve as model prisons for the rest of the country. [. . .] So that these central establishments would answer the purpose, not only of model prisons and fields of experiment for the national system of discipline, but would also serve as nominal schools for the instruction and education of governors and other prison officers.' (The Earl of Chichester, in House of Commons, 'On gaols and houses of corrections', *First Report from the Select Committee of the House of Lords Appointed to Inquire into the Present State of the Several Gaols and Houses of Correction in England and Wales. . .*, May 1835.)

'The erection of a Model Prison in or near the metropolis, upon the most approved system of separation, suggests itself as a legitimate and desirable appropriation of a few thousands of the public money – for there can be no worse economy than system of prison discipline like those which at present so manifestly tend to perpetuate and foster crime.' (*The Bradford Observer*, 26 April 1838.)

'The Earl of Chichester, as the Chairman of the Sussex Quarter Sessions, has sent a communication to all the Quarter Sessions throughout England, calling on the Magistrates to send in memorials to the Government, asking that several model prisons should be built near London, that the various plans of prison discipline might be fairly tried, and that which tended best to reclaim the offender selected and generally adopted throughout England.' (*The Observer*, 6 January 1839.)

'The Proposed Model Prison. It is reported that negotiations are on foot for the purchase of a piece of ground at Barnsbury park, Islington, on which is to be erected the new Government model prison. The site is near Copenhagen house, with a cold bleak atmosphere and a deep clay soil, which renders the ground generally damp, but, standing upon a hill, it is capable of effectual drainage.' (*The Observer*, 18 August 1839.)

'About a mile northward from King's Cross, London, and adjoining the Caledonian Asylum, is the site on which the Marquis of Normanby, on Friday, laid the foundation of a new model prison, the design of which is to carry out more effectually the plan of separate confinement.' (*The Manchester Guardian*, 15 April 1840.)

'The inmates of the new "model prison", when it is erected, will, it is asserted, be picked prisoners, selected for the purpose of trying the merits of the new system. The prisoners, however, must not think that the discipline is founded on less confined principles than heretofore.' (*The Satirist, or Censor of the Times*, 19 April 1840.)

'THE ART OF LEGALLY TORMENTING. At the new Model Prison, building near the Caledonian Asylum, in the new North-road, we are told the following arrangements are to be carried into strict effect. We cannot help thinking the discipline a kind of torture very unworthy of a Christian country.' (*The Age*, 27 September 1840.)

'This new prison, as its name imports, is intended as a model by which the houses of correction or penitentiaries in England are in future to be erected. [. . .] With the exception of some of its details, it will be constructed upon the same principle as the Eastern Penitentiary, in the state of Pennsylvania, near the city of Philadelphia, but not upon so large a scale. [. . .] As the strictest economy is observed, architectural beauty has not been much regarded. The Woods and Forests have no control over the model prison, beyond passing the accounts, which are paid at the treasury.' (*The Manchester Guardian*, 3 October 1840.)

'It appears that the change in the government has had no effect on the arrangements for erecting and completing the Model Prison, or preventing the realization of the cruel and inquisitorial designs of its originators.' (*Cleave's London Satirist and Gazette of Variety*, 5 March 1842.)[10]

This starting point takes us to the period immediately following the prison system's penal transformation, formalized in France by the revolutionary penal code of 1791. It was a time when, in principle, prisons became not only places of detention but also correctional facilities where the served sentences had a transformative purpose. Prisons then became the core of the repressive system, competing with – and sometimes combined with – exclusionary sentences (or even elimination) based on expulsion from Metropolitan France ('transportation', 'deportation', and later 'relegation'), particularly to penal colonies. One should not overlook that the rise of imprisonment coexisted with the persistence of other punitive measures. Challenging the 'dominant narrative of the history of punishment, which has foregrounded the rise of prisons and penitentiaries as the key means of effecting governance and enforcing social discipline in the nineteenth century and later', Clare Anderson has persuasively shown that a global history of convicts should embrace 'convict mobility' as well. In Portugal, for instance, a new penitentiary constructed in Lisbon in 1873 was supposedly designed around individual confinement, yet overcrowding became so severe that authorities soon resorted to penal transportation to African colonies. In France, too, the new punitive power configuration did not exclude forms of continuity with the repression of the *Ancien Régime*. But it was now organized around confined surveillance rather than public torture, as its champions were crediting imprisonment with both economic and moral virtues.[11]

That being said, Baltard's earlier reference to imitation raises an important periodization issue. Even facilities existing prior to the 1791 turning point were sometimes retrospectively referred to as 'model prisons'. It is in this sense that the prison known as 'La Force' in Paris, which opened in 1780–2, was singled out as a 'model', both for its design and for the separation of prisoners into different categories. This stood in stark contrast to the general ghastliness of the places of detention highlighted by the famous philanthropist John Howard (1726–90), credited as the author of the classic text *The State of the Prisons in England and Wales* (1777). French historian Christian Carlier, in his book on the French prison of Fresnes (which I will reference in chapter 5), described La Force in Paris as France's first model (royal) prison.

Its fate foreshadowed that of later penitentiaries, as a few decades after it opened, 'the model prison had become a dreadful place'. In neighbouring Belgium in the 1770s, the House of Force in Ghent, which Howard praised before it quickly disappointed him, served as a model for the development of the French *maisons centrales* (prisons intended for long-term sentences). These 'houses' were themselves inspired by the reformatory in Rome. Foucault referred to the trio of Ghent, Gloucester in England, and Walnut Street in the United States (see below) as '"models" of penal detention', though he also described them as not 'innovations or points of departure'.[12]

The contradiction was only an apparent one. A model does not emerge out of nothing; one way or another it necessarily draws inspiration or derives from a precedent. One could therefore get caught in an endless genealogical search if one were to go looking for the original source. Setting aside a model proposed by the monk Jean Mabillon (1632–1707) in his 1690 text published posthumously in 1724, Foucault singled out Amsterdam's Rasphuis, a house of correction dating back to the late sixteenth century, as the 'oldest of these models, the one that is generally regarded as having inspired all the others'. Though critical of Foucault's work, Pieter Spierenburg also reckons that 'the Amsterdam rasphouse may have been the first truly criminal prison in world history'. As I have already suggested, we will not be going back that far. Nor will I reopen the thorny historiographical debate about the periodization and conditions of the emergence of the penitentiary system (with some arguments stressing economic transformations, others state formation, and so on), even if this fascinating aspect continues to be the subject of disagreement. We will start at the precise moment when the expression 'model prison(s)' flourished, concomitant with the prison system's penitentiary turn.[13]

From this perspective, a model prison is one that, in addition to its traditional deterrence and detention functions, claims it will actually reform prisoners, 'improve' their souls and bodies, and correct their behaviour for the presumed benefit of society as a whole. By various means (atonement, coercion, imitation, introspection, instruction, retribution, work, reward, and so on), such a prison promises to 'rehabilitate' in a moral, legal, and social sense. But this is only a minimal definition, since in its fullest sense a model prison is supposed to be much more than that: a 'model of the ideal society' in miniature, a microcosm of a perfect society. Obviously, these proclamations should not be taken literally, nor should their true meaning be misunderstood. 'Humanizing' detention conditions was not the issue at hand; the crucial point was to ensure that imprisonment served a purpose, rather than being mere aimless detention. Nevertheless, it is in their name that 'model prisons' have served as beacons or standards for their country, sometimes even their continent, if not the world.[14]

This definition, although inclusive, only marginally addresses repressive 'models' whose sole purpose was, and still is, neutralization. A notable example was the Ngaragba Prison (Central African Republic) in the late 1980s. It was described as a 'model', but only in the sense that it was a condensed representation of the prevailing political regime. Far from being isolated, this prison was an integral part of the social dynamics and power relations of that time, which were characterized by arbitrary authority, clientelism, and violence. The same could be said of the Makala Prison (Democratic Republic of Congo), which a 2012 article paradoxically described as both a 'model prison' and 'the antechamber of hell'. The model prisons I will be examining in this book embody the penitentiary ideals of the early nineteenth century, those ostensibly intended to fulfil the functions of correction, reformation, and rehabilitation, as well as those that epitomized a curative, therapeutic, or remedial orientation, echoing medical paradigms. Other forms will not be included, or will be mentioned only in passing, such as agricultural penal colonies like the one in Mettray, France, which Foucault called 'a prison, but not entirely', a 'punitive model', but 'at the limit of strict penality'.[15]

That being said, the choice remains tricky. It is hardly possible to discuss all of the so-called 'model prisons', even in cases where the name is obviously appropriate. Women's prisons, and especially children's prisons, are often at the forefront in this respect. My selection is based on several criteria: examples should reveal broader patterns or processes; overly similar cases should be avoided, with a view to highlighting a variety of configurations or circumstances; examples should provide insight into little-known situations, while not neglecting better-known cases that cannot be ignored; and, finally, there should be some examples that look beyond Western countries. The resulting selection is open to criticism, and admittedly somewhat arbitrary, since the spatial and temporal spectrum of this field is extremely vast, as is the potential bibliography. As the situation in English-speaking countries has been well covered in the historical literature, I chose to highlight lesser-known examples, partly based on sources in languages other than English. All the same, the selection will hopefully offer a fairly comprehensive overview. To help set the scene, it is worth briefly reviewing the essential references of the early nineteenth century. While this period is certainly the most well known, it provides crucial context for our exploration.

Women and children first!

During the nineteenth century, women were the embodiment of all the hopes placed in moral education. If there was one principle of separation that persisted even when rule enforcement proved unstable, it was certainly the separation of the sexes. Women were not always exonerated from their offences, and were sometimes accused of being covertly behind many male crimes, yet, generally speaking, they benefited from relative penal leniency. Their misdeeds were often attributed to weakness of character rather than genuine malice. 'Reformation' essentially consisted of teaching domestic values.

In any case, women's prisons have been no exception to the recurrent cruel irony that purported penal models tend to result in deplorable detention conditions. A stark example in the twentieth century is Madrid's Ventas Prison (1931–69), the most overcrowded women's prison in Spanish history. The Republican Director General of Prisons, Victoria Kent, originally intended it as a 'model prison' facilitating rehabilitation, as part of the Second Republic's progressive penal reform. However, the establishment was dramatically transformed under Franco's regime, as was Barcelona's Modelo (see chapter 6). Far from its reformist ideals, it became a warehouse for female inmates, including minors, packed in under terrible conditions.

But it was children, especially the poor and marginalized, who became the focus of the burgeoning penal ideal, and remained its last refuge even after it had been exhausted. Less directly accountable for their actions, children were also considered more malleable, susceptible to influence, for better or worse. At the turn of the twentieth century, and even more so on the eve of the First World War – a time when demographics were a crucial military factor – they were regarded as valuable 'capital' that should not be wasted, at least in the case of working-class children.

In France, there has been no shortage of more or less atypical initiatives, from La Rochefoucauld-Liancourt's unrealized project to create a 'test prison' (*prison d'essai*) for young inmates in 1814 ('Too utopian?' wonders historian Jacques Bourquin, before answering: 'In any case, it was a project that went against the tide'), to the recent *Établissements pénitentiaires pour mineurs* (juvenile correctional centres). There was also the 'special home' for young prisoners founded in 1847 by Charles Lucas, the prison school in Oermingen a century later after the Liberation of France, and the Fleury-Mérogis centre for young prisoners in the late 1960s (chapter 10).

In neighbouring countries too, euphemisms were often employed to avoid the unpleasant word 'prison', as with the British 'juvenile reformatories'. It is not without irony that historian Geneviève Heller chose 'This is not a prison' as a title for her book on the Vennes 'house of education', near Lausanne. However, such linguistic precautions did not prevent the history of these institutions from being marred by scandals. The penitentiary of Saint-Hubert, which opened in 1844 and served as a model for other establishments of the same type in Belgium, closed just over a century later following a trial that laid bare the brutality of its practices.[16]

From Panopticon to Auburn, via Cherry Hill

Famous ever since it was resurrected by Foucault, the Panopticon (to which Jeremy Bentham's name is inextricably linked – not without some injustice to his youngest brother Samuel, who played an equal role in designing it both theoretically and practically) is now so well known that there is no need to dwell on it. As the editor of *The Panopticon Writings* asserted: 'There is probably no building that has stirred more philosophical controversy than Bentham's Panopticon.' However, two aspects are worth recalling, since Foucault's examination was as selective as it was brilliant.[17]

While the Panopticon was regarded at the time 'as not much more than a bizarre little utopia', as Foucault himself admits, the extent to which it was actually a matrix is a matter of dispute. Some authors, attempting to qualify or even invalidate its influence, have emphasized that no real prison has ever truly resembled it, if only for economic reasons. In this respect, the influence of the Panopticon model on actual constructions would have been marginal at best. Other authors, such as architects Augustin Rosenstiehl and Pierre Sartoux, see a profound influence providing an almost unwavering – if occasionally unconscious – source of inspiration right up to the beginning of the twenty-first century. It all depends on how the radial blueprint that became so visible in the nineteenth century is viewed in light of the Panopticon: was it a continuation or a departure? Either way, a number of prisons are thought to have been more or less inspired by that model developed around 1786, starting with Geneva's Tour-Maîtresse (1825) and London's Pentonville (1842), to which the first two chapters of this book are devoted. Between these two dates, it is also worth mentioning La Petite Roquette in Paris, 'the first explicit implementation of panopticism in France', according to Michelle Perrot. Other examples in France include the prisons of Niort (1853) and Autun (1856). In the rest of Europe, one could point to Le Nuove in Turin (Italy, 1870 – synonymous with modernity at the time, its name would become a symbol of torture under fascism) or Arnhem (Netherlands, 1880s, famous for the renovation of its dome by architect Rem Koolhaas in the late 1970s). In the Americas, two examples are Stateville Prison near Chicago, built in the late 1910s ('When the State of Illinois has finished her new three and one-half million dollar prison, features once thought essential to penal housing will be forgotten', *Scientific American* boldly asserted in 1917), and the Presidio Modelo in Cuba, built in the mid-1920s.[18]

On the other hand, it is also worth noting that although the term 'panopticon' is now generally associated with the ultimate in coercive surveillance, the original idea was much more ambivalent. The aim of this generic, multi-purpose utilitarian project was to eliminate counterproductive, degrading, morbid prisons (or workplaces) and transform them into places of regeneration. The Bentham brothers were concerned about hygiene and transparency, and they wanted the inspectors themselves to be supervised. Their project included some pioneering aspects, along with others that were strange or even fanciful. In short, it remained an unrealized scheme, which was impractical in some respects, yet pivotal (albeit belatedly).

Almost as famous (and even more famous in the United States) are the Auburnian and Pennsylvanian models, which epitomize the advent of corrective punishment. Despite many common features, the opposition between them – that is, between 'separate system' and 'silent system' – shaped European prison debates in the nineteenth century. The historiography on this subject being abundant, I will limit myself to a few essential points.[19]

The pioneering Philadelphia (or Pennsylvania) model is based on day-and-night solitary confinement. On the rare occasions when prisoners left their cells, they wore masks to prevent them from recognizing each other. When it first opened in 1773, the Walnut Street Jail was a conventional colonial prison. Following the American Revolution, it underwent partial conversion in 1790, including the construction of a new building within its grounds, referred to as a 'Penitentiary House'. While the structure was designed to provide short-term solitary confinement for newly arrived inmates, this was not representative of the systematic penitentiary practices it would later establish. The Walnut Street facility continued to be characterized by collective detention, with multiple prisoners sharing cells. Although the Quaker administrators viewed their approach as 'reform', including particular efforts to improve hygiene, the prison's regime was primarily one of silence, labour, and prayer aimed at inducing penitence. Despite its reputation as the United States' first correctional institution – and its treatment as a model for other states – Walnut Street's conditions quickly deteriorated. Overcrowding, frequent escapes, arsons, and riots plagued the facility, revealing the limitations of its design. Walnut Street was not exactly a 'modern' or 'groundbreaking' penitentiary, but rather a 'proto-prison', as Ashley Rubin has termed it – an experimental yet flawed institution that embodied the tensions and contradictions of early American penal reform. It was as a replacement that the Philadelphia model subsequently took shape in the 1820s. The first prison built according to the new model was the Western State Penitentiary (1826) near Pittsburgh – an experiment so calamitous, the prison had to be demolished and rebuilt after a short time. This was followed by the model's most famous incarnation, the Eastern State Penitentiary at Cherry Hill (from which it took its nickname), on the outskirts of Philadelphia. As soon as it opened in 1829, Cherry Hill attracted visitors from several continents, inspiring new prisons from Belgium to Scandinavia to Prussia. This is why this penitentiary is generally considered to have been the world's most famous or influential, revered by its admirers as a masterpiece of design, with little regard for the destructive effects of the near-permanent solitary confinement it imposed. It officially closed in 1970 or 1971, but as far back as the early twentieth century it was already considered permanently obsolete, just like its rival in Auburn.[20]

In Auburn Prison, which opened in 1818 (chronologically between Walnut Street and Cherry Hill) while still under construction, prisoners were locked in their tiny cells at night and worked in large workshops during the day. They were not allowed to communicate, and any breach of this enforced silence was subject to physical punishment, particularly flogging. Many scholars have situated Auburn in the context of the development of North American capitalism and its structuring of the labour market and factory system. In contrast to the Pennsylvanian method of individual artisanal production, which was unprofitable from a commercial perspective, the Auburn system sought to exploit the productive potential and economic function of captive factory-style labour. This model seems to have struggled to spread in Europe. Its influence was mostly confined to the United States, at least if we accept the views expressed by experts at the time. At the first International Penitentiary Congress (Frankfurt, 1846), the Auburnian system received virtually no support, while its rival largely dominated. However, this lack of success in Europe must be qualified. Its influence there was palpable at an early stage. Long before the debates of the 1830s between supporters of the Auburnian and Philadelphian systems, the issue had been settled for half of French prisoners. In factory-like '*maisons centrales*', the prison space was organized around forced labour. The punitive aspect of this labour became increasingly apparent under the July Monarchy (1830–48), as its profitability became less obvious. Still in operation today, Auburn has recently come to be associated with solitary confinement measures imposed on repeat violent offenders.[21]

As already suggested, these models were themselves innovations based on a legacy. The architect of Cherry Hill, John Haviland (1792–1852), who designed a radial scheme with lasting global influence, drew on earlier English and Irish models. The circulation of models subsequently intensified through travel, visits, and reports. The International Penitentiary Congresses – which officially began in London in 1872 but were preceded by meetings in Frankfurt (1846) and Brussels (1847) following private initiatives – were a preferred forum for the leading figures of the emerging 'prison science'. As Nir Shafir showed, their purpose 'was not only to circulate ideas and people but also to determine which models were the most effective through comparison'. But adopting a model did not mean replicating it identically. Circulation often involved adaptation and alteration, especially when the model was crossing national and even continental borders. This was also not a one-way North–South process, at least not from the second half of the nineteenth century. The architect of La Santé (chapter 3), Émile Vaudremer (1829–1914), mentioned the prison in Lima in his notes. Likewise, the Saint Petersburg Prison (chapter 4) had a certain influence on the one in Fresnes, France (chapter 5). Norman Johnston's book *Forms of Constraint* gives a number of examples of cross-fertilization and comparison that are sometimes counter-intuitive. For example, he points out that the presence of workshops at the end of corridors in the Buenos Aires Prison recalls the layout of Japanese prisons built at the same time.[22]

'Peripheral' model prisons

Foucault likened the success of the coercive formula based on discipline, surveillance, and imprisonment to that of the steam engine. As Stephan Scheuzger points out, this view did not avoid the pitfalls of a 'diffusionist' conception based on an overly linear and one-directional way of seeing the relationship between centres and peripheral areas ('the West and the rest'). Recent research has shed new light on the ways in which penal prisons spread across the continents. Even before the mid-nineteenth century, the new 'modern' prisons being built in capital cities were serving as symbols of modernity and prestige in addition to their practical functions. However, in most countries, the presence of these buildings was the exception rather than the rule, with major disparities between geographical areas.

According to historian Florence Bernault, there is no such thing as a model prison, especially not one particular to the African continent, a situation that mirrors the absence of a specifically colonial utopia in that part of the world. 'False penitentiaries', as she calls them, are an expression of a 'conquest prison system', dedicated to the reproduction of colonial power through political repression, racial discrimination, and economic extraction. The most recent collective reference volume does not mention any model prisons as such in Africa.

Elsewhere, European and American penitentiary utopias of the early nineteenth century gave rise to various achievements, especially in Latin America, as we will see through several *modelos* (see counterpoint III). In South-East Asia, where the Philippines under American trusteeship was at the forefront of prison reform, the Bilibid Prison in Manila was considered a model prison in the 1910s and 1920s. Known for the concerts given by its brass band, it even became a tourist attraction of sorts.

Generally speaking, prisons imitating Western models were intended to signal that a system was modernizing, such as those built in the Near and Middle East in the 1920s and 1930s, many of which were completed late. One example is Qasr Prison in Iran, which began operating in 1929 and was dedicated to political prisoners. Designed by a Russian architect based on European models and incorporating Persian architectural motifs, it was intended as a symbol of the new imperial state and its modern judicial system. Borrowing from the Benthamian and Philadelphian models, it impressed its first occupants not only with its imposing security arrangements, but also with its cleanliness, décor, and facilities. Now a museum (we will elaborate on such a conversion in counterpoint I), it served as the country's main political prison until the 1970s, and had a reputation for extreme harshness. Ironically, one of its promoters ended up imprisoned there.

Challenging conventional wisdom, Kent F. Schull has shown that the Ottoman authorities invested significant resources in modernizing their prison system from the 1850s to the 1920s, during the Empire's final decades. Although penal reforms progressed slowly, their efforts were not wholly unlike those of their American and European contemporaries. A prime example is the 1871 'model prison' in Istanbul's Sultanahmet district, which officials designed with the explicit intention of replicating it across all provincial centres. Though this initiative failed to take hold, the Hamidian era saw a revival of these efforts after the implementation of the 1880 Prison Regulation. Administrators then began building similar 'model' prisons throughout the Empire, with Abdülhamid II actively promoting them internationally as showcases of modern architectural design and state-of-the-art facilities. By the 1910s, even Edirne's prison textile factory had been held up as a model for comparable facilities across the Empire.[23]

Although the decision to adopt either the Auburnian or Philadelphian system was based on a variety of distinctive factors such as the role that work would play, the impact it would have on the body, or the costs it would entail, the opposition between them played out on a foundation of common principles: enforced, silent labour as a presumed means of correcting behaviour, and separation. One should therefore be careful not to exaggerate the actual differences between the two models. After initially being praised, both systems were eventually condemned for their cruelty. Their core principles were eventually abandoned after attempts to combine the two models. As chapter 3 will show, when La Santé prison opened in Paris, it included two sections: one inspired by Philadelphia and the other by Auburn. Besides, the prison regime represented by these 'models' was not necessarily any 'better' than those in other places or in the past. The ideal of correcting offenders, encapsulated by the term 'reform', was based just as much on the critical view that prisons were overly lenient and therefore ineffective as it was on criticism of abuses of power that occur discreetly. The rhetoric of reform, which contrasted it with idle captivity, was adaptable to the imposition of strict order and harsh discipline.

Albany Penitentiary, described as a 'model prison of the world', illustrates this well. Opened in 1848 in the wake of the American reform movement and amid socioeconomic upheaval, this pioneering regional prison quickly became a model to be imitated locally and beyond. From the outset, the motivation for building it was in no way sentimental, but rather economic. Designed to handle petty crime at a low cost, the prison was built by the inmates themselves. Work was central to the model, serving not only a disciplinary purpose (ensuring obedience), but also an economic one (offsetting the cost of incarceration). In fact, the prison soon became profitable. Strict order was maintained. Punishments were severe, and combined with the careful nurturing of religious feeling. Albany Penitentiary is a prime example of the reversal mentioned at the beginning, closing in

1931 after a half-century of decline. It had become a symbol of repressive archaism and corruption, as judges were bribed to keep it afloat by filling it with prisoners serving long sentences.[24]

All in all, it seems clear that if there is such a thing as a 'carceral utopia', it is more in the sense of a 'non-place' than an 'ideal place'. But to put things into perspective, we need to revisit the utopian impulse behind the plan to create 'model prisons'.

The strange non-death of prison utopia

Historians of nineteenth-century prisons often use the term 'utopia'. This is hardly surprising, as it was a century of political and architectural ideals, exemplified by Jean-Baptiste André Godin's Familistère de Guise, inspired by (but also different from) Charles Fourier's Phalanstère. Prisons were no exception, apart from the fact that no one claimed for themselves the word 'utopia', which rather served as a term of denigration. From the 1830s, 'utopians' and their pipedreams were fiercely mocked by supposedly wise reformers. The fact remains that the 'carceral system' did include 'invincible utopias', as Foucault argued in *Discipline and Punish*. He presented 'utopian duplication' as one element of the 'fourfold system' defining the 'carceral system'.[25]

There was indeed a utopian impulse among some thinkers of the time. It initially took the form of idealistic philanthropy, and later evolved into a more secular belief in the potential of scientific and technical progress. This new kind of utopian narrative was central to what Jacques-Guy Petit calls the 'second philanthropy'. It revived a monastic tradition that exalted enclosed places as 'laboratories of perfection'. In a similar vein, Michael Ignatieff explains that prison utopias expressed a 'modernizing rationality', although he is quick to point out the 'gap between rationalist utopia and prison practice'. While this gap is undeniable, utopia cannot simply be reduced to an illusion that contrasts with reality, as one conventional definition suggests.

As Norbert Elias put it, utopias are best understood as 'logical extensions of a genuine science of the social', standing 'between illusion and reality, between wish and analysis'. Without yielding to any enchanted vision, we must try to identify 'the reality of utopia' without viewing it as a merely imaginary plan devoid of any tangible effect on social relations, even if this effect reveals an unbridgeable gap between intentions and outcomes. Has prison discipline really achieved the miracles that some commentators have ascribed to it? Of course not. But it has partly shaped the daily life of many prisons.[26]

Generally said to date from the mid-1810s to the late 1830s, the utopian period extended outside the perimeter of prison. As strange as it may seem today, the staunchest advocates of penitentiaries considered them not only symbols of modernity, but also quintessential utopian places, ideal sites for the social reform they were seeking more generally. 'It is difficult for those of us who are critical of modern prisons to imagine a time when these institutions were, for humanitarians and reformers, the new hope of a better society,' wrote Patricia O'Brien. To contemporary eyes, prisons would seem to be the most inappropriate places for a 'progressive' purpose of that kind. There was a time, however, when the search for the right kind of prison was part of a broader prison reform movement that was itself conceived as a special means of addressing the 'social question' – though 'resolving' often meant containing the effects rather than removing the causes. The prison utopia was at the forefront of the 'great project' to transform the poor, which took shape in the nineteenth century. Strict and extensive, the prison system was also ground-breaking. Preceding not only the introduction of schools and asylums, but also the advent of workers' housing estates and Christian patronages, the dream of a model prison was the first attempt to educate and normalize the masses. In the view of both utilitarian and philanthropic reformers, prison was an *in vivo* social laboratory, a school, convent, and factory all in one, a place whose general scope and configuration was considered optimal.

According to historian Catherine Duprat, these benefits were merely rhetorical. The new form of discipline was essentially a call to order. 'In the nineteenth century there were actual crèches, savings banks, and social housing, but there was no model prison.'[27]

There remains no consensus on what this 'non-existence' implies. Certainly, even at the height of the philanthropic era, education lagged far behind the establishment of order through separation, work, and silence. However, before discussing the failure of this utopian projection, evident in the gap between discourse and deeds, it is important to understand the meaning of that discourse. As suggested earlier, this utopia was not universal; it was not designed for everyone. As an expression of a class worldview that contained its share of contradictions and antagonisms, it was conceived by the elite for the masses. What the discourse of wealthy members of the upper class presented as education, regeneration, or reform was little more than an attempt to inculcate dominant bourgeois norms and defend the established order, as made clear by the repressive tendency that followed the 1848 revolution. Under the guise of knowledge and wisdom, this discourse stemmed from a social anxiety based on well-understood socioeconomic interests. The model prison was arguably the product of a utopian movement, but this movement must not be confused with any kind of disinterested generosity, or the wish to implement socially fair punishment. The aim was to moralize the common people, the lower classes, willingly or by force, and to inculcate in them the values of booming industrial capitalism – work, property, savings, punctuality, productivity, sobriety, and so on – in order to keep them in their place. In short, it was the exact opposite of emancipation.

From that perspective, could one say that model prisons were a paradoxical success, as an effort to bring people into line, suited to the idea of prison as an 'omni-disciplinary' institution? Even from this point of view, there is still a long way to go. As Patricia O'Brien put it: 'The new prisons were not models of social order and discipline, reflecting and enforcing a broader social order. They were most often centres of contained disorder and occasional chaos. Discipline, isolation, and rehabilitation had a rhetorical reality and an institutional one.' And yet this difference between 'realities', however big it may be, is not necessarily proof of failure. The notion of discipline encapsulates a fundamental tension: it may refer to an effort to cultivate productive, law-abiding citizens, or it may function as a means of inflicting what John Pratt calls a 'carefully calibrated level of suffering'. Through the question of model prisons, what we need to revisit is the issue of whether the failure of prisons is true or untrue. To do this properly, it is necessary to look beyond prisons, be they 'models' or not.[28]

Foucault pointed to the blatant failure of the prison utopia, which he sometimes dated as beginning in the 1820s, and sometimes dated to the 1840s, the period in which *Discipline and Punish* ends, setting aside a few leaps he made into his own time, that is to say, early 1970s France. Though historians have revised some of Foucault's interpretations, they generally agree on a similar periodization. One can stop at the end of the 1820s if one is linking it to the end of the first philanthropic cycle in Europe. Or one can extend it to around 1840, when the focus shifted back to prison's expiatory function based on solitary confinement, increased repression, and doubts about its educational virtues and the usefulness of forced labour. One could also extend the date even further, as did Michelle Perrot, describing the period from 1815 to 1848 as 'the era of the prison triumph', or Dominique Kalifa, who argued that the 1840s and 1850s saw the collapse of the 'prison utopia'. The occurrences of the phrase 'model prison(s)' in the English press confirms this periodization (see Graph 1). In France, one can even more generously include the era covering the last quarter of the nineteenth century, marked by a strong resurgence of the term 'model prison', following the great parliamentary inquiry of 1872–5, which led to a law on individual confinement for local jails, and subsequently to the activities of the Société générale des prisons, founded in 1877 (see Graph 2).

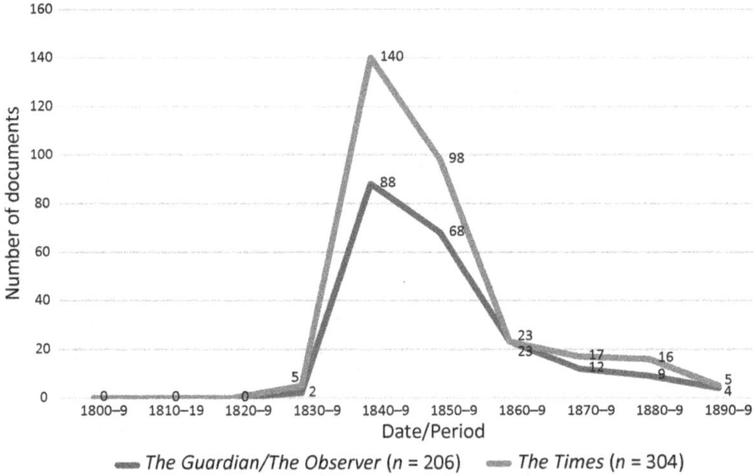

Graph 1 'Model prison(s)' in British newspapers during the nineteenth century

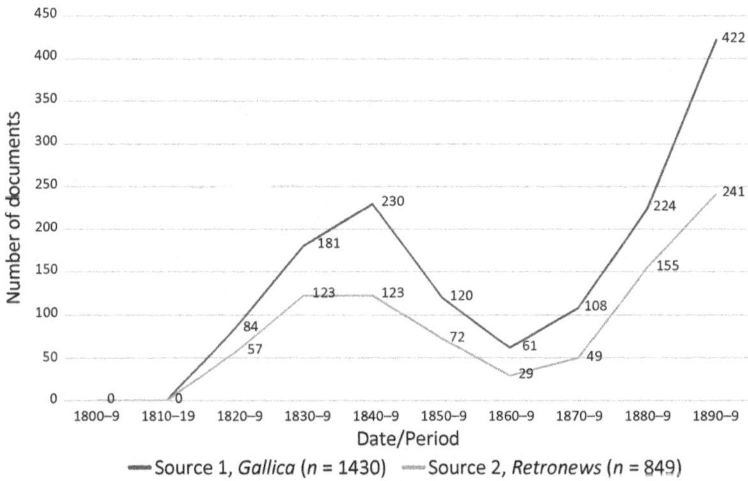

Graph 2 'Model prison(s)' in French newspapers during the nineteenth century

This period would extend to 1885, when several measures were introduced to circumvent prison or limit its influence, especially banishment and conditional release, followed six years later by the introduction of probation. By the time these measures were enacted, enthusiasm for prison had long since waned. Favour had shifted to exile sentences, as well as to the expansion of agricultural penal colonies – emphasizing the presumed virtues of the land and open air as opposed to confinement.[29]

In short, it has long been evident that the prison utopia has been a failure of sorts. This brief history of model prisons, gripping though it may be, is not exactly a suspense story. My aim is not to determine whether or not the prisons explored here ever really lived up to their claims. This question has already been settled: the answer is no. Nevertheless, the persistence of so-called 'model prisons' deserves special attention. What does the very notion of a model prison mean once the prison utopia that was its driving force is long gone? How can we make sense of what Alain Brossat called this 'strange prison utopia which, contrary to all the evidence, continues to link confinement, punishment, and the reform of "guilty lives"'? Why has this 'living-dead utopia' not disappeared? And its persistence is not solely discursive. It is regularly revived in the form of legal rules, architectural designs, institutional settings, technical equipment, and professional routines. As this book will show, all of these elements keep repeating the past in a kind of eternal return, but with a distinctive twist each time.[30]

In order to explore the extensive history of model prisons, I combine two different but complementary approaches, with a view to covering and collating specific cases and broader patterns.

The first path consists of (twelve) chapters, each focusing on a place (one prison) and year (when it opened or began operating). This chronological progression will take us from the early nineteenth century to the first decades of the twenty-first, through selected, specific examples. The aim of these chapters is not to recount, even in outline, the complete and complex history of each institution. That would obviously be an impossible mission. It is rather to highlight key elements that characterize them, while exploring why and how they were regarded as 'models' in the first place, and examining the utopian rationale behind that type of carceral institution.

This core approach is supplemented by a secondary one that takes the form of (six) 'counterpoints'. Admittedly the musical analogy is imperfect, but it captures the way these sections support and enrich the chapters while standing on their own. The counterpoints can be read in order or randomly, alongside the chapters or independently. Unlike the chapters, they are not in chronological order, some bringing readers back into the present, others offering historical retrospectives. Their purpose is to provide thematic or transversal overviews, sometimes introducing new perspectives that cut across periods and places. In particular, they help shift the discussion from 'model prisons' to 'prison models', and from the theme of 'utopia' to the related, opposite themes of 'heterotopia' and 'dystopia'.

Chapter 1

La Tour-Maîtresse, Geneva (Switzerland, 1825)

Tour-Maîtresse Prison (1851–62)
Source: Bibliothèque de Genève (Geneva Library), vg p 0073

After visiting Geneva's new Tour-Maîtresse Prison in June 1832, seven years after it had opened (as well as another new penitentiary in Lausanne), Alexis de Tocqueville sarcastically dubbed it a '*bijou* prison [*bonbonnière*]'. The famous Count had been sceptical even before his visit. From a distance, as early as 1831, he had already perceived those two facilities to be 'more like palaces than prisons' – suitable for Switzerland perhaps, but certainly not for France: too costly, too cosy. His on-site inspection only confirmed this view: 'Discipline whose gentleness and meticulous details are only suitable for a *bijou* prison like the one in Geneva: full bed, baths every month, library, recreation on Sundays, restraints on punishments, wages. Everything is as neat and tidy as a boudoir for a lady of fashion.'[1]

'Everyone praises the penitentiaries of Lausanne and Geneva,' Tocqueville writes. But the Count disapproved of a deluxe prison that took such good care of its inmates, not least because of its small size (except for the cells, which he considered too large), being designed to hold only a few dozen inmates. The term '*bijou* prison' resonated so profoundly with Louis-Mathurin Moreau-Christophe (a lawyer by profession who supported Tocqueville in his defence of solitary confinement, nicknamed 'the anti-philanthropist' by historian Jacques-Guy Petit) that he would later use it himself. It is well known that then, as now, prisons that were perceived as excessively 'lenient' or 'comfortable' were often singled out by elites seeking to coercively impose moral standards on the labouring classes, at a time when the latter were considered 'dangerous classes'. On the whole, however, Tocqueville's assessment of La Tour-Maîtresse was not without nuance, particularly given his unfavourable view of French prisons at the time ('I have no trouble saying that I find this prison infinitely superior to all the establishments of the same kind that I have visited in France'). He praised several aspects of the new Swiss prison, including staff supervision, health conditions, and specific features such as the way visits were organized. And while he found the regime too lenient, he went so far as to make the comment: 'If the Geneva penitentiary is not yet a good prison, it is at least very close to being one.'[2]

Named after the bastion tower that was incorporated into its architecture, Tour-Maîtresse had a reputation as a 'model' prison, causing it to attract the attention of philanthropists and other supporters of prison reform in Europe, earlier than

London's Pentonville Prison (chapter 2), and even prior to the Eastern State Penitentiary in Philadelphia, which did not open until 1829. When Tocqueville and Gustave de Beaumont were sent on their famous trip to the United States, Tour-Maîtresse (like Millbank in England, which we will encounter in chapter 2) was more influential in Europe than its American forerunners Walnut Street and Auburn. It owed this to a number of distinctive features, which legal scholar Robert Roth analysed in his landmark study, where he makes passing mention of the fact that prison reform had historically been the preserve of small political communities, or even micro-states: so after Amsterdam and Philadelphia, now it was Geneva, marked by a strong Quaker influence. The distinctiveness of Tour-Maîtresse was encapsulated by a detail in how it was characterized: the prison was specifically referred to as a 'penitentiary', in French a *prison pénitentiaire*. This adjective alone signalled a new era, at least in terms of penal doctrine. The optimism surrounding the construction of the prison did not prevent debate and opposition, including disagreement about the relevance of this term.[3]

First and foremost, Tour-Maîtresse represented an 'imperfect but indisputable' implementation of the panoptic project – 'imperfect' because, strictly speaking, it was only an 'apparent semi-panoptic' that did not fully comply with the principle of constant surveillance, yet 'indisputable' because it was the 'first European panoptic creation', according to Michelle Perrot. This is why it was in reference to the Panopticon that it was presented in a short film by Caroline Cuénod. The 'father' of Tour-Maîtresse was Étienne Dumont, who passed away in 1829, not long after the completion of his work. A theologian by training, Dumont admired and emulated Jeremy Bentham, a personal friend whose works he published in French translation. Personifying a synthesis or convergence of English utilitarianism and Genevan Calvinism, he was a moderate who, frightened by the progress of the French Revolution, made only a brief appearance in the Constituent Assembly at the beginning of 1793. He was, so to speak, the travelling salesman of Bentham's 1787 text *Panopticon*, whose French version (1791) we owe to his zeal. Bentham's contribution to the design of the Geneva prison was therefore indirect, and also only partial. Let us not forget that under the guise of perfect rationality, Bentham's project was actually utopian and contained an element of fantasy. Dumont was more pragmatic. He sorted things out, for example giving priority to the function of confinement over the principle of visibility promoted by his mentor. *Panopticon*'s influence on Tour-Maîtresse was nonetheless decisive, especially as the architectural and doctrinal aspects cannot be separated. From the outside, the mere sight of the prison was intended to act as a deterrent for potential offenders.[4]

The Geneva prison was by no means built on a whim. On the contrary, it was conceived over a long period and gave rise to a level of reflection that few prisons – and, indeed, few social institutions here or elsewhere – have attracted. This unique characteristic set it apart from other prisons of its time. This goes to show just how misguided it would be to attribute its failure to haste or indifference. The designers of the Geneva penitentiary were well aware of the previous incongruity between what had been intended and what had been achieved in the area of prisons. Their intention was to finally reconcile intention with realization. The promoters of Tour-Maîtresse were aware of the previous experiment of Walnut Street. They also enquired into similar contemporary experiments, starting with Millbank. If there was in fact an element of utopia in this project, as there was in others, this should not be taken to mean that its promoters were chasing a fantasy. The project was intended to be rational (and eventually 'scientific'), based on architectural, mechanical, statistical, and medical knowledge.[5]

Tour-Maîtresse was not just a model prison, but also a 'symbolic prison'. In the eyes of its promoters among the enlightened elite of Geneva, it possessed a special value. Its construction was intended to symbolize an ideological, political, and even moral shift, corresponding to the advent of a new era of social progress. It was supported by a parliament that had become predominantly progressive, in an intellectual climate of intense bourgeois-liberal sociability. The intellectual influences were manifold, combining Calvinism, utilitarianism, liberalism, Rousseauism, Quakerism, progressivism, philanthropy, and Anglophilia, as Geneva intellectuals kept abreast of the latest developments in British prisons. Legalism too: not only was the prison brought about by a well-crafted law passed in March 1822, but its opening three years later was accompanied by another law that could be viewed as something of a 'penitentiary bible'. In this respect, Dumont advocated an unusual position: prison reform should precede, not follow, penal reform. A virtuous prison was an essential requirement for any sensible criminal law. What better way to express the central place that prisons now occupied in the arsenal of punishment?

The regime that was supposed to prevail within the prison walls also merits some attention. While the Philadelphia paradigm was generally dominant in Europe, Tour-Maîtresse was theoretically governed by an updated Auburnian system. Tocqueville did not consider this to be a genuine import of the American penitentiary system, as interaction between prisoners during the day was not prohibited in Switzerland. Yet this new system was perceived as 'highly perfected', to the extent that distinguished European observers like Carl Mittermaier and Charles Lucas regarded Geneva as a distinct prison model in its own right – on a par with, and even superior to, Auburn and Philadelphia – due to its having synthesized their best features. Since then, it has tended to be regarded as an Auburn-like system reconfigured through a classification scheme that, even before Pentonville, laid the groundwork for the progressive system that includes the varying of imprisonment conditions based on the stage of incarceration, and the possibility of sentence reductions for 'good behaviour'. It was therefore a pioneering prison, even if its innovative nature remained largely theoretical. By the early 1840s, the prison had largely embraced the usual Auburn-style approach based on silent group work during the day and individual confinement at night. In this regard, one should not be misled by the term 're-education', which already betrayed a class perspective. Harsh discipline prevailed under that guiding principle. Significantly, the prison's first warden (from 1825 to 1842), Christophe Aubanel, was a former policeman and a supporter of the panoptic system. Though physical punishment was apparently limited, enforcement relied heavily on measures like 'absolute silence, shackles, uniforms, and of course disciplinary sanctions'.[6]

From '*bijou* prison' to four-star hotel

'*Bijou* prison', 'boudoir'. . . Tocqueville showed a flair for analogy unmatched by his successors. In the nineteenth century, new prisons were often likened to palaces when being criticized for their 'comfort' and even their 'luxury'. A major French parliamentary inquiry between 1872 and 1875 quoted a man called Blanqui who, in 1848, had described Loos-les-Lille Prison in northern France as a clean, well-ventilated, well-heated, well-stocked palace. In short, a much more enviable place than the 'squalid basements inhabited by the spinner labourers of Lille'. As one might guess, this was not the revolutionary Auguste Blanqui, but rather his elder brother, economist Adolphe Blanqui. His words expressed a version of the principle of 'less eligibility', which says that in order for prison to be deterrent, a prisoner's life must be harder than that of the lowest paid 'free' worker.

In the twentieth century, conservatives were more inclined to compare prisons with leisure facilities or holiday camps. But today the most popular comparison is to a hotel, usually including a star rating: they are given three, four, or even five stars in the wildest exaggerations. Exactly when this hotel theme emerged is difficult to pinpoint. In any case, the modern world has breathed new life into the genre in two ways: first, by placing actual hotels inside penitentiaries, as in the cases of the Russian prison Kresty-2 (chapter 4) and the totally atypical San Pedro Prison in Bolivia; second, by converting former prisons into hotels – the opposite of Paris's Conciergerie, the royal palace that became a prison during the Revolution (counterpoint I). The former function of these buildings is readily used as a 'marketing pitch' for tourists.[7]

So was Tour-Maîtresse really a *bijou* prison? This mocking comparison says more about the social position of the person who drew it than it does about the prison. It is an understatement to say that one could find places that were more welcoming than those penitentiaries. All the more so since Tocqueville's judgement came on the brink of a shift in perception, when the 'liberal' years were fading and disappointment was settling in. The apparent legalism of the early days gave way to intimidation. After several amendments, the progressive prison law of 1825, which had coincided with that new institution, was ultimately supplanted by a harsh new law in 1841. Inside the walls, overcrowding became evident almost immediately after the prison opened, and all attempts at education were abandoned. Even the gradual arrival of doctors and psychologists at the end of that period was an ambivalent process. By this time, Geneva's model prison had long since lost its ephemeral prestige.

The proponents of this prison wanted to leave a lasting impression. Yet the result was quite the opposite. Once it had lost its ideological grounding and social basis, Geneva's achievement swiftly faded into obsolescence. Indeed, the contrast between the 'penal dream' and the 'penitentiary achievement' was so stark that it led to the demolition of Tour-Maîtresse in 1862, less than four decades after it had opened – a decision that speaks volumes beyond the written accounts. Moreover, not only was it quickly dismantled, but also its demolition was primarily motivated by urban planning considerations, with minimal debate or deliberation. Intellectuals keen on prison discipline had started turning their attention to agricultural penal colonies. In short, Tour-Maîtresse's existence was as brief as it was pioneering. In the end, it left so little enduring legacy that its history has largely been forgotten. All momentum for reform was lost, and when new projects emerged in the 1860s and 1870s – including those by Tour-Maîtresse's architect Samuel Vaucher-Crémieux – they were quickly abandoned. In 1872, a Geneva lawyer put it this way: 'Those interested in prison reform should no longer look to Geneva for a model.'[8]

Chapter 2

Pentonville, London (England, 1842)

Pentonville Prison in 1842
Source: Chronicle/Alamy

According to historian and architect Robin Evans, Pentonville Prison was 'not only the most advanced prison, but the most advanced building of its time'. He further explains that this 'national monument' has left its mark not just on the history of prison architecture, but also on architectural history in general. By all accounts, Pentonville is indeed one of the most imitated prisons of all time. It was nicknamed 'Model Prison' while being designed, even before getting its official name, and the label stuck after the new London institution came into operation in 1842. As soon as it opened, Pentonville became the new 'penitentiary Mecca', the 'darling of prison reformers and a place of pilgrimage for architects of the day'. These words say it all. Significantly, in his book *A Just Measure of Pain*, Michael Ignatieff made it the subject of the first chapter, simply entitled 'Pentonville'.[1]

Authors eager to distance themselves from Foucault have been keen to argue that this prison and its radial layout actually had a far greater impact on subsequent prison developments than Bentham's Panopticon, which essentially remained on the drawing board. For example, Clive Emsley notes that 'the development of prisons, and particularly of the new penitentiaries, often advanced with only passing reference, if any, to Bentham's plans'. However, this detail should not downplay Bentham's influence on Pentonville in its intention (if not its shape): to turn 'an issue of psychology into an issue of mechanics', as Evans pointed out, 'to make architecture the instigator of virtue'. Paraphrasing Montesquieu, it could be said that from this perspective, power was supposed to be exercised through the proper arrangement of things – not of the legislative system or even the institutional organization, but rather the material arrangement in the most physical sense. What Jacques-Guy Petit wrote about that same period in France applies even more to Pentonville: the 'utopian prison', he explained, 'consists in this case not so much of the idea of a moralizing prison, but rather the belief, similar to Bentham's theories, that the moral improvement of prisoners can be determined by a machine-space [*espace-machine*]'. This image echoes Ignatieff's judgement that Pentonville 'was run like a machine'. It was a machine designed to break bad habits, but it would soon break down itself.[2]

Pentonville's extraordinary influence acted at four levels: national, imperial/colonial, European, and global. Nationally, the UK Parliament was so pleased with the feedback on Pentonville that within a few years, dozens of prisons or prison extensions had been built on the same model. One example is Hull Prison, which Pentonville's designer – Joshua Jebb, an architect and engineer by training – decided to revamp after visiting it. By 1849, Hull included a twenty-two-cell 'model' unit. This 'transplant' was not an unqualified success: three years later, the prison governor himself confessed that he preferred Dublin's Mountjoy Prison, from which he had just been transferred. Yet Mountjoy, opened in 1850, was itself modelled on Pentonville and also designed by Jebb. This shows that the entire British prison system was redesigned along the lines of Pentonville, with some fifty facilities built or renovated from the 1840s to the 1860s, including the Belfast House of Correction. According to Evans, 'The model became the norm.' Moreover, Pentonville was part of a network of self-designated 'model' institutions (covering education, housing, and sanitation) that were designed not only for replication but also for innovation, experimentation, emulation, and exhibition. As Tom Crook has argued, these institutions must be understood together as 'a key technology of social reform'.[3]

In imperial and colonial terms, Pentonville served as a prison paradigm for the British Empire, which itself played a major role in the global spread of the corrective penal system. Malta was a forerunner in this respect, compared to Burma, for example, or even India, where the influence of the London model became apparent only later. Corradino Prison, which opened in 1850, was built at the turn of the 1840s on the Pentonville model. However, its purpose was not really to combat crime. There was already an existing prison meeting that quantitative 'need'. The real aim of the new prison was to assert imperial authority and ensure sovereignty over colonized subjects overseas. It was a matter of reproducing colonial domination, even if this meant making some adjustments to the prison framework, particularly to add elements of local Catholic culture. This example is a reminder that reproduction does not necessarily mean identical replication pure and simple. Importing a model, including

Pentonville in relation to the earlier Pennsylvania standard, has generally involved changes to suit local conditions, or adaptations to keep up with technological progress. As Mira Rai Watts points out when concluding her case study of Bengal, 'Several decades of experimentation in the subcontinent resulted in prisons with loose ties to the Western world, with physical and operational formats decidedly different from those of Western prisons.'[4]

Pentonville also stands as a paradigm at the European level, even if concrete achievements were slow to follow. Analysing the power relations among various actors in Prussia between 1820 and 1860, Thomas Nutz explains that in the early 1840s, Frederick William IV made prison reform a key issue in the midst of a debate over the respective merits and shortcomings of the Philadelphian and Auburnian systems. Typically for that period, the new monarch believed modern prisons were a sign of scientific and technical progress, like railways and steel bridges. Moreover, in a politically turbulent era, the fight against crime was a good way of asserting royal authority and Christian responsibility. The Prussian king visited Pentonville in 1842, before it had even opened, and returned enthusiastic, becoming one of the continent's strongest advocates for the Pennsylvania system. That same year, contrary to the counsel of some of his advisers, he ordered that all new Prussian prisons should follow Pentonville's example, as part of a complete overhaul of a system that would now be designed to compete with France and England. In particular, he called for a new prison to be built in Moabit, Berlin, that would be based on the London model in every respect: cell size, water supply, exercise yards, and so on. Other projects were to be added, and negotiations were even initiated with Joshua Jebb himself. But they were broken off for financial reasons, and then the revolutions of March 1848 brought these ambitions to a screeching halt. Ten years later, shortly before his death in 1857, the monarch barely managed to impose solitary confinement at 'his' model prison in Berlin.[5]

A half-century after the American models, Pentonville became the centre of international prison tourism. Visitors flocked from countries all over the world, including Russia and China. Tsar Nicholas I asked for the blueprints in order to study them. Representatives of the Qing dynasty visited the prison in the 1860s and came away in awe: this deep impression was to be repeated in the case of Beijing's first model prison, built at the turn of the twentieth century (chapter 7). Pentonville has influenced the design of prisons from Lima to Saint Petersburg, from Tokyo to Melbourne, from Buenos Aires to Conakry.[6]

This historical development is all the more remarkable if one considers, as historian Ernest Teagarden noted in the late 1960s, that the prison was supposed to be a one-off 'Victorian experiment', the prison system having been somewhat neglected in an era known for its (legislative) reform. In fact, Pentonville was not exactly the first of its kind. It was a reaction to the failure of buildings of the late eighteenth and early nineteenth century. Particularly hated was the squalid Newgate, the country's most (in)famous prison in the mid-eighteenth century. Angry London crowds had attacked this longstanding symbol of oppression during the Gordon Riots of 1780. Indeed, Newgate was seen as the epitome of hell on earth, with inmates crammed together under appalling conditions. (Its American namesake, officially 'State Prison of the City of New York', which opened in 1797 and was also designed as a model prison, quickly acquired the same reputation, and closed just three decades later.) Then came Millbank, the first national penitentiary, also in London on the site of the future Tate Britain gallery. Ironically, Millbank was already considered a showcase prison. The Penitentiary House Act, passed by Parliament in 1779, provided for the creation of new penitentiaries to subject certain categories of offenders to a structure that would both punish and correct them. This led to the construction of Millbank, which was modelled on the Ghent Reformatory. Despite many obstacles (including competition from colonial penal transportation, which was considered less costly, and initially worked in tandem with imprisonment), Millbank eventually made Newgate a symbol of a bygone era, even before Pentonville. Completed in 1816 but not fully operational until 1821, this impressive polygonal building was the first prison in the nation to use solitary confinement for inmates considered most amenable to reform. It soon became a disaster, however. Poorly designed from the outset, Millbank grew synonymous with physical illness and mental disorders (not to mention death). It was even shut down for a year in 1824 due to a scurvy epidemic, before being transformed into a depot for convicts awaiting transportation to Australia. Throughout the 1820s, inmates continued to rebel against its iron discipline. And so Pentonville was intended to succeed where Millbank had failed. . .[7]

Pentonville's impressive design and layout made it highly influential. When it opened, ten years before the Crystal Palace was built for the Great Exhibition in 1851, 'no other prison or penitentiary had ever been so meticulously contrived'. The aim of Pentonville was to usher in a new era, a specifically corrective one, in the context of prisons newly becoming the central penitentiary instrument over transportation to the colonies, which was declining at that time and would be abolished in 1867. The main proponent of the Pentonville model was prison inspector William Crawford. Supported by reformers and philanthropists, he had an earlier model in mind: the Eastern State Penitentiary, which had impressed him when he saw it during a visit to the United States as a military engineer. Joshua Jebb instead took Cherry Hill as his main reference, though he modified the model by incorporating other elements, for example from the reformatory in Rome and from the Panopticon. Even so, the principle of separation and even visual and acoustic hermeticism reigned supreme, both inside and out. Unlike the Panopticon, which Bentham thought should be open to the outside world, here closure to the world was clear. Out with the principle of publicity, in with actual secrecy. Nothing was left to chance within the walls, from heating to ventilation and lighting. Hygiene was paramount, so the corrupting effects of promiscuity had to be brought to an end. Order was seen as the only healthy thing, and the prison had many individual exercise and walking yards. There was also a certain educational ambition, which meant literacy training, but more importantly religious and moral instruction. Prison work, on the other hand, 'had been turned into an affliction, deliberately pointless, thereby breaking the vital connection between labor and industrial production at that time – and further splitting prisoners off from the rest of the population'.[8]

The principles advocated by John Howard – health, amendment, safety – were once again being applied, though not without some practical difficulties. For example, hygiene presupposes a minimum of openness, which is not easy to reconcile with the closure required for the atomization of the individual. Besides, times had changed, and while the legacy of the cardinal virtues was palpable, they were now somewhat different. New imperatives – classification, inspection, separation – were being superimposed over the old ones. The watchword 'reform' was replaced by 'treatment'. The reform of souls and bodies was newly driven by an aim of 'rationality'. The structure itself was designed to make the exercise of power and control over human beings more rational. If the cells had a water point, this was certainly for reasons of hygiene, but also for the smooth running of the place in general. The guiding principle was to instil psychology into Pentonville's mechanics, in order to turn it into a 'factory of virtue' – meaning harsh surveillance. Yet it was still possible to break out, as prisoner George Hacket demonstrated in 1850 when he made a sensational escape, baffling authorities and the press.[9]

Cutting-edge as it was, Pentonville's design was based entirely on 'functional austerity'. Its operation was meticulously regulated, as a 'total institution', in Erving Goffman's sense. As for the idea that the building's relatively reassuring, if not appealing, façade reflected its interior, Robin Evans calls this an 'architectural deception', given the harshness of the discipline within the prison walls, 'replacing the terror of physical pain with the bewilderment of solitude'. Its clearest expression was the rigid enforcement of the law of silence. Just 'a gesture, a sign, a smile or a whisper' was all it took to be sent to the 'dark cells in the basement' as additional punishment. The walls framed an ascetic and arduous life of work and prayer under constant surveillance. Solitude and silence induced apathy at best, regularly leading to madness or suicide. Cold and hunger were the norm, and corporal punishment was commonplace. During walks, prisoners were roped up and hooded in 'mask hats'. 'What we called deterrence or reform then, we would now call brainwashing,' claimed historian Ursula Henriques in the early 1970s. Before Foucault, she argued that reformers did not want punishment to be reduced, but rather made more refined and effective.[10]

The cruel irony is that if Pentonville was 'one of the controversial symbols of the age', this was not just because the principle of solitary confinement gave rise to mixed or conflicting views, as in the United States. It was also because, like other model prisons before and after, it was attacked from two opposing sides. While some judged it too harsh, others accused it of being too lenient, as Thomas Carlyle's criticism illustrates.[11]

Thomas Carlyle against 'model prisons'

In his 1850 satirical tract *Model Prisons*, Thomas Carlyle recalls his visit to a London penitentiary. 'Surely one of the most perfect buildings in London,' he writes sarcastically. In this vivid and ferocious attack on the 'liberal' prison, Carlyle (in a sense the anti-Dickens on the subject, the latter having strongly criticized the Philadelphia system after a visit in 1842) describes the prison as a 'palace' – a term also often applied to Reading Prison, opened in 1844 after Pentonville and later made famous through 'The Ballad of Reading Gaol'

(1898) by Oscar Wilde (who had been transferred there from Pentonville). From the refectory to the layout of the cells, from the teaching conditions to the purity of the air, Carlyle wrote, not without a good dose of exaggeration, 'everything is excellent, the ultimate in care and ingenuity; in my life I have never seen such a clean building; there is certainly no duke in England who lives in a mansion of such perfect and complete cleanliness'.

Obviously, Carlyle's 'enchanted' description was by no means an endorsement. His vitriolic irony expressed a reactionary critique of the 'syrupy and disastrous jargon of philanthropy' as part of a more general contempt for the absurdity of democracy. The text would attract withering comments from Marx and Engels, mocking 'a fury much greater, yet all the cheaper for being directed against those officially expelled from established society, against people behind bars; a fury which sheds even that little shame which the ordinary bourgeois still for decency's sake display'. At no point did Carlyle name the prison, and it has long been assumed to have been Pentonville, but there is some evidence to suggest that he was actually referring to the Westminster House of Correction, alias Tothill Fields, a prison of a much lower standard. One can only imagine the ire that Pentonville would have aroused in him. . .[12]

The myth of Pentonville was very soon tarnished. The model institution quickly came to resemble a warehouse for the disposal of 'unproductive' people and 'dangerous' classes. It is an understatement to say that it never managed to 'manufacture goodness in quantity' as it had promised. From the second half of the nineteenth century, Pentonville was condemned as a place of torture because of the cruelties inflicted there (particularly the use of the treadmill), but also because of the harmful effects that the separate confinement system had on the human mind. Internal prison documents prove that mental health issues were grossly downplayed in official statements and annual reports. As Catherine Cox and Hilary Marland wrote:

> When viewed through the prism of the mental disturbances that plagued separate confinement from the start, the Pentonville experiment failed. [. . .] Far from being a place of order, rationality, discipline, and unchallenged state power, the prison was marked on a day-to-day basis by the struggle to manage mania, delusion, depression, and despair. And in the end, the worryingly high incidence of mental disturbance – provoked or made worse by the prison's discipline – was a key factor in the rejection of the purest form of separation.

By the time a landmark sociological study was conducted in the late 1950s, the myth of Pentonville as a model prison had long since faded. Instead, it came to represent a bygone era of punishment. Meanwhile, hopes had shifted to young offenders' institutions and their efforts to present themselves as 'educational' centres.[13]

Pentonville's achievement looks anachronistic from today's perspective. The high regard in which the principle of separate confinement was held at the time, despite ongoing struggles over its strengths and weaknesses, was a historical culmination, but also the beginning of the end – 'the end of the movement for penal reform as Newgate had marked its beginning'. From this perspective, Pentonville heralded the collapse of the rehabilitative ideal (legally buried in 1877) and the emergence of the repressive trend that was to dominate the second half of the century. In *The Fabrication of Virtue*, Robin Evans championed the idea of 'uncoupling' the role of architecture and the goal of reform. He argued that, given the degree of innovation at Pentonville, the prison's failure could not be blamed on faults in its architectural design, since the experiment was the ultimate in the field and beyond. In any case, from that point on, the rhetoric of reform and amendment increasingly gave way to scepticism. When Wormwood Scrubs opened in 1875 (the last major English prison built in the nineteenth century, it was only completed in 1891), one could see that an effort had been made to soften its outward appearance as a penitentiary and blend in more with its surroundings. The point was no longer to stand out as a monument, but to be forgotten.[14]

Like Wormwood Scrubs, Pentonville was earmarked for sale by the British government in 2007, but the plan was subsequently scrapped. Unlike Reading, which was shut down in 2013 in order to be sold, the prison was still open ten years later in one of London's most deprived areas. Accounts from people who have spent time within its walls, including official spokespeople, describe an appalling situation. Once a symbol of pride, Pentonville has become a token of shame. Echoing the highly critical tone of a recent report by the Chief Inspector of Prisons (which Carl Cattermole of *The Guardian* called 'one of the most damning accounts I've read about British prisons – fiction included'), a former inmate, who wrote a survival guide for future prisoners after serving time in five penitentiaries, concluded in 2015: 'I've been in Britain's grimmest prisons, but Pentonville's the worst.' A few years later, the situation was still dire, and the slump seemed worse than ever. Today, to put it mildly, architects will need a great deal of imagination to contemplate 'unlocking Pentonville' through an 'architectural liberation' guided by values of social justice and emancipation.[15]

Counterpoint I

Models of (re)conversion

> For 115 years, Lukiškės Prison was guarded by high walls and barbed wire, but today the site is open to the public. From prison to artistic venue, a new version – Lukiškės Prison 2.0 – is home to 250 creators and artists, and a place where curious spirits can learn and explore. Sit down for a refreshing drink, attend a concert or take a tour to get a glimpse of life in the former prison. This unique space has become a star on the silver screen as well. The location easily transforms to depict various spaces, and has even served as the backdrop for Stranger Things season 4.

This description from the website Go Vilnius, which depicts the Lithuanian prison's 'rich history' as a journey 'from confinement facility to cultural venue', exemplifies a particular category of prison transformation. Lukiškės Prison is representative of a fundamental paradox in penal history: facilities that achieved recognition only after their operational failure. When they opened, these buildings were not regarded as model prisons – not even in rhetoric or on paper. In fact, some of them were particularly terrible places. Yet they have become post festum 'models' of a special kind: models of (re)conversion. In other words, these former prisons only found success or appreciation after they ceased to be places of detention and assumed a different role, as residential buildings, places of work, or recreational areas. In Vilnius, historian Nicolas Offenstadt described his mixed feelings when facing the festive conversion of Lukiškės Prison, given the institution's dark history as an antechamber to the Nazi massacre of Vilnius's Jewish population and later as a site for Soviet repression of Polish resistance movements. The site's modern transformation does not erase its history, which is documented and commemorated there, but it may, over time, risk fading from collective memory. Either way, the conversion of prisons reveals much about modern societies' ambivalence towards their carceral past.[1]

Historically, many prisons were themselves the result of functional conversions, particularly from religious establishments such as convents and monasteries. But the process has also worked in the opposite direction. As two historians ask rhetorically: 'Among visitors to Mont-Saint-Michel, who would know that the abbey was a prison until the early 1860s'? This circular historical trajectory – from religious building to prison to cultural venue – demonstrates how architectural spaces can be repeatedly re(de)fined, while their physical structures remain partly unchanged.[2]

At first glance, three distinct types of prison (re)conversion can be identified: commemorative, cultural, and commercial. While these approaches may appear mutually exclusive, arguably they are often complementary, even intertwined.

Some conversions have led prisons to assume prestigious new roles, as demonstrated by France's École nationale d'administration (ENA, now Institut national du service public), a renowned higher education institution that trains high-ranking civil servants. Initially based in Paris, in the early 1990s it was relocated to the site of Strasbourg's former Sainte-Marguerite Prison, which had served as a correctional facility from the 1730s to the mid-twentieth century. Similarly, the École nationale de la magistrature in Bordeaux, which trains magistrates, occupies a compound that has centuries of military and carceral history, and includes the Pennsylvania-style Thiac Prison, which opened in 1846 next to the courthouse. An academic building worth mentioning is the Maison des sciences de l'homme in the heart of Paris, which housed the École des hautes études en sciences sociales (EHESS) from 1970 on. It was built on the site of the former Cherche-Midi Prison, modelled on Auburn before it was demolished in 1966.[3]

Germany offers particularly illustrative examples of commercial recycling, driven in this context by the decline in the prison population since the 2000s and the subsequent closure of jails in several regions. In 2013, *Der Spiegel* reported that in some areas, prisons in valuable locations were being sold to private investors who planned to turn them into hotels, luxury apartments, or art venues. One entrepreneur purchased the former Stendal Prison in Saxony-Anhalt for 37,000 euros before investing over two million more in converting it into around thirty apartments. In Baden-Württemberg, two wealthy businessmen invested five million euros in turning the former prison in Offenburg into a hotel, preserving its original character in order to provide guests with a thrilling experience. In Martin Luther's home town of Eisleben, a former women's prison faced an uncertain fate in the 2010s, with proposals ranging from a budget hotel for pilgrims to a sex club. These transformations might seem anecdotal or even frivolous, but they provide valuable insights into prisons in the public sphere and popular imagination, as well as into the ability of private interests to profit from any opportunity.[4]

In recent decades, the conversion of former prisons into hotels or museums has become increasingly common. Some cases are particularly spectacular, such as the former Ushuaia penitentiary – the world's southernmost prison in the deep south of Argentina – where actors dressed as inmates serve as tour guides. But there are dozens of examples around the world, ranging from Armagh Prison in Northern Ireland – built around 1780 and later renovated according to Pentonville principles in the 1840s and 1850s (chapter 2) – to the Saintlo Ottawa Jail Hostel (formerly Nicholas Street Gaol until the early 1970s), to Broad Street Prison in Nigeria, which was repurposed as a multi-functional leisure centre in 2010. Some former prisons have been transformed into luxury accommodation or fancy hotels, such as the Malmaison in Oxford, England, and the Four Seasons Istanbul in Sultanahmet, Turkey. In France, a prime example is the conversion of the former Béziers Prison into a three-star hotel. Slovenia's Hotel Celica in Ljubljana was once a military prison, but is today a youth hostel with a cultural bent, featuring vibrant interiors, now housing artists rather than guards and inmates. Some establishments strategically exploit the symbolic power of their names, as in the case of Alcatraz Hotel in Kaiserslautern, Germany, and the Liberty Hotel in Boston, United States. In Australia, Melbourne's Pentridge Prison has retained its original designation despite its transformation into an entertainment venue.[5]

Some conversions, whether completed or merely proposed, are particularly striking in the way they are quick to incorporate the weighty history of dictatorship and/or colonialism into new commercial or touristic incarnations, paying little attention to the need for an appropriate transition. In the early 2000s, Hong Kong authorities sought to repurpose Victoria Prison, which was still operating in its incongruous location among high-rise buildings and skyscrapers. Initially conceived as a commercial and touristic development similar to Covent Garden, it ultimately became an arts centre. In Valparaíso, Chile, the former prison Cerro Cárcel, which held political prisoners during Augusto Pinochet's regime, was transformed in the 2010s into the Parque Cultural de Valparaíso, an official cultural venue. Uruguay's Punta Carretas Prison provides another spectacular example. Within a few years of closing – an event that served as a powerful symbol of political demilitarization – it had become a temple to consumerism, housing dozens of shops. By the mid-1990s, it had come to exemplify the zealous embrace of neoliberal globalization and a forceful break with the past. Victoria Ruetalo interprets this as a reverse allegory of class struggle: whereas the prison once excluded inmates from society by confining them *inside* an isolated space, the shopping centre now excludes the poor by keeping them *outside*.[6]

There are several conversion projects worthy of special consideration, even though they were abandoned, suspended, or altered. In France in 2010, Avignon's city council purchased the former Sainte-Anne Prison (adjoining the Palais des Papes), which had been vacant since closing in 2003. The council intended to sell it to a multinational hotel corporation that was proposing to transform it into a luxury hotel. But when the agreement fell through, only minor renovations were carried out, in order to provide an unconventional setting for a contemporary art exhibition in 2014. It was ultimately converted into a residential estate. In such cases, written traces and physical remains of the carceral past are usually removed: the primary aim of the conversion is not to commemorate, and this past is often treated as a burden to shed.[7]

But in some cases, the approach is quite the opposite. In France, the Conciergerie is probably the oldest and most well-known example. This former medieval palace was transformed into a prison for the Parliament of Paris in the late fourteenth century. It remained an important detention facility during and after the French Revolution, and continued as a prison until 1934, though part of it was turned into a museum as early as 1909. Less well known, but more unusual, is the case of the GwinZegal art centre in Guingamp. Resulting from the bold restoration of one of France's first cellular prisons, which had become more or less derelict, it opened in 2019, and became a national art and culture education institution in 2021. Guingamp Prison was originally built from 1836 to 1840. Designed under the influence of prison inspector Charles Lucas, it was a small local jail that was supposed to epitomize new penitentiary ideas. The press kit available at the inauguration of the art centre suggested that the conversion entailed both rupture and continuity, since the prison originally had a supposed 'humanistic' aim, as the cultural venue also has today. This is a questionable stance that raises thorny ethical questions, if only because the word 'humanistic' is vague.[8]

More than a decade ago, social scientist Michael Welch embarked on an unusual transcontinental exploration of former prisons converted into museums, from Buenos Aires to Sydney, from Johannesburg to Seoul. His resulting book, *Escape to Prison*, reveals not so much penitentiary utopianism as the ambivalence of modernity: prison museums claim to represent progress and rationality, yet their exhibits simultaneously confront visitors with histories of suffering and social control. Connecting this phenomenon to 'dark tourism', in which sites of historical violence are repackaged as heritage attractions, Welch further argues that such encounters are inseparable from commerce and commodification. As he notes, Eastern State Penitentiary exemplifies the trend. This iconic institution has been welcoming eager visitors since 1994. But who would ever have imagined that 'America's Most Historic Prison' would not only house an educational-cultural centre, but also host 'Halloween Nights' marketed as an 'immersive experience', with tickets starting at forty dollars? Alcatraz still stands as another pre-eminent example, attracting approximately one and a half million visitors annually since it became a tourist destination in 1972.[9]

Citing these figures, Alana Barton and Alyson Brown highlight the inherent ambiguity of this process, particularly when it comes to prisons that are still in operation, such as Dartmoor in England or Kresty in Saint Petersburg, Russia, which was temporarily opened to visitors (chapter 4). Paradoxically enough, the transformation of prisons into museums – or the 'museumification' of prisons – might have the effect of increasing rather than diminishing the general public's ethical indifference to incarceration, since it could dull critical reflection instead of sharpening it. This is especially problematic in profit-driven contexts in which people are hardly encouraged to give thoughtful consideration to these spaces, whose function is (or was) far from trivial. Exhibitions can also surreptitiously convey a biased message in favour of (more) prisons. As Justin Piché and Kelvin Walby point out, 'in most cases, the meanings produced in former prisons transformed into museums in Canada reproduce the idea that incarceration is necessary for the protection of society, and that today's contemporary confinement practices are more humane and respectful of prisoners' rights than in the past'. It is to avoid such pitfalls that French historian Philippe Artières calls for a 'critical patrimonialization' of former prisons, with a view to educating, not entertaining.[10]

Chapter 3

La Santé, Paris (France, 1867)

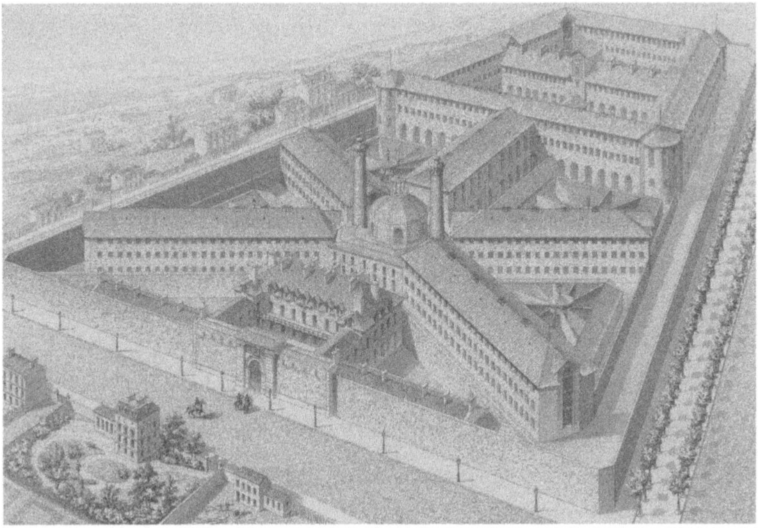

E. Gaudrier, La Santé Prison, 1880s (aerial view)
Source: PWB Images/Alamy

July 2014. La Santé prison in Paris was emptied of its inmates, who had been transferred to other jails. Five years of renovation work were about to begin on a facility that had often been threatened with closure, but was still standing. Known for its dilapidation, condemned on numerous occasions, sometimes even deemed to epitomize the ills of the entire French penal system, La Santé could no longer accommodate prisoners in conformance with European Union rules on safety and dignity. French newspaper *Le Monde* called this temporary closure a 'turning point in the history of French prisons'. As a remnant of the reform movement of the mid-nineteenth century, La Santé has the image of an obsolete anomaly a century and a half later. It was in this prison that the '*affaire Vasseur*' began in January 2000, a political uproar that, unusually, brought French prisons into the media spotlight for several months. *Le Monde* published advance extracts from a book by Véronique Vasseur, the prison's former head medical officer. In what would soon become a bestseller, she wrote: 'La Santé is a city within a city, full of dirt, misery, disease and depravity. . . Illogical, irrational, incomprehensible, it's a world apart, cut off from life.' Politically, the book was actually quite innocuous. It blamed no one in particular for all of that misery, and lacked a critique of capitalism and the state, which had been the cornerstone of prison censure three decades earlier. But its impact was undeniable. Lawsuits were filed in the period between its publication and the beginning of renovation works, and in 2006 a crumbling wing was closed.[1]

This state of decay was a reversal of the image that prevailed at the time when the prison opened. As early as 1983, French sociologist Michel Fize noted:

> In the years following its inauguration on 20 August 1867, the Maison d'Arrêt et de Correction de la Santé was considered to be a 'model prison'. It offered the best conditions in terms of ventilation, hygiene, cleanliness, light, space . . . and security. This is why it was praised so highly. All observers commented that the new prison was astonishingly modern, and undoubtedly one of the most, if not the most, beautiful in Europe. Everything was advanced: prisoners had real beds, they could wash, there was heating [. . .], they had gas lighting. What's more, the prison had a kitchen equipped with the most modern facilities, a sewerage system – quite exceptional for the time – and large, bright workshops. In short, it was comfortable![2]

In a book published more than thirty years later, Fize presents the history of La Santé in terms of two shifts: 'from architectural splendour to gradually ugly buildings', and 'from the "good prison life" to appalling detention conditions'. La Santé is now infamously emblematic of the tragic fate of model prisons, which were once celebrated (at least by those who championed and designed them) but were soon to be reviled. Its seemingly contradictory name ('*santé*' meaning 'health') adds a symbolic layer to this historical contrast. It was thus named because it had access to what was then the Hôpital de la Santé (later renamed Sainte-Anne), and more broadly to reflect the hygienist drive of the time: to put an end to dirty prisons in a dirty city. La Santé was not the first 'model prison' of its kind in France. It followed in the footsteps of Petite-Roquette, and especially those of the Mazas Prison, which opened in 1850 and was soon described as a terrible place by various critics, including French statesman Georges Clemenceau, a physician by training. (Inspired by Pennsylvanian architecture, the prison was demolished prematurely less than half a century after it opened.) Mazas was the most direct influence on the layout of La Santé, but thanks to the skill of architect Émile Vaudremer, its design possessed a certain originality, if only in the peculiarities necessitated by the sloping terrain. Although it was Vaudremer's first achievement in that field, his design was widely praised, even after the failure of the experiment had become apparent. La Santé prison 'immediately became part of the corpus of remarkable buildings of the nineteenth century', as architectural historian Caroline Soppelsa writes. She adds:

> Surprising as this idea may seem to us today, in the mid-nineteenth century, La Santé prison was in fact a veritable laboratory for architectural innovation in the field of comfort in collective housing, which at that time was still confined to military barracks and hospitals, long before these technical advances appeared in the housing of the working classes. [. . .]

> At La Santé, the prisoners had central heating, individual toilets, bathing facilities, an ingenious collective food-provision service using underground networks, and a pneumatic guard-call system comparable to that used for servants in large bourgeois houses. . . All these features contributed to making the Vaudremer prison the most modern penal institution of its time.

According to Fize, it was an 'exceptional establishment in every respect'. Among other end-of-century improvements, he mentions that the pneumatic call-button was replaced with an electronic one.[3]

Adding to its uniqueness, La Santé also had a dual nature, in two senses. First, it was both a place of confinement (*maison d'arrêt*) and a penitentiary (*maison de correction*). This ambivalence was an idiosyncrasy of the French prison system at the time. Initially, it was almost two prisons in one, each having its own reference model: a Philadelphian section for remand prisoners, and an Auburnian section for convicted prisoners at the end of the century. (The former influence would prevail overall.) Administratively, both were under the same local authority. Physically, they were separate but linked by a connecting building that contained the infirmary and the chapel. Ultimately, they remained quite distinct, and arrangements were made between them to prevent all types of communication, even visual. Hence the architectural *tour de force* that turned a weakness (the sloping ground) into a strength: although the two sections were quite separate, the administrative building was on the same level as both of them.

Second, the prison stood in the shadows of both Jeremy Bentham and Antoine Lavoisier. Bentham's influence was on surveillance: the circular room on the ground floor of the central building was equipped with a window that provided a nearly panoptic view, while the chapel was visible to all. Meanwhile, the convicts' quarters were equipped with corner turrets designed to provide a panoramic perspective. The prison space had to be under tight and continuous control. And then there was Lavoisier's influence, visible in the physics of flows that determined the architectural design. Everything here had to do with movements, transfers, leaks, mixtures, circulations, pressures, and thresholds. Lavoisier himself took a personal interest in La Santé. In 1780, he designed a ventilation system, and devised an automatic waste drainage system that involved digging a canal around the prison. The latter system was groundbreaking in a city that was not to adopt mains drainage until the late 1880s. (It would, however, have the undesirable effect of serving as a conduit for the rats that were multiplying in Paris at the time.)[4]

La Santé was (intended to be) a dual-purpose prison because it was designed as a healing facility in addition to being a punishment machine. This was the dream of the early nineteenth century: to make prisons into healthcare facilities, on the model of the modern hospital; to turn prisons into 'moral infirmaries', where physical hygiene and moral virtue would go hand in hand.[5]

On modern hospitals and model prisons

Prison: a place of punishment and correction. Hospital: a place of treatment and healing. In contemporary descriptions, the division of roles seems clear. Since the closure of asylums – hybrid places that were part-prison and part-hospital – we have been faced with two institutions that have very different missions, though they do not serve essentially opposite purposes. Yet one of the achievements of critical historiography in the 1970s, beginning with David Rothman's *The Discovery of the Asylum* (1971), was to show how the modern histories of the hospital and the prison – distant legacies of Christianity – are inextricably woven into the broader history of confinement and discipline. From Holland's Rasphuis to France's Hôpital Général to England's Bridewell, the first houses of correction were a mixture, or at least one could say that a clear-cut institutional separation had not yet taken place. It should come as no surprise that a later edition of John Howard's famous book included an appendix on 'hospitals'. Less than two centuries later, Michel Foucault and colleagues described the hospital as one of the 'three great schemes' that contributed to the development of the penitentiary, the other two being the cell and the workshop. Since then, historians have painted a more hesitant picture, with Jacques-Guy Petit pondering: 'fortress, hospital, lazaretto, factory, monastery, panopticon? The French prison system has long been in search of its meaning and function.'

Without delving into a complex history, let us just focus on one point. With its therapeutic transformation between the late eighteenth and early nineteenth centuries, the function of hospitals in the modern sense (a place of healing, not just hospitality) became a defining element of so-called 'model prisons'. The exhortation of French physician Pierre Cabanis to turn prisons into 'infirmaries of crime' was only one of the most prominent expressions of a widespread hope. Far from being strictly separated, the two institutions are part of a shared historical movement. Both were conceived as 'healing machines' to combat contagion, as French psychiatrist Jean-Étienne Esquirol called them. The principles of both were set in stone through architecture.

In the second half of the twentieth century, when the therapeutic definition of 'confinement' revolved around the theme of 'treatment', this reflected the hope of converting the 'sordid business of punishing' into the 'fine profession of curing', to use Foucault's expression. It was the basis for legitimizing a prison whose legitimacy was increasingly called into question during the critical wave of the late 1960s. As early as 1887, Peter (Pyotr) Kropotkin, with his experience of imprisonment in Russia and France, was already turning the argument on its head: 'I do not mean, of course, that

> we ought to substitute lunatic asylums for prisons. Far be it from me to entertain this abhorrent idea. Lunatic asylums are nothing else but prisons; and those whom we keep in prisons are not lunatics, nor even people approaching the sad boundary of the borderland where man loses control over his actions. Far be from me the idea which is sometimes brought forward as to maintaining prisons by placing them under pedagogists and medical men.'[6]

La Santé was untimely in at least one respect. When it opened in the waning years of the Second Empire, the historical apogee of the quest for the right kind of prison had already passed. Moreover, the prison authorities adopted solitary confinement (only partially in practice) at a time when it was being discredited as ineffective, unfair, and especially too costly. Abandoned in 1853, it did not make a comeback until two decades later, when the 1875 French Prison Act on 'individual custody' was passed. La Santé was therefore either late or early, depending on your point of view. This question of timeliness reflected another, more far-reaching matter: the decline of the philanthropic ideal, crushed or transformed by renewed repression in that period, when prisons were being abandoned to the sole function of coercion. This shift also reflected a reduction in the range of penal options, with the parallel rise of deportation and transportation – methods that were not mutually exclusive, since imprisonment could serve as a springboard for deportation, as in the case of French revolutionary figure Louise Michel, who was sent to New Caledonia in 1873.

Within the walls of La Santé, the authorities administered the usual disciplinary 'potion' that characterizes a total institution by definition: moral (religious) instruction, work, and silence in the case of convicts, and the control of space, time, movement, and speech. The prison did its best to maintain its reputation for innovation as long as possible. For instance, in 1873, it became the site of the first central prison infirmary in the Seine department, equipped with 'modern' surgical facilities. Twenty years later, the École supérieure pénitentiaire, the leading national training centre for prison guards, was also established there. Getting a bit carried away, albeit with some caveats, Michel Fize used generous and sometimes florid expressions to describe how the 'good life' at La Santé lasted for several decades, right up to the First World War. He goes so far as to say that it was a time when life in the prison was 'beyond reproach'.[7]

In the early twenty-first century, La Santé prison holds a special place in the popular imagination, for a number of reasons. Its peculiar name is obviously one of them. Another is the list of personalities who have been imprisoned there, from revolutionary political prisoners to celebrities, not to mention some prominent CEOs of the 1990s. Its 'special section', which housed prisoners benefiting from a 'special (prison) regime', served as a model for other French prisons in the twentieth century, thought it did not have the aura of legend that surrounded Sainte-Pélagie, where many writers and artists served sentences, including Aristide Bruand, Gustave Courbet, and Gérard de Nerval. From the late nineteenth century, it also housed another separate section for prisoners sentenced to death. One could see the silhouette of the guillotine outside its walls from the end of the nineteenth century to the late 1930s, and the last execution took place there as late as 1972. Furthermore, since the closure of Petite-Roquette in 1974, La Santé has been the only prison within the city limits of Paris. It has remained because of its proximity to a hospital, as mentioned, but also because it is close to the Paris law courts. Nevertheless, its demolition was being considered as early as the late 1950s, by which time it had long ceased to be regarded as a model prison. Demolition was considered again in the following decade, when Fleury-Mérogis prison was built (chapter 10), and it was discussed yet again in the 1980s because of its dilapidation.[8]

In some ways, La Santé is part of France's cultural heritage. It is still up and running after reopening in 2019. During its closure, a familiar refrain was heard: the conservative press was furious, repeating the old theme of the 'four-star' prison, while mainstream progressives kept their fingers crossed. 'Let's hope La Santé will become a model once again, and this step forward will improve prison conditions in France,' wrote the lawyer and former French Minister of Justice Robert Badinter, after whom the new local multimedia library was named. It is hard to share his confidence. Although history may not prove anything, in this case it at least encourages scepticism. As a matter of fact, a year after the prison reopened – and two decades after the '*affaire Vasseur*' – *Le Monde* reported some of the same old issues, including overcrowding on the prisoners' side and understaffing on the employees' side. But some things are changing: the walls of the prison governor's office are now decorated with posters of the punk rock band The Clash.[9]

Chapter 4

Kresty, Saint Petersburg (Russia, 1892–3)

Kresty Prison (aerial view, 2016)
Source: Andrew Shiva via Wikipedia Commons (CC BY-SA 4.0)

2016: a major prison overhaul is underway in Saint Petersburg. Thousands of inmates are about to be transferred to a brand-new prison, already billed as the largest in Europe, even larger than the gigantic Fleury-Mérogis in France (chapter 10). This one has a capacity of 4,000 and is largely automated. It is said that there will be no watchtowers, but it will have lifts, a concert hall, a sauna, as well as a shooting range for surveillance staff. In short, it will virtually be a miniature city, which even manages to revive one of the oldest clichés, the hotel analogy, though this time there is an element of truth to it: a guesthouse for visitors will be integrated *within* the prison walls. The name of this prison complex sounds a bit like the title of a B movie sequel: Kresty-2.

According to a dispatch from Agence France Presse in 2014: 'The new Russian facility is due to replace Saint Petersburg's infamous Kresty Prison, a red-brick landmark that has housed some of Russia's most high-profile prisoners during its 120-year history.' This replacement is also a removal – a move to the outskirts of the city. It is no coincidence that this second 'cross' (*krest* in Russian, in both the architectural and religious sense) is located in a remote suburb of Saint Petersburg, some thirty kilometres away, unlike the first one, which sits in the heart of the city and is visible to tourists taking summer river cruises down the Neva. This displacement reflects a general trend of relocation to the periphery that can also be observed in many other countries, often for purely economic reasons, land being cheaper outside urban centres. But there was also a more urgent motivation in this case. In the run-up to the 2018 World Cup, the central location of the old, overcrowded Kresty Prison – constantly referred to as 'infamous' or 'gloomy' – was inconvenient, even embarrassing, both materially and symbolically. The prison closed for good in 2017.[1]

Panopticon; or, the Inspection-House was written in Russia, Samuel Bentham having arrived there in 1780 before his brother Jeremy paid him a long visit in 1786–7. Their original aim was to establish the famous Panopticon there, but this did not exactly happen, although not for lack of trying. A little-known panoptic institution was built in Saint Petersburg in 1807–9 on the banks of the Okhta River, but it was made of wood and destroyed by fire in March 1818. As Roger Bartlett has shown, Saint Petersburg was actually the site of the only panoptic building to be constructed under the supervision of the Bentham brothers themselves. Known as the 'Panoptical Institute', 'Panoptical

Institution', or 'Okhta College of Arts', the establishment was completed in 1809 and began accepting apprentices. This technical boarding-school, which had workshops devoted to ship design, was arguably a disciplinary institution, but not a prison. When it comes to prison, Russia did not get the Panopticon, but it got Kresty.[2]

Located in the Vyborgsky District, Kresty was an unusual prison, at least by Russian standards. Its name derives from the cruciform design of its red-brick buildings – an adaptation of the radial model dear to John Haviland. Those buildings converged on the St Alexander Nevsky church, which was closed by the Bolsheviks in the wake of the October Revolution. By most accounts, this design was the work of architect Antony (Anatoliy) Tomishko, who had been deeply impressed by Germany's Moabit Prison. However, architect and historian Norman Johnston wrote that Émile Gilbert, the designer of the French Mazas Prison, was involved, even drawing the blueprint in 1884. As for the actual construction, like some American prisons, it was built at least in part by the inmates themselves.[3]

Built during the reign of Alexander III, Kresty was initially known as the main detention centre for remand prisoners. Supposedly a pre-trial, short-term jail, it soon became a Tsarist political prison for real or perceived opponents of the regime, while also holding ordinary criminals. It subsequently never really stopped being used as a political prison, notably after the Revolution of 1905. Numerous activists, radicals, and liberals were incarcerated there, from Bolshevik leaders, including Leon Trotsky, who had already experienced Madrid's *modelo* (counterpoint III), to Alexander Kerensky, head of the Provisional Government after the February Revolution. It retained this role of political repression throughout its history. Countless dissidents of all kinds were locked up there, especially during Stalin's purges. In the early 1930s, a zoologist arrested along with other scientists gave an account of this special prison (from which he said hardly anyone was ever released) under the control of the secret police. Prisoners were crammed into single cells, under appalling, unhygienic conditions, with no water or toilet, only a washbasin – as was the case in many other prisons, including some in France much later. Suicides were common in that den of terror. In *The Gulag Archipelago*, Aleksandr Solzhenitsyn refers to Kresty several times. At one point, he estimates that in 1932 alone, it is likely that up to a thousand prisoners were summarily executed there.[4]

And yet, when it officially opened in 1892 or 1893 (the date even fluctuates between 1890 and 1894 depending on the source), Kresty's reputation as a model prison was well deserved. Not only was it the largest in Europe, housing some 1,150 inmates – a very large number for the time – but it was also exceptionally modern in light of the country's standard of living. Lenin, who relied on prisons as revolutionary breeding grounds, famously said: 'Communism is Soviet power plus the electrification of the whole country.' As it happened, Kresty already had electric lighting, hot water, and a state-of-the-art ventilation system. Olga Strelkova, in her article examining the past, present, and future of the prison – and dispelling a few myths along the way – reports that a monument to John Howard stood in Kresty's courtyard.[5]

A model, an experiment, and a symbol: the Shlisselburg Fortress

Based on the memoirs of Vera Figner, a 'populist' who was imprisoned in the fourteenth-century Shlisselburg Fortress from 1884 to 1904, historian Philippe Artières has told the story of its renovation. He describes it as a 'model', as well as an 'experimental' and 'symbolic' prison. These characterizations should not mislead us about the terrible reputation of this island-based political prison, where influential figures of anarchism and communism such as Mikhail Bakunin and Sergey Nechayev were locked up. In the 1880s, this fortress became the symbol of Tsarist imprisonment. In the late

> nineteenth century, it was nicknamed the 'Russian Bastille'. Its rules were extremely strict, although they varied depending on the period: isolation, constant surveillance, no talking, no noise, no writing, and so on. Another socialist activist, Emma Goldman, described this 'House of the Dead' as 'the even more dreadful tomb of the political enemies of Tsarism' compared to the already dreaded Peter and Paul Fortress. 'How cruel and perverse the human mind which could create a Schlüsselburg!' she wrote in the 1920s (using the German spelling). 'Verily, no savage could be guilty of the fiendish spirit that conceived this appalling tomb. Cells built like a bag, without doors or windows and with only a small opening through which the victims were lowered into their living grave. Other cells were stone cages to drive the mind to madness and lacerate the heart of the unfortunates. Yet men and women endured twenty years in this terrible place. What fortitude, what power of endurance, what sublime faith one must have had to hold out, to emerge from it alive!'[6]

The opening of this prison is part of local, national, and international history. Locally, Kresty was not built from scratch. It was based on a jail for short-term sentences that had been in operation since the late 1860s – itself a converted wine warehouse dating back to the 1730s – in the context of the abolition of serfdom. But the previous jail soon proved overcrowded and unhealthy. Hence the reconstruction that began in the 1880s to create a prison based on isolation: this would be Kresty.

The construction of Kresty is also part of Russia's history of national prison reform. In this connection, Bruce Adams has pointed out similarities that bring Russia closer to the United States and Europe, countering the temptation to narrowly portray it as representing unqualified, backward 'alterity'. For example, the first Russian charitable prison society (the 'Prison Aid Society'), established in Saint Petersburg 'with enthusiasm and fanfare', dates back to 1819, the same year as the French

Société royale pour l'amélioration des prisons. And similarly to France at the same time, Russian prisons were under the supervision of the Ministry of the Interior. Although a new version of the Criminal Code was passed in 1845, it was the general abolition of corporal punishment in 1867 that marked the real advent of the penal prison in Russia and the beginning of the reformist movement in penal matters. After these initial measures, the country underwent a second round after 1879. A series of commissions found the silence imposed as part of the Auburn system to be cruel and antisocial. Between 1870 and 1890, numerous construction projects and renovations were carried out to solve the problem of overcrowding, before Kresty became a model for other prisons in the country – and beyond. It served as a template for Lukiškės Prison in Vilnius, Lithuania (completed in 1904 [counterpoint I]), and had a certain influence on the design of Fresnes in France a little later (chapter 5).[7]

The international context is also crucial to understanding the opening of Kresty. The prison was brought into service shortly after the Fourth International Prison Congress of June 1890 took place in Saint Petersburg – Russia's so-called 'window on the West'. Attended by representatives of twenty-six countries, the event aimed to show the world that Russia was as advanced as other nations, even when it came to prisons. Like his foreign colleagues, the delegate from the Russian prison authority stressed the importance of hygiene (including the access to baths), ventilation, heating, lighting, and (religious) education. Following the first congresses in Frankfurt (1846) and Brussels (1847), and a visit by Tsar Nicolas I to England, a committee had already been set up to design a cellular prison in Saint Petersburg based on the Pentonville model (chapter 2). But the project was abandoned for economic reasons: transportation to Siberia was deemed more cost-effective. As a rule, the West served as a reference. Russian reformers were explicitly inspired by European and American models, and sought to make the most of the Auburn and Pennsylvania systems.[8]

There was an element of anachronism in this. Russia embarked on a modern prison system at a time when enthusiasm in Europe was waning, giving way to a period of reflection on alternatives to imprisonment, or at least ways of limiting its use. The extent to which this Russian 'modernity' was achieved is of course a matter of debate. As always, there was a gap, if not a gulf, between actual practice and official goals. While Bruce Adams emphasizes the tangibility of progress in penal matters to challenge the dismissive stereotypes surrounding pre-1917 Russia, his analysis remains nuanced, demonstrating how reforms were only partial and limited in scope. At Kresty and other places of detention, the promised individual confinement was short-lived due to overcrowding. What is more, Kresty would become an (O)GPU (Soviet secret police) facility in 1923, and its name would come to be associated with Stalinist abuses, the adjacent clinic being used as a torture chamber. During the 1960s, Kresty would become officially known as 'Investigative Isolator No. 1 of the Administration of the Federal Service for the Execution of Punishments for the City of Saint Petersburg'.[9]

A century after opening, Kresty's reputation – which occasionally extended beyond Russia's borders, such as when Greenpeace activists were imprisoned there in the mid-2010s – was appalling. After criminologist Roy King visited it in 1992, he reported that he found it extremely dilapidated. Built to hold 1,150 prisoners, then more than 3,000 after a refurbishment in the 1960s, it held 7,200 by the end of 1992. Cells measuring 7.5m^2 were packed with ten prisoners or more (even as many as fifteen), in suffocating conditions. More recent estimates have put the number of inmates at 10,000 to 12,000, making it one of the most overcrowded prisons in the world – the ultimate irony for what was supposed to be a beacon of individual custody. Nils Christie describes the awful overcrowding in the 1990s, and, in particular, the incidence of tuberculosis, which had reached epidemic proportions. In 1997, the Mayor of Saint Petersburg expressed shock after visiting the place. Vladimir Putin himself is said to have been disturbed by his visit to Kresty in 1999; he went so far as to plead for prison reform before the State Duma in 2001, a prelude to the creation of Kresty-2.[10]

In 1996, a museum that had been created within Kresty's walls a few years earlier was opened to the public. During 'weekend tours', you could visit the prison and its chapel, while Kresty was still an active prison, or rather a 'penal dustbin', as a journalist called it in 2001. At one point it was even 'the most popular prison tourism destination', according to a survey. That said, as long as this repository of human misery remained in operation, the city's website itself advised people to avoid it.[11]

The museum closed around 2010, supposedly only as a temporary measure, but the closure proved to be permanent. The fate of the original Kresty Prison then hung in the balance for years. In 2025, it was finally sold at auction to a property development company for over one billion roubles (more than £10 million). Describing its renovation as 'one of Saint Petersburg's most ambitious urban planning projects', the new owner pledged to breathe new life into the building by establishing a museum – ostensibly to preserve the prison's 'memory and history' – alongside a hotel, restaurants, and art galleries. Questions remain about the project's ability to serve as a meaningful memorial, rather than a commercialized attraction. As for the second Kresty, it is not hard to guess what its future holds. As Felix Ackermann writes, the transition was telling enough: 'The change over [*sic*] from Kresty to Kresty II has clearly revealed two important features of Putin's rule in Russia: state corruption and state violence.'[12]

Counterpoint II

Envisioned model prisons

It is a like never-ending quest. Just when you think the myth of the good, virtuous prison has finally run out of steam, new attempts are made to square the circle in the name of architectural innovation or functional improvement. The three examples that follow, which never got off the drawing board, share the declared desire to move beyond 'panopticism' and mere coercion. They reveal that the dream of the virtuous prison persists despite centuries of failure, adapting its rhetoric to contemporary sensibilities while reproducing many of the same fundamental contradictions.

In the early 2000s, a small British group, led by a 'social entrepreneur' with a background in the humanities, designed nothing less than a '21st-century model prison'. 'Our purpose is simple,' explained Hilary Cottam, director of the Do Tank: 'to design a new building to support a revolutionary regime at no extra cost and to slash reoffending rates by providing individual learning programmes.' Their slogan, 'learning works', was more than an abstract celebration of the virtues of education. It was an implicit reference to 'nothing works', coined by American sociologist Robert Martinson in the 1970s. Against Martinson's will, the unfortunate ambiguity of the phrase was later instrumentalized by neo-conservatives opposing social programmes and rehabilitative measures in prisons. By contrast, the British group's design promotes learning and training, based on what they call a 'live–work–learn model'. According to project architect Simon Henley, who gained an understanding of the realities of incarceration by visiting several prisons, the aim is to reverse the thinking behind the Panopticon and the radial model that he believes stems from it (farewell, Pentonville). This means fostering location-based activities (or 'nodes') within a facility made up of semi-autonomous physical units known as 'houses'. On the model of scattered housing, each of these units would accommodate a few dozen inmates, while others would even be placed outside the perimeter as part of their transition to freedom. The scheme is designed to avoid excessive fragmentation and provide a sense of community or group identity.[1]

This scattered layout is not meant to be similar to patterns inherited from the second half of the twentieth century. The aim is rather to depart from them. Along with a courtyard architecture, a chessboard structure is used as a diagram to 'radically rethink the prison', pairing black squares (as 'interiors') with white squares (as 'exteriors'). It is designed to allow a fluid circulation of people without needing to create a central roundabout. Its purpose is to channel the energy of prisoners and staff into useful activities, while ensuring a degree of internal freedom in a setting that is restricted but open, austere but not oppressive. The plan includes various facilities and amenities in cells and communal areas, with a library containing twenty thousand books available for borrowing, and cells linked to an internal computer network, ensuring the proper circulation of knowledge.

Structural differences aside, it could be argued that this concept(ion) does not differ from panoptic and radial designs as much as its proponents claim. First, it shares one of their essential characteristics: multivalence, adaptability. In keeping with Bentham's project, albeit unintentionally, the explicit aim is to design a generic model that applies not only to prisons but also to hospitals, universities, or supermarkets. This presents the risk of a lack of functional differentiation. Second, confidence in the 'invisible pedagogy' conveyed by the design is highly reminiscent of Pentonville's architectural wager. Moreover, the accompanying rhetoric that boasts the merits of this model prison for the new century is hardly charitable or humanitarian in tone, even when it evokes rehabilitation and the prevention of recidivism. Instead, it speaks the language of efficiency, management, profitability, and the rationalization of time and space. This also operates at the level of real estate and geography: the imagined prison has a small footprint of just one hectare, so as not to encroach too much on otherwise valuable land. Hilary Cottan made it clear that it was still a prison: 'The surroundings are no longer mentally and emotionally repressive, but they are spartan. This is a place that you would not choose to visit more than once. That single visit should equip you with skills, internal discipline and the potential for personal transformation.'[2]

During the same period, young French architect Caroline Charpentier took up the challenge by creating a little-known alternative prison design called Kanoptikon – from *kanôpos*, the name of both an Egyptian city and a funerary urn. Her whole aim was to counter the 'anti-urbanity' of prisons with a facility that would function as a 'micro-city' inside the walls, and an 'urban landmark' on the outside. From this perspective, instead of being concealed, a prison should be visible and well integrated into its surroundings. The design proclaims the importance of verticality, in contrast to a horizontality deemed pathological. This would take material form in a 56-metre tower, conceived in explicit opposition to Bentham. Designed as a 'communication tool', it would be a visible symbol in the city. Charpentier's starting point is that existing prisons, even so-called 'modern' ones, lack any ecological perspective or genuine consideration of the relationship between prison and city, for narrowly defined security reasons. Her approach stands in stark contrast to the prison building programmes that have prevailed in France since the 1980s, which have heavily relied on compartmentalization and fragmentation. The aim of the Kanoptikon is to give the prison a certain *urbanity*, in both senses of the word.[3]

To this end, footbridges and walkways are favoured as symbols of connection (between outside and inside, between the individual and the community), as are familiar spatial markers of urban life like signs. The architect explains that, contrary to traditional principles of prison architecture like atomization and separation, the whole programme is driven by an ideal of openness. Instead of surrounding and isolating the individual, the prison is organized like a miniature city, though its functionalities are certainly reduced. Spaces like a lecture hall or a room dedicated to culture or art would be placed at the interface between inside and outside in order to open up the building. In the same spirit, unlike the architectural model based on the nave, this prison provides for 'autonomous housing modules' inspired by Mauzac Prison (chapter 11).

A third prison that was dreamed up but never realized was supposed to be located in Saint-Julien-sur-Suran, in France's department of Jura. It was conceived as a modest-sized institution designed to rehabilitate individuals deemed harmless, with a focus on instilling a sense of responsibility. Free of bars or barbed wire, the prison was even to be connected to a shopping centre where inmates could work as they approached the end of their sentence. The aim was ostensibly consensual: to limit reoffending (the prison was even to be (nick)named 'Together Against Recidivism'), and to provide decent detention conditions, thereby reviving a village in demographic and economic decline. However, the project was particularly controversial, sowing discord among local residents. This turmoil temporarily ended in March 2012 with a public consultation ending in a vote, with 54% rejecting the proposal. This narrow defeat reflected a political divide. The fact is, it was an unusual plan, to say the least.

This prison initiative was not a public undertaking, but a private and very personal one. It did not come from the Ministry of Justice or the prison authorities – who greeted it with gritted teeth at every level – but was rather conceived by an unconventional ex-prisoner. Pierre Botton was a businessman who once had the ear of the media and some decision-makers. Nothing had predestined him to campaign for better prisons before he was convicted of a serious white-collar crime in the 1990s and subsequently underwent a traumatic incarceration. After the Ministry of Justice (quite surprisingly) approved his proposal to create a new model prison, the Syndicat national des directeurs pénitentiaires (National Union of Prison Directors) published an opinion piece in January 2012 warning of the risk of prison privatization. This article sought to shine a light on an opaque, exceptional process that could have had serious consequences in a realm where the profit motive was gaining ground. Challenging the proposed building's very characterization as a 'prison', the union called for it to be reclassified as a private rehabilitation structure, so it would not be mistaken for a public institution. A national spokesman publicly lambasted a 'somewhat incongruous, opaque project', an 'unidentified penitentiary object'.[4]

Yet this entrepreneur's dream seemed to be off to a good start. In the early 2010s, the opening of this unconventional prison was even announced for the near future by a supportive, even benevolent right-wing government. Botton was a friend of Nicolas Sarkozy, who was then President of France. He therefore had enough social capital to win support from large companies, politicians, and various business leaders and celebrities who promoted his project on television. The former businessman had come a long way since his descent into hell. In 2012, a decade after participating in the activities of a group called Mialet – bringing together former 'VIP inmates' (white-collar criminals, that is) – he published a book entitled *Moi, ancien détenu, bâtisseur de prisons nouvelles* ('Me, a Former Inmate, Builder of New Prisons'). Two years earlier, he had set up an association, 'Les Prisons du cœur', which was supported by several large French corporations. When it was presented in July 2011, his prison proposal had the support of foundations linked to major French companies. As a result, despite strong local and national opposition, the former money-maker had so many resources that he actually came close to building a model prison in accordance with his own wishes. Alas: even though Botton was heard by a special parliamentary committee exploring ways to combat prison overcrowding in 2012, his project was shelved at that time, with some harsh words from the new Minister of Justice about it being a fanciful, unreliable project.

These three projects illustrate various attempts at what could be called the contemporary resurrection of carceral utopia. Despite their divergence from traditional prison architecture, they share some of the fundamental contradictions that have plagued prison design since its modern inception. These unbuilt prisons reveal a persistent pattern in penal history: the belief that architectural innovation and wise design alone can overcome the fundamental contradictions of incarceration. From Bentham's Panopticon to contemporary 'humanistic' projects, every generation confronts the same essential issues: how to reconcile coercion with rehabilitation, security with dignity, isolation with reintegration. The failure of these projects to materialize is perhaps as instructive as their designs, suggesting that the good (not to mention the perfect) prison remains an unattainable ideal, not only because of a lack of 'resources', but also because the institution itself cannot reconcile its conflicting social aims. Other attempts at groundbreaking prisons continue to be made, with varying degrees of sophistication. But they fall prey to what geographer Olivier Milhaud calls the 'spatialist temptation': that is, the delusion that a shrewd and fair organization of space can in itself resolve social contradictions and pathologies, when in reality it can do little more than reflect them.[5]

Chapter 5

Fresnes (France, 1898)

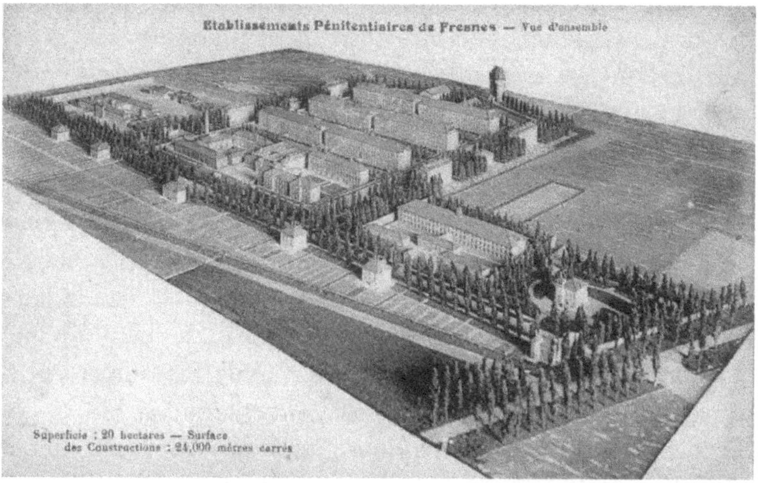

Fresnes Prison (early twentieth century)
Source: *Criminocorpus*, Christian Carlier series

Fresnes Prison is a monument in the truest sense of the word, a crushingly large building over one hundred years old. Apart from the cells, everything here is very big, very long, very high, and very vast. Imagine . . . a central corridor, 245 metres long, with a waxed wooden floor, vaulted like a Romanesque church. Not only does this corridor endlessly extend into the depths of the prison where the solitary confinement cell hides, but it is interrupted at regular intervals by gates, which are always closed.

> [. . .] [These gates] conform to the shape of the vault, almost six metres in both height and width. A towering gate of more than thirty square metres is no joke. It subjugates you, and this is what it is made for.

In her 2006 book about madness in prison – or rather prison madness – journalist Catherine Herszberg described a hellish place. When she voluntarily spent a few months inside that symbol of the criminalization of mental disorder, it was a physical and moral ordeal. Fresnes Prison is certainly no ordinary place. It is so imposing that it overshadows the eponymous town: the very name 'Fresnes' instantly conjures up images of a fearsome prison, one that, by a cruel irony, is bordered by 'Rue de la Liberté'.[1]

Over the years, there have been many first-hand accounts of the harshness of the Fresnes Prison system and the humiliations involved in surviving behind its bars. In 1933–4, pacifist activist Jeanne Humbert depicted the underground dungeon as 'a hole, a hovel, where no farmer would put his pig'. A decade later, in 1945, writer and journalist Henri Calet described a despicable world that was a 'tolerable camp' only in comparison to Ravensbrück, Auschwitz, or Dachau. In the mid-sixties, lawyer Denis Langlois, a conscientious objector placed in military detention at Fresnes, wrote about the appalling conditions in the '*cachot*', the prison dungeon. Later, in his book *Même à mon pire ennemi. . .* ('Even to My Worst Enemy. . .'), anarchist bank robber Louis Beretti described the tense atmosphere created by the silence and strict discipline that still prevailed there in the early 1980s. He and many other critics (Jean Genet wrote some of his novels there) tell a story of endless suffering. During the Nazi occupation, Fresnes Prison was used as a death antechamber, for temporary detention prior to deportation to concentration and extermination camps. Many members of the Resistance were executed in what served unofficially as a political prison, during both the Occupation and the subsequent Liberation purge.[2]

Paradoxically enough, many of these accounts point out that Fresnes was originally designed as a model prison. In this respect, it was part of the utopian period of the early nineteenth century. The authors of a brief history of Parisian prisons write:

> Opening with the destruction of a prison symbolizing the political power to be brought down, the period was characterized by the utopian invention of the 'good' prison. In Paris, this utopia was exemplified by the building of four new prisons in less than a half-century (Petite and Grande Roquette in 1836, Mazas in 1850, and La Santé in 1867–8), at least three of which were considered to be 'model prisons' when they opened. The period ended with the failure of this 'penitentiary Paris', when the new 'model prison' for the Seine department was deliberately built outside the capital, in Fresnes, a small suburban farming village with fewer than a thousand inhabitants at the time.

Fresnes Prison therefore marked a change of geography, but it also has its place in a linear history. Let us take a look at some of its characteristics.[3]

The first, as I have just mentioned, is geographical. Fresnes is located in the countryside, not in a city. It heralded the gradual relocation of prisons to the outskirts of urban centres, or even far away from them. The official reasons for this shift were security and hygiene, but there were also economic and even aesthetic motives. For Paris, a city destined for greatness (in Universal Exhibitions in particular), it was a matter of getting rid of its 'scum' or 'rabble'. In a way, Fresnes dispelled the dregs of society by transferring them to a less expensive, less visible place. The prisons inside Paris were seen as a blot on the landscape, a stain on the glittering capital, hindering the development of certain districts. At the same time, there was a growing belief in placing prisoners in a supposedly invigorating natural environment, as opposed to the 'corrupting' city.

Fresnes, however, has curious political origins, especially for a place that opened at the height of the Third Republic and claimed to be a model 'republican' prison. Christian Carlier, who has studied the origins and development of Fresnes in depth, writes that the 'cellular potion of which Fresnes was to be the elixir' was brewed in a 'cauldron of former Orleanists, opportunist republicans, narrow-minded conservatives, fervent Catholics and implacable enemies of the republican left'. Champions of the new prison included such atypical figures as Louis Lucipia, who chaired the local prisons committee within the French departmental council. There is no question that the man knew a lot about prisons. As a former prisoner himself, in 1872 he was handed a death sentence that was later commuted to hard labour and then exile. Though sceptical about the very notion of 'moralization', he was a supporter of the abolition of children's prisons, and advocated a healthy environment and the practice of gymnastics. Fresnes Prison is also the work of the lawyer and politician René Bérenger, whose name was closely associated with the French laws on parole (1885) and suspended sentences (1891). Carlier writes of the two men: 'Bérenger and Lucipia: between the great Orleanist, Catholic, conservative public figure who reluctantly supported the Republic, and the Fourierist, internationalist, Communard activist, there was as much difference as between the carp and the rabbit. Fresnes is the product of this unholy marriage, so we can understand its monstrous side.'[4]

Another important aspect is compliance with the law. Fresnes was the 'most flamboyant application' of the 1875 law on individual custody, and in fact it was one of the few prisons – if not the only one – to enforce it, making it 'the exception that proves the rule'. This undoubtedly explains its overzealousness to some extent: Fresnes conformed to the cell model 'to the point of caricature', causing it to be described as the model's 'epitome'. Beyond the law of 1875, which was rarely applied in every detail, this excessive zeal can also be explained by the fact that the cell model, which was intended to have become the norm in the 1840s, had only been implemented partially and sporadically in places where it was supposed to have been fully applied, such as La Roquette and La Santé. Hence the idea that Fresnes was something of a belated victory for advocates of the separate system, who had fought for the strict application of cellular isolation. However, in practice, the individual separation of prisoners would turn out to be 'all just for show'.[5]

Although the Deputy Home Secretary declared 'it is impossible to imagine anything that would more fully realize the idea of a prison for our time', there was an element of anachronism in Fresnes. Its construction certainly stemmed from the return of the individual confinement model, but the golden age of that model was over, as we saw in the case of La Santé (chapter 3). The cell model had been increasingly influential from the end of the Restoration through the 1830s, but it had not become widespread until the early 1840s. Then the traditional classification of prisoners returned in the 1850s. The cell as an 'individual prison' – which Jacques-Guy Petit praised as 'well suited to liberalism and bourgeois individualism, while at the same time serving the needs of suppression through its severity' – was widely and strongly rejected by philanthropists. Those most hostile to 'cellular madness' even viewed it as a form of torture. The cell system was revived only because the debates surrounding it had died down to some extent in a new political landscape. The Second Empire had come and gone, and by the late 1870s, only left-wing members of Parliament were committed to opposing individual confinement. This revival was as sudden as it was brief, and in the 1880s the 'fever of individual confinement' subsided almost completely. This led some authors to argue that the 'model prison of Fresnes was already backward when it was built'. As an 'anti-panopticon of sorts with its large rectangular buildings and very long corridors, it was closer to the old convent and dungeon models than to new prison technology based on the "visibility trap" and transparency'.[6]

This leads us to another defining element, which relates to architecture. Architect Henri Poussin championed small, separate but connected buildings, breaking with the radial layout. He proposed a new spatial organization based on rectangular blocks containing cells. Known as the 'telephone pole', this layout places rows of cell blocks perpendicular to a central corridor, which in Fresnes leads from the chapel at one end to the disciplinary wing at the other – quite a contrast. Perhaps surprisingly, more traditional inspirations also seem to have played a part. In any case, Fresnes was not built on a whim. In Vimont's words, it represented 'the culmination of a century of reflection on the ideal prison', even if this particular product may seem crude, reducing a prison conception to its simplest expression. Fresnes Prison was 'about individual confinement and nothing else', according to Carlier and his co-authors. The focus was on the cells, and more generally on a hygienic and functional layout that avoided all the dreaded forms of contagion like epidemics, homosexuality, and recidivism, even though it had to optimize the flow of people and things at the same time. History was already repeating itself, and in terms of equipment and amenities, Fresnes was in step with the times, if not ahead of them. It had state-of-the-art water, heating, lighting, and electricity; there was even a goods lift on rails to convey food. Right-wing journalists condemned the excessive luxury of 'Fresnes Palace', as if the workers outside had reason to be jealous of the inmates. In 1903, the French daily *Le Matin* called it 'very special resort'. The 'luxury hotel' analogy was a common one, used by the mayor himself during his inaugural speech. Even the guards were denigrated as 'well-to-do' (despite their modest salary, though it was relatively high compared to other prisons) by a local population unanimously hostile to this 'criminopolis', as it was labelled by the title of a book published the year before it opened.[7]

Inspiration in all directions

When it comes to prisons, inspiration is likely to come from all sides, flowing in and then out again. Although Fresnes was considered architecturally groundbreaking, its designer was inspired by the Russian prison in Saint Petersburg (chapter 4). And Norman Johnston traces the 'telephone pole' layout back to England's Wormwood Scrubs Prison, which he sees as a forerunner of Fresnes. In turn, Fresnes is said to have inspired other projects, not only in France (especially Baumettes Prison in Marseille), but also abroad, including on the American continent, from Rikers Island in New York – another prison hailed as a model when it opened, prior to turning into a debacle – to Punta Carretas in Uruguay, which we encountered earlier (counterpoint I). For Johnston, Fresnes is even 'by far the most influential prison built in France', and by extension Henri Poussin was one of the most innovative and prominent prison architects, along with William Blackburn, John Haviland, and Joshua Jebb. However, Johnston points out that Fresnes was little imitated prior to the Second World War. It was not until the 1950s that it became a standard model, whose appeal lay in its security features, not in any correctional virtues.[8]

The nickname 'criminopolis' also refers to the imposing size of the building. Fresnes was supposed to replace several Paris prisons: Grande Roquette, Sainte-Pélagie, and Mazas, which closed in 1898. The size of the building initially planned (1,800 cells or 6,000 places were to be created) was widely criticized as much too large, especially for an individual confinement prison, and it was regarded as a step backwards in terms of correctional efficiency. After several controversial blueprints, a set of prison buildings was finally built, which by 1911 was housing twice as many people as the town of Fresnes, constituting 'a territory outside the community, something of an island developing a specific form of sociability'. This excessive size added another ingredient to the anachronistic nature of Fresnes. It began operating at a time when prisoner numbers were falling, to the extent that the prison was initially difficult to fill. Originally designed for short sentences (it served this purpose until the 1930s), prisoner turnover was high.[9]

Fresnes also had a number of unusual features, such as its hospital exclusively for the prison population, the only one of its kind. It was an institution that straddled the line between prison and hospital, two institutions whose histories have always been intertwined. The hospital in Fresnes later came to embody this entanglement in its own way. In 1983, a decade before the 1994 law that placed prison healthcare exclusively under the aegis of the French public health system, it was overseen by two ministries (both justice and public health), making it not only a special medical unit under the sole supervision of the local prison authority, but also a public hospital in its own right. It remained a national institution after 1994. From 1945 to 1962, Fresnes was also the site of the first penitentiary staff training school, and prior to that it contained a post-secondary school from 1927 to 1934. From the early 1950s, it also housed the Centre national d'observation, responsible for assigning a profile to every prisoner based on an examination, with a view to preventing recidivism and detecting incipient threat.[10]

Fresnes has always been a prison like no other, at least in France. Yet its trajectory is typical of the fate of model prisons. Although it opened at a time when the prison system had fallen into disrepute, it was supposed to be successful. As the authors of *Fresnes, la prison* wrote: 'Hygienic, functional, organized around individual cells, reserved for a specific category of inmates, Fresnes seemed to have everything going for it, and everything needed to succeed in its extraordinary dual mission to punish and correct: punishing to better heal, excluding to better include. At "Fresnes-la-belle", a *model prison*, the future of penitentiaries looks bright.' Nevertheless, this perfectly 'rational' yet inhuman 'totalitarian universe' (as Carlier called it) would soon lose any flattering reputation it may have enjoyed. As early as 1912, a report by the General Inspectorate, a source unlikely to be suspected of dishonesty, euphemistically stated that 'Fresnes Prison itself, the only specimen of modernism in the Seine region's prison system, is far from realizing the ideal for which it has been hailed'. Like other prisons based on individual confinement (often described as 'tombs' or 'catacombs' at the time), it remained a crushing machine, 'a site of physical and moral death'.[11]

At the time of its centenary in 1998, Fresnes no longer had any supporters. Even *Le Figaro*, a conservative daily that had always specialized in disparaging prisons as four-star hotels, conceded: 'Looking at the bricks of Fresnes Prison, it is hard to fathom that when it was built exactly one hundred years ago, it was considered a model.' Some fifteen years later, when Fresnes Prison came to be viewed as a hotbed of jihadist recruitment of 'radicalized' inmates, this did nothing to improve its reputation. A recent newspaper article, titled 'Plongée dans l'enfer de la prison de Fresnes' ('Plunged into the Hell of Fresnes Prison'), quotes an inmate who has spent fourteen years behind its bars: 'At Fresnes, we're still in the 1800s' – the nineteenth century in other words, but stripped of its penitentiary ideals.[12]

Chapter 6

Cárcel Modelo, Barcelona (Spain, 1904)

Cárcel Modelo, Barcelona (1904)
Source: Unknown author, 'Arquitectura española contemporánea', *Arquitectura y Construcción* año VIII, 149, 1904–5, p. 137

'A modern prison – the Spanish more openly call it Cárcel Model, or model prison – successfully resolves the problem of economy in space, labor, and surveillance,' wrote Victor Serge in 1930, in a slightly ambivalent tone. What exactly a revolutionary like him meant by 'successfully resolves' will be discussed in our conclusion. For now let us just say that the author of *Men in Prison* – who had moved to Barcelona in 1917 after serving five years in prison (some of that time spent in La Santé) – probably had in mind Catalonia's 'Centre Penitenciari d'Homes de Barcelona', better known (in Catalan) as 'La Model'. However, as he suggested, the 'model' designation was not exclusive to Barcelona's new prison. It appeared in the name or nickname of several of the 'modern' correctional prisons built throughout Spain between the 1860s and 1900s (mostly after 1874 under the Restoration) that were based on individual cells, but did not exclude other methods of punishment.[1]

Among them, Barcelona's Cárcel Modelo – which opened in 1904 outside the city limits in the town of Sants, which would later be absorbed by urban expansion – was not the first of its kind, having been preceded several decades earlier by models in Vitoria (1861) and Bilbao (1873). Though it was designed to hold about 700 to 800 inmates, it was not the largest model prison, that distinction going to Madrid's Modelo, which opened two decades before its Catalan counterpart. Even the controversy that surrounded the Barcelona project was not unprecedented, as was the near-silence of the local press when the prison finally opened. Construction was admittedly prolonged: work began officially in 1887 and effectively in 1888 (the same year the first Barcelona Universal Exposition was held), but it took more than fifteen years to complete. The facility was not entirely finished when it opened, with one wing remaining to be built, which would be reserved for convicts (as opposed to remand prisoners). Despite these problems, the debate it generated was not as fierce as that inspired by the earlier Madrid prison project. Therefore, what characterized Barcelona's 'model' was not innovation, size, or controversy, but rather two distinctive aspects, one theoretical and the other empirical. Theoretically, it was conceived as the culmination of a half-century of penal debate, especially from an architectural standpoint. Empirically, its historical trajectory and configuration proved exceptional, particularly during the Spanish Civil War. As a site and microcosm of this highly troubled period, historically Barcelona's Modelo has reflected Spain's social and political struggles.[2]

In general terms, it can be said that Barcelona's Modelo was based on the same basic principle as others of the same breed: a conservative correctional ambition (founded on moral, and especially religious, indoctrination) that would later evolve towards the therapeutic rhetoric of 'treatment'. But Barcelona's specimen was distinctive from the outset: among the prisons that were labelled 'models' because they embraced the system of separate cells, it stood out as the 'model of all models'. Although the cost needed to be lower than that of the Madrid prison in order for the project to be approved (hence the use of relatively cheap materials like local bricks), the architectural layout was designed to meet the highest European standards – prisons in Leuven, Brussels, and Berlin serving as examples – in terms of space, ventilation, and both natural and electric light. Even the toilets were innovative: they were designed so that they could not be used as a communication channel. In the view of this new prison's main supporters (lawyers Pere Armengol i Cornet and Ramon Albó y Martí, as well as architects Josep Domenech y Estapà and Salvador Viñals), it would represent a departure from the chaos and insalubrity of traditional jails, like the old, dilapidated Reina Amàlia Prison located in a former convent in Barcelona's infamous El Raval district. It would establish a new benchmark based on isolation, hygiene, and religion (partly relying on a Catholic patronage system), where inmates would be under constant surveillance from the central rotunda, in conformance with Bentham's panoptic principle. Surveillance was crucial in the design of the cells themselves: the door had a small conical peephole that allowed the prisoner to be watched unawares. As authors like Pedro Fraile and Pelai Pagès I Blanch have noted, the Barcelona Modelo had so many innovations – even with respect to other model prisons – that it opened as the country's most modern prison, the one that best reflected the penitentiary principles developed by reformists and philanthropists over the previous decades. In a text describing his first encounter with Dostoevsky's novels while serving time as a political prisoner (he was imprisoned in 1923 for two months), Ignazio Silone recalls: 'The "Carcel Modelo" was indeed, in certain respects, a truly model prison.'[3]

Though it might seem like the correctional ideal had been extinguished several decades earlier in England and France, it is hard not to return to the theme of prison utopia. 'Barcelona's prison was a model one, built in a star shape, like an eighteenth-century utopia,' recalls architect Ricardo Bofill, who was imprisoned there under Franco's dictatorship. A 'redemptive utopia', several historians confirm, but one that failed from the outset. Complaints about poor detention conditions emerged shortly after the prison opened, and increased after the First World War, when overcrowding became endemic and ruined the ideal of individual confinement. Moreover, though Barcelona's Modelo was officially designed to hold remand prisoners and rehabilitate ordinary criminals (it served as a criminological playground for psychologist Joaquim Fuster during Primo de Rivera's dictatorship in the run-up to the Spanish Civil War), it was extensively used for political repression, especially against left-wing activists. This shift made it a deeply ambivalent space, since its use was still technically in keeping with the project's ostensible purpose: 'improvement'.[4]

The Elmira–Ocaña Connection

Opened in 1876, the New York State Reformatory in Elmira was then regarded as a groundbreaking penal model. This particular model was based on a so-called 'progressive system' underpinned by indeterminate sentencing – adjustable according to the 'progress' demonstrated by prisoners, who were typically young adults deemed capable of reformation. The institution maintained this reputation as a model into the early 1890s, influencing similar experiments across the United States in the early twentieth century (before it 'proved to be just as barbaric as the older prisons from which young adults had been diverted', as Ashley Rubin recalls). It was this system that Fernando Cadalso sought to introduce in his own country.

As Inspector General of Prisons, Cadalso represented Spain at the 1910 International Penitentiary Congress in Washington, where the cellular model – precisely the one on which Barcelona's recently opened Cárcel Modelo had been built – came in for sharp criticism. Thanks to a study grant, in 1912–13 he was able to travel to the United States and visit Elmira. Upon his return, he championed the establishment of the Reformatorio de Adultos in Ocaña, Toledo. This facility opened in 1914 in a former central prison that had been repurposed. It was not a mere copy of Elmira; the model was adapted to local culture, particularly to the prevalence of Catholicism. Nevertheless, the institution adopted the same principles: adjusting detention conditions based on behaviour, emphasizing manual labour and moral education, and avoiding both strict solitary confinement and forced labour that lacked any educational dimension. It even introduced the possibility of conditional or early release, a provision viewed with suspicion by conservative jurists and officials, who deemed the experiment too 'American'.

However, the institution – partially destroyed by a fire in 1922 – soon faced familiar challenges, compounded by underfunding. It struggled to demonstrate a genuine reduction in recidivism. By the time the Reformatorio was dismantled by the Francoists as a symbol of supposed liberal and Republican 'leniency', its reputation among progressives had already been tarnished.[5]

Long before the Spanish Civil War, the prison had already become a tool for quelling social unrest, primarily targeting revolutionary unionism (anarcho-syndicalism), but also radical Republicans (such as educator Francisco Ferrer) and Catalan separatists. This reflected the repressive tendencies of the successive regimes that governed Spain from the end of the nineteenth century. Shortly after it opened, the prison witnessed intense struggles over the status of political prisoners and demands for improved detention conditions. A riot erupted in 1919, with prisoners demanding better food and hygiene. But the following year, after General Martínez Anido was appointed as civil governor of Barcelona, the repression intensified. Conditions temporarily improved with the proclamation of the Republic in the early 1930s, but prison revolts continued to occur. The Spanish Civil War transformed the situation entirely. The conflict exacerbated existing tensions and contradictions, deepening political divisions within the prison system. The gap between theory and practice widened dramatically. While the Catalan Republican authorities who controlled the prison upheld their commitment to the original vision of a model correctional institution, it became an arena of mass repression.[6]

What is hard to fully comprehend in hindsight is that, at the outbreak of the war, some inmates saw the prison as an enclave, sometimes even a safe haven, as well as a touchstone of Republican legality in a context of violence and confusion where illegal private detention spaces were flourishing. After the prison was temporarily emptied in mid-July 1936 following an assault by armed anarchists, the anti-fascist prison committee that assumed control of the premises on behalf of the Generalitat of Catalonia (against the central authority in Madrid) reasserted the founding principles that had been distorted in practice. A 'humanistic' ideal of rehabilitation (as opposed to mere coercion) was pursued once again. Prison guards were even renamed 'reform auxiliaries'. The situation was absolutely exceptional: the prison staff consisted of revolutionaries (all factions of the 'Republican front' were represented, although the anarcho-syndicalists were in the majority), and for a while, the facility was virtually self-governing. The revolutionary left considered Barcelona's Cárcel Modelo central to the reconstruction of the Spanish state it advocated.

But the situation changed drastically between mid-1936 and mid-1938, by which time the prison's configuration starkly contrasted with its original intent, despite all efforts to uphold its founding principles. As French historian François Godicheau points out, the Modelo no longer epitomized the project to rehabilitate a few hundred prisoners in a Catalonia who had resisted fascist oppression. It had become the centrepiece of a brutal system in which severe overcrowding prevailed, even though there were more political prisoners than ordinary offenders (not to say that the boundary between the two groups was strict). All trace of any coherent prison programme had once again vanished. Different rival groups shared the facility, in a situation that was politically explosive. Gallery 1 was controlled by the anarcho-syndicalist Confederación Nacional del Trabajo (CNT), gallery 2 by the communist Partido Obrero de Unificación Marxista (POUM), and gallery 3 by officers loyal to General Franco. Galleries 4 and 5 were mixed, housing ordinary criminals and anti-fascists deemed deviant, while gallery 6 was nicknamed the 'monastery' because far-right religious inmates made up the majority.[7]

As suggested, in this particular prison (there were many of them in Catalonia, and concentration camps as well), the Republican authorities maintained an official line that tacitly denied the very existence of the status of political prisoner. A distinct political identity nevertheless emerged: 'anti-fascist prisoners'. It is worth quoting the full conclusion of François Godicheau's study, as it eloquently explains how crucial Barcelona's Modelo was to the tangled web of this period's political divisions:

> The history of the Modelo during the war reflects all the divisions that characterized the complex situation in Catalonia: pro-Franco camp versus Republican camp, central government versus Generalitat of Catalonia, communists versus anarchists and members of the POUM, CNT leadership versus radical anarchists, the state versus the revolution, and Republican legitimacy

versus illegal forms of repression. We can also find conflicting views between the police and the judiciary, the POUM and the CNT, national and foreign anarchists.

But the significance of this history lies in the emergence of a relatively distinct and autonomous political group within the prison, capable of polemicizing and confronting external organizations, even those to which they were supposed to belong, and the state.

The Modelo was not only a place that reflected the complex situation of the home front during the civil war; it was the site of a political struggle in its own right, the arena of a complex power struggle, made up of offensives and compromises, like other Republican institutions of the time, particularly the army, the judiciary, and the police.[8]

Under Franco's dictatorship, when the number of prisoners quickly reached staggering levels (depending on the source, the figures range from 8,000 to 13,000 in the early 1940s), Barcelona's Cárcel Modelo was an abomination. It could be called a 'model' only in the sense of being a concentrated reflection of the regime's abjectness. As historian Ricard Vinyes has recounted:

> When, in 1944, Mavis Bacca Dowden, a British woman accused of spying for the Allies, walked through the gates of Barcelona's model prison, she was briefly told how things worked: 'Here, you own nothing except what you have eaten, and not even that . . . because you will probably throw it up.' An accurate phrase that sums up the foundation on which the entire structure of fascist prison power was built: total dispossession, both material and moral.[9]

At the end of that same year, 1944, George Orwell reviewed a book by an 'unwilling witness against Franco's Spain', namely Belgian journalist Charles d'Ydewalle, an erstwhile supporter of Franco who was nonetheless imprisoned for reasons that remain unclear. It provided a glimpse into the 'horrors of the model prison' in the early 1940s:

> He was incarcerated first of all in the Model Prison in Barcelona, which had been built to hold 700 prisoners and at this time was holding 8,000. Later he was placed in a concentration camp among refugees of many different nationalities. Here the conditions were comparatively sympathetic: it was possible to buy small luxuries; one could choose one's hut mates, and there was international rivalry in the matter of digging tunnels under the barbed wire. It was the Model Prison that opened or partially opened Mr d'Ydewalle's eyes to the nature of the regime.
>
> At the end of 1941, nearly three years after the ending of the civil war, people were still being shot, in this prison alone, at the rate of five or six a week. In addition there was torture, presumably for the purpose of extracting confession, and on occasion the torturer 'went too far'.[10]

During the 1950s and 1960s, corporal punishment remained commonplace, and summary executions frequent (it is estimated that more than 1,600 prisoners were brought out of this prison to be put to death), culminating in 1974 with the strangulation of anarchist activist Salvador Puig Antich. Barcelona's Modelo was a place of agony where inmates sentenced to death by a military court awaited Franco's orders. According to historian Amélie Nuq, former 'residents' of the Asilo Durán youth reformatory, traumatized by the discipline imposed there, described their own establishment as 'an institution whose horror was surpassed only by Barcelona's Model Prison, the archetypal political prison under Franco's dictatorship'. Incarceration could result from political dissidence, but also sexual deviance and mental disorders. Women suffered exceptionally harsh repression there.[11]

Following the end of the dictatorship and Spain's transition to democracy, prison riots occurred as conditions continued to deteriorate due to inadequate investment and severe overcrowding.

In 1977, prisoners formed the Coordinadora de Presos en Lucha ('Coordinating Committee of Prisoners in Struggle'), which demanded a blanket amnesty and fundamental reforms to prison rules and practices. Although the prison's closure was first considered in the mid-1970s and announced by officials in 1987 (three years after a major riot) because a new prison called Cuatro Caminos was just about to open near Barcelona, the Cárcel Modelo remained operational. The situation further deteriorated in 1990 when another riot prompted violent repression, leading inmates to file a class action lawsuit. Despite these protests, meaningful reform remained elusive. Throughout the 1990s, Catalonia mirrored a broader European trend, as prison populations surged in the context of the 'punitive turn'. In short, Spain's democratic transition failed to restore the 'noble' ideals that had originally inspired the Cárcel Modelo. This failure became starkly apparent when Human Rights Watch was denied access to the facility, which by then was housing 1,900 prisoners in spaces designed for only 800.[12]

The European Committee for the Prevention of Torture and Inhuman or Degrading Treatment or Punishment (CPT) was able to describe worrying conditions, owing mostly to overcrowding. In April 2013, it issued a report following a June 2012 visit to Barcelona's Modelo, which received special attention. It was not the committee's first inspection:

> In several previous visit reports to Spain, dating back to 1994, the CPT has underlined the deleterious effects that the high levels of overcrowding have had on the conditions of detention for prisoners held in La Modelo Prison. As the Committee has pointed out, an overcrowded prison entails: cramped and unhygienic accommodation; a constant lack of privacy (even when performing such basic tasks as using a sanitary facility); reduced opportunities in terms of employment, education, and other out-of-cell activities, due to demand outstripping the staff and facilities available; overburdened healthcare services; increased

> tension and hence more violence between prisoners and between prisoners and staff. All these negative factors have been observed by the CPT over the years at La Modelo Prison.

Viewing some conditions as unacceptable, the committee reiterated the objective of placing no more than two people in each cell – not quite the individual confinement initially promised. Although the 2013 report positively commented on some improvements, it also alerted public authorities to the prison's partial disrepair, worsened by massive overcrowding that adversely affected both inmates and staff. It called on public authorities to implement a clear strategy to reduce prisoner numbers, recommending gradual action ('phased reduction'), but implemented immediately. Other concerns related to healthcare, solitary confinement, and allegations of ill-treatment. In 2014, more than a century after it opened, a collective book recounted the prison's history, emphasizing the struggles that had taken place there. The crude reality of the Modelo prison was humiliation and torment. Therefore, the authors advocated demolishing it without building a replacement, since a new prison would inevitably repeat the same failures.[13]

The fate of the Modelo, a prison that became increasingly architecturally incongruous with its urban surroundings, remained uncertain for years. Should it be demolished or preserved as a cultural centre? Should it be commemorated or erased from memory? The site attracted property developers, while residents of the gentrified Eixample district long campaigned for its demolition. A conversion plan was approved in 2009, but the prison did not close until 2017. Soon after, an academic once incarcerated there as a political prisoner in the 1970s organized an exhibition showcasing its century-long history, which was followed by various artistic initiatives. An architectural competition was organized with a view to refurbishing the old prison. The option that finally prevailed was to preserve part of the prison building and better integrate it into the surrounding urban fabric, while also creating a park-like green space, and providing community facilities including a nursery, an elderly daycare centre, and a sports and culture complex, probably with some sort of commemorative plaque or other memorial. Meanwhile, as part of a transformation process that is still underway, the prison has been renovated and repainted so that guided tours can be organized.[14]

Counterpoint III

Modelos

As the preceding chapter suggested, the designation '*modelo*' was originally much more than a superficial label or thoughtless nickname. It reflected a philosophical and architectural carceral ideal that, shaped by British and French models, spread throughout Spain and later across the Spanish-speaking world. Initially influenced by Pentonville Prison, this label became widespread, reaching beyond prisons located in capitals and other major cities. It was more or less systematically applied to several of the nearly thirty modern prisons built in Spain between the 1860s and 1900s that (theoretically) had individual cells, such as those in Cieza (community of Murcia) and Bergara (Basque country). However, apart from Madrid (1884) and Barcelona (1904), only a few – especially those in Bilbao (1873) and Valencia (1903) – retained the designation over time and continued to be known as *modelos* in the national collective memory.

Madrid's Modelo stands as a particularly significant example. Designed by architect Tomás Aranguren to hold approximately a thousand inmates, it was Spain's largest new prison. Following legislation passed in 1877 (after other short-lived bills over the three preceding decades), the prison was officially inaugurated in 1883, and began operations the following year. It represented

Spain's first implementation of a mixed panoptic-radial system of individual confinement, setting the standard for prisons in the rest of the country. Despite the notorious reputation of Madrid's former Saladero Prison (which incidentally took its name from the pig-salting operation for which the building was originally used), the construction of the new cellular prison generated intense debate. Author Benito Pérez Galdós even incorporated the controversy into his acclaimed novel *La Desheredada* (1881), although the Cárcel Modelo he refers to (where the protagonist Isidora is imprisoned) did not yet exist. This debate began as early as 1876, with parliamentary discussions focusing particularly on the cellular system. Famous social reformer Concepción Arenal strongly opposed the project during the early 1880s, citing economic considerations and suspicions of corruption, criticisms echoed by the liberal press. At a conference held at Madrid's Athenaeum in June 1884, Francisco Lastrès, a conservative member of Parliament and fervent proponent of individual confinement, delivered an impassioned speech hailing the 'colossal progress' represented by this new institution. Yet Madrid's modelo fell into disrepute long before it was destroyed by an aerial bombardment in November 1936. (It was replaced by Carabanchel Prison after 1940.) According to Michael Schnepf: 'By 1888, *La Cárcel Modelo* had become the laughingstock of Madrid and the entire Spanish penal system.'[1]

Spanish *modelos* like Catalonia's Mataró Prison (built 1854–63) were inspired by both the panoptic model and the radial model with a central rotunda. Spanish delegates had visited Pentonville in the 1850s, following various legislative reforms during the 1830s and 1840s aimed at implementing a correctional perspective, including a new penal code in 1848 and a prison law in 1849. This dual influence emerged amid intense debate about the strengths and weaknesses of the 'separate system' based on strict individual confinement. Although royal decrees from 1844 tended to approve the cellular design, and support for cellular architecture in official Spanish circles increased following the 1846 International Penitentiary Congress, the 1847 decree that established the framework for national model prisons did not explicitly endorse this system. Moreover, despite a prison programme being agreed upon in 1860, practical achievements remained limited. What typically prevailed within the walls of prisons was a military-influenced blend of coercive and interrogatory surveillance.[2]

If we exclude the earlier case of Valladolid in the late 1840s, which was similar to Ghent's workhouse and did not actually serve as a prison, the first official *modelo* was in Vitoria. When this new prison began operations around 1860, it was one of the smallest institutions of its kind. Some thirty years later, a French officer described it in positive terms, if only in comparison with the French system. He approved of its three galleries arranged in a Latin cross formation, its spacious and airy cells, and the visible efforts being made to improve the inmates' moral standards. Drawing attention to the insight gained by 'studying a more modest prison, perfectly equipped and suited to the needs of a small town', the visitor wrote in 1891:

> In order to avoid the effects of prolonged isolation, which he considers harmful to southern temperaments, the director ensures that prisoners held in cells are visited frequently and are taught reading, writing, and the principles of arithmetic. [. . .] It would be desirable for the departmental administrations to resolutely apply the [French] law of 1875 [on individual confinement] and construct small buildings similar to the one I have just described. We would then, without excessive expenditure, have model establishments in which order could be easily maintained and which would ensure, along with legitimate punishment for offences committed, the serious rehabilitation of the guilty.

Ironically, Vitoria's Modelo was reportedly modelled on the French prison in Bordeaux, which was already in a deplorable state at the time. (Its influence proved extensive nonetheless, as it had earlier inspired Santiago's Cárcel Penitenciaría in the 1840s through French architect Auguste Charme, who advised the Chilean authorities.)[3]

Despite being (or precisely because it was) largely forgotten at the turn of the twenty-first century, Valencia's Modelo merits special attention. According to José María Pérez Fernández, writing in 2000 when the building was derelict and the target of looting after it closed in 1992, this spectacular structure deserved preservation because of its construction technique, historical and artistic value, and its status as possibly Spain's only remaining symbol of the philosophical and legal ideal it had once represented. Stemming from the reform legislation passed in 1877, its construction began in 1889, but the prison did not open until 1903. Both its physical configuration and its underlying principles – particularly the emphasis on light and brightness – followed Madrid's precedent and anticipated the building that would be constructed in Barcelona. Valencia's prison exemplifies the attempt to combine individual confinement, central surveillance, redemption through work, and the supposed benefits of religious and educational hope. Moreover, it represents a model of 'rationalist architecture', prioritizing utility and efficiency through an optimal alignment of form and function.[4]

Later, the *modelo* designation spread well beyond national borders, and by the early twentieth century it had come to be used throughout the Spanish-speaking world, even though no singular mould or archetype unified all these instances. Despite receiving little academic attention, perhaps the most (in)famous of them is the visually impressive Presidio Modelo in Cuba. Replacing a penal colony, this prison was only in operation for about four decades, yet one of its most enduring features was its use as a tool to suppress political dissent. Built between 1926 and 1931 under the rule of Gerardo Machado on what was then known as Isla de Pinos (now Isla de la Juventud), its explicit purpose was to crush progressive opposition – so much so that critics dubbed it a 'model of atrocities'. Architecturally, it bore the visible influence of the panoptic model, drawing inspiration from the notorious Stateville Correctional Center in the US state of Illinois, as well as from Latin American institutions in Buenos Aires and São Paulo. The Cuban 'model' became famous for holding the Castro brothers in 1953–5, first in the hospital wing, then in solitary confinement. (In a letter, Fidel Castro described the prison as a 'fantastic school' from which to prepare the revolution.) It remained operational after the Cuban Revolution and served as a tool of repression during the sixties. The prison closed in 1967, and the building became home to a technical school, joined by a museum in the 1970s, when the Island's name was changed. In 1978, Fidel Castro even planned to establish a communist educational centre on the site. But the building was eventually abandoned, although it was awarded the status of 'national monument'. 'The symbolic role played by this prison in the making of Cuba cannot be overemphasized,' Ricardo Salvatore and Carlos Aguirre argued.[5]

In parts of South America, prison reform debates emerged earlier than historians have long assumed. As Stephan Scheuzger has noted, just weeks after Chile's 1818 independence, an article was published already advocating the abandonment of the old confinement system inherited from the '*bárbaros españoles*', and praising new prison experiments, particularly Philadelphia's Walnut Street. From the 1830s onwards, the Creole intellectual and political elite vigorously debated rehabilitative ideals, as well as the respective virtues and drawbacks of different models (Panopticon, Philadelphia, Auburn). It was in this context that Santiago's penitentiary was legally established in 1843 under a conservative government (following intense debate, particularly about costs), as a means of addressing the confusion and disorder prevailing in existing detention facilities, where surveillance was so poorly organized that escapes and riots were commonplace. This Philadelphia-inspired prison was built between 1844 and 1849 and became partially operational during that time, but construction continued until 1860. Here as elsewhere, one finds an ambiguous blend of progressivism with conservatism and utilitarian concerns about the maintenance of order, inherent in the correctional approach. Unsurprisingly, historians describe this experiment as a complete failure. The correctional model based on individual confinement collapsed almost immediately due to overcrowding by both ordinary criminals and political prisoners – a situation that worsened following the liberal revolutions of 1851 and 1859. The Talca penitentiary established in 1860 encountered similar problems. Factory-style labour – supposedly a way to 'regenerate' inmates – became central for both disciplinary and economic reasons, since the inmates' products generated profit.[6]

In Brazil, the first prison modelled on the Pennsylvania system – a so-called 'house of corrections' (*casa de correção*) – was officially inaugurated in Rio de Janeiro in 1850, but its construction had begun as early as 1834. This, too, originated in events of a more distant past that had been concurrent with (not merely following) the prison discourse among imperial powers. Reform movements in Brazil began as early as the 1820s, shortly after the empire had gained independence – predating Tocqueville's and Beaumont's famous reports on American prisons. Discussions about the English prison reform movement began in the early 1830s under the auspices of the philanthropic Sociedade Defensora da Liberdade e Independência Nacional (Society for the Defence of Liberty and National Independence). However, Rio's penitentiary – designed according to a radial blueprint inspired by modern prison architecture – was dogged by a protracted and erratic building process. Fifteen years after construction had begun, only one wing was operational, and of the four planned 200-cell wings, just two were ever completed. This is a good example of the weakness of certain reform initiatives, and of the consequences of their high cost for newly independent states in the making. Besides, the Brazilian 'model' did not escape the general trend: 'The Casa de Correção, conceived as the pioneer of the reformatory project, turned into a house of disease and death.'[7]

Perhaps the most renowned of these supposed models in Latin America is Bogotá's Cárcel Nacional Modelo, which opened in 1876. A century later, this Colombian prison had acquired a fearsome reputation, operating in direct opposition to any noble principles, having become a deadly battleground between guerrillas, paramilitaries, and traffickers. A 2004 report by the International Federation for Human Rights reviewing twenty years of work in Colombia stated that all the prisoners judges had spoken to when visiting the Cárcel Nacional Modelo about a decade earlier had said they had been tortured during their detention. Yet initially, until the 1930s, the prison was a symbol of modernization. The penal and prison reforms of this period can be understood as components of capitalist development, with legally warranted discipline supplanting religion as the foundation of social control. From this perspective, the punishment system's actual function included managing surplus populations relative to the labour market.[8]

This interpretation also applies to the Penitenciaría Nacional, which opened in 1877 under a liberal government in Buenos Aires. Outwardly designed according to the Pentonville model, with internal management inspired by Auburn, it served as an exemplar throughout the continent, and was presented nationally as a symbol of progress and modernity alongside technical achievements like railways and the hydraulic infrastructure. Its blueprint was even exhibited at the 1878 Paris Universal Exhibition – that same year, Argentine delegates attended the International Prison Congress held at Stockholm. Built under the influence of both American correctional ideology and developing European positivist criminology, it was also inspired by notions of pathologization and medicalization – twin aspects of the 'treatment' doctrine. Day-to-day life primarily revolved around hard labour and religious indoctrination, supplemented by basic education; 'a place of penance rather than a site for reformation'. The aim of modern prisons – and more broadly, a penal system designed to benefit the ruling elite – was to discipline the workforce, which at that time was predominantly rural. The development of factories and prisons occurred in parallel rather than in succession. As Ricardo Salvatore and Carlos Aguirre have observed, 'the existence of factories did not seem to condition the acceptance and propagation of the penitentiary model. As the Argentine case shows, the penitentiary's workshops were a model of organization to which no private establishment could aspire (there were few private workshops as large, productive, and disciplined as the Penitenciaría Nacional).' Prison reform occurred amid the transformation of Argentina's working class, influenced particularly by massive European immigration (perceived as problematic) and generally precarious labour conditions that risked fostering popular sedition.[9]

Uruguay's Punta Carretas Prison on the outskirts of Montevideo – previously discussed in relation to conversion models (counterpoint I) – also served as a model for the Latin American region when it opened. A symbol of the new century in both aesthetic and practical terms, it was inaugurated with great ceremony by the republic's president in 1910. It was designed as a high-security prison, with facilities based on cutting-edge technology: not only electricity, but also modern workshops, a barbershop, a bakery, a pharmacy, and even a pasta factory. But within decades, it had completely changed. By the 1950s, the prison was already being seen as the antithesis of what it was intended to be, having become a focus of protest, and overcrowded due to severe political repression.[10]

Obviously, the overused *modelo* designation did not have the magical power to align reality with original intentions. The term became increasingly incongruous, as abuse and suffering within prison walls intensified. The designation was eventually abandoned. Among Spain's newest prisons, none has dared adopt the name '*modelo*'. Conversely, certain prisons that observers would have considered 'models' in South America at that time did not necessarily bear this designation, even unofficially, and were only known as penitentiaries or correctional houses. For instance, São Paulo's Penitenciária do Estado, originally built in the late nineteenth century, underwent a radical restructuring in the 1910s and was regarded as one of South America's most advanced facilities. Although it was occasionally described as São Paulo's *cárcel modelo*, its official name was changed to Instituto de Regeneração, reflecting the era's penal reform ambitions. Similarly, some prisons were named '*panóptico*' without actually embodying panoptic principles, as in the case of the Panóptico Nacional in Bolivia, and Penitenciaría de Lima in Peru (commonly known as El Panóptico), whose architecture drew from radial rather than panoptic designs.[11]

One point gets repeated often in mainstream discourse on prison reform: that the concept 'model prison' contains an inherent contradiction. Institutions designed as showcases of enlightened penal reform have consistently devolved into sites of suffering that contradict their founding principles. Conventional analysis suggests that this persistent gulf between idealistic rhetoric and institutional reality reveals how these prisons have served aims quite different from their stated purposes, becoming instruments of political control rather than vehicles for rehabilitation. But this interpretation overlooks a crucial fact, namely that reform and rehabilitation are not separate from or opposed to control and discipline – they are, in fact, the same phenomenon viewed through different lenses and from different class perspectives. What reformers and philanthropists term 'rehabilitation' is precisely the inculcation of discipline and the assimilation of legitimate social norms. The case of Latin American penitentiaries illustrates this dynamic clearly. For instance, in Peru, where Lima's penitentiary was completed in 1862 and 'considered a model for its time', the 'failure of the penitentiary goal of reforming criminals is only one side of the story. The other side is its success in reinforcing the authoritarian nature of the Peruvian state and of the modernization project pursued by its elite.' When the penitentiary model was introduced to Latin America, it underwent a transformation that scholars often characterize as the dilution of Enlightenment ideals, particularly under the influence of positivist criminology in the late nineteenth century. However, this transformation simply made even clearer what was already obvious in the European models: prison reforms fundamentally served as mechanisms to categorize, stigmatize, and control populations deemed socially inferior or dangerous. Moreover, in South America, prison 'modernization' did not displace brutal punishment, but instead coexisted with other forms of repression, as exemplified by Brazil's island penal colony of Fernando de Noronha.[12]

Chapter 7

Model Prison No. 1, Beijing (China, 1912)

Model Prison No. 1, Beijing (1917–19)
Source: Sidney David Gamble, via Wikipedia Commons

Like the Spanish *modelo*, this Beijing prison built in the early twentieth century was a model by name. First called 'Capital Model Prison', it came to be known as 'Capital Prison No. 1' after the Republic was proclaimed. Indeed, this prison's first characteristic was that its construction spanned two political regimes. Designed under the Empire during the final years of the centuries-long reign of the Qing dynasty (1644–1911), its blueprint was approved in 1909. Construction began the following year, and after an interruption during the 1911 revolution, the new prison was established in late 1912, under the Republic. Practically, it was made to serve as a blueprint for other buildings of the same type, not only in Beijing, but also in other major political and commercial centres. Symbolically, although a legacy of the fallen late Qing dynasty, it was a touchstone for the social legitimacy of the new political regime.

This event was part of a broader change in the Chinese penal system, one that took place later than in Europe, but at a brisk pace. Bridging the falling Empire and the new Republic, this shift was both intellectual and institutional, legal and practical, verbal and physical. As in the Western nations that were held up as benchmarks at the time, the advent of the Chinese modern prison paralleled the official abolition of corporal punishment in 1905. Torture, decapitation, tattooing, branding, and execution had previously been commonplace, when prisons had mainly been for defendants on remand. Even though China's prison system had already been the most extensive and coordinated in the world since at least the fourteenth century, prisons played a major role in the renewed penal system established in the early twentieth century, as did fines and the death penalty, which now took place behind prison walls. The construction of new prisons was part of this broad overhaul of the penal system (around forty were built by the end of the 1910s, particularly in provincial capitals and ports open to foreign trade), under strong Japanese influence. That project obviously had its share of inertia, hindered as it was by the weight of tradition and the overlap between old and new practices.[1]

An 'institutional icon' (to use Jan Kiely's expression), Beijing's Prison No. 1 was not the earliest embodiment of China's new punitive approach. That distinction belongs to the Wuchang Prison in Hubei Province, also known as the Hubei Model Prison. Although it did not open until 1913, construction began as early as 1907 – before work had started on Prison No. 1. But as its name suggests, Model Prison No. 1 raised the banner the highest, symbolically at least. Claiming to meet the highest international standards in terms of infrastructure (lighting, ventilation, etc.), it served as a model for various buildings across the country over the decades that followed, starting (logically enough) with Beijing's Model Prisons Nos 2 and 3. Activity reports, which obviously portrayed it in a very favourable light, were sent to other prisons to bring them up to the new standard. Model Prison No. 1 became so costly that private sponsorship was needed to complete it.[2]

The radial design of the prison – with its double fanned-out structure linked by an administrative building and its corridors running from two central points – was a variation on the Pentonville model. Moreover, the figure of John Howard was sanctified by the prison's first director in the room where prisoners gathered to hear sermons. He included the English philanthropist's portrait among five figures depicted on the wall, alongside Confucius, Lao Tse, Muhammad, and Christ. This was a sign of the Japanese influence, the director having studied in Japan and also worked in its prison administration. After running Beijing's first model prison, where he trained more than 300 wardens in a special institute, he was promoted to director of the Chinese prison administration, which on the eve of the Second World War oversaw more than 120 new prisons, not to mention hundreds of local jails.[3]

The Japanese influence

Historians have described Beijing No. 1 Prison as a kind of Western–Japanese–Chinese hybrid. Unlike the trend that prevailed when Japan was under China's influence at the beginning of the Meiji era (1868), the Japanese influence on the modernization of Chinese prisons at the end of that era (1912) proved to be direct and decisive. (Douglas Reynolds argues that the 1898–1907 'golden decade', characterized by Sino-Japanese cooperation, was historically more significant than the apparent rupture of 1911–12.) It was exercised through the expertise of lawyers, scholars, and architects commissioned for this purpose, as well as through the training of Chinese officials in Japan, including Wang Yuanzeng, the first director of the Model Prison. In 1908, China appointed Japanese prison expert Ogawa Shigejiro as an adviser to oversee the construction of Beijing's model prison. This appointment was part of a much broader context. As Mark Finnane summarizes: 'Chinese emissaries abroad from the 1860s and Chinese students in Japan and elsewhere from the 1890s brought back to China the blueprints for a transformed criminal justice system. The material impact of this communication of ideals was a very ambitious prison-building program, whose planning began before the 1911 revolution and continued beyond it. Like so many blueprints elsewhere, the achievement was imperfect, but the Beijing Model Prison and others like it spoke to the abiding influence of the prison as a mark of a modern society by the time of the First World War.'

In Japan, at the height of the Meiji era in the early 1870s, the first draft of a prison law effected a shift towards the objective of correction and rehabilitation, along with a reduction in suffering. 'In 1878, the second International [Prison] Congress, which was convened in Stockholm, much praised Japan's innovations,' Clare Anderson notes. However, in practice, one kind of cruelty replaced another within the walls. As Daniel Botsman explains, the championing of the modern prison – that is, incarceration supposedly aimed at correction and reform – certainly changed the form of punishment in Japan, but it also made it more systematic and broader in scope. Though the country's first modern prison dates back to 1874, it was Tokyo's Sugamo Prison, completed in 1895, that is said to have served as the Asian reference point for Beijing's Model Prison No. 1. Influence of this kind tends to have a rebound effect, absorbing some local heritage every time. The Chinese Criminal Code, passed in 1910, was based on the Japanese Criminal Code, which in turn was inspired by the German Criminal Code. As for the new Japanese prisons (made of brick and even stone instead of wood, such as Taihoku in the colony of Taiwan, considered a jewel in the crown by the Japanese elite), they were influenced primarily by France (the Japanese central prisons were modelled on the French '*maisons centrales*') and England (through the British colonial prisons in Hong Kong and Singapore), and secondarily by the United States, where emissaries were dispatched in the 1870s.[4]

The question of influence raises a historiographical dilemma. As in the case of other prisons like Kresty (chapter 4), two symmetrical mistakes may threaten accurate understanding. The first is the exaggeration of otherness. There is the temptation to treat the Chinese situation as exotic, absolutely foreign, as if it had nothing to do with Western trends. But this danger can be quickly dispelled, because the broad similarities are quite obvious, even if these differ in their chronology. Anyone venturing into Chinese prison territory with *Discipline and Punish* as their only compass will certainly have to adapt, but without being overly disoriented. Although recent major historical studies make little reference to Foucault, their descriptions reflect the advent of a disciplinary model in terms of both its conditions of emergence and its empirical manifestations, such as the dissemination of examination as a 'normalizing gaze'. Docility and utility went hand in hand. Central to this objective was prison labour (sewing, printing, building, etc.) carried out in workshops that were located, as in the new Japanese prisons, at the end of the corridors, where prisoners usually worked in chains. The prison was virtually self-sufficient, with most everyday items produced on-site, and some prison workshops even making a profit selling their products outside the prison. The Ministry of Justice even organized an exhibition of objects made by prisoners in 1915, an event that was subsequently made permanent. Besides, Model Prison No. 1 printing house was producing documents for the Ministry of Justice. More generally, the guiding principles of the new penal approach were familiar: the goal of transformation through instruction and inculcation; the analogy between prisons and schools or hospitals; the idea that the prison was a yardstick to measure the level of civilization; or simply the emphasis on hygiene, if only to ensure the smooth running of the prison. There were also material extensions of Western inventions, such as English-style pews to prevent prisoners from exchanging words and glances during collective sermons.[5]

The second pitfall, on the other hand, is to exaggerate the level of imitation, to trace everything back to the reproduction of Western models, as if it were a simple case of copy and paste. This pitfall is probably more difficult to avoid, if only because the Chinese reformers themselves explicitly and frequently mentioned the influence and adoption of American and European penitentiary models, especially after the disaster of the Boxer Rebellion. The Qing dynasty had sent emissaries all over the world to study new foreign prisons. In a 1919 article published in the French *Revue pénitentiaire*, a Chinese author who earned his PhD in law in France stated that 'Modern prisons are built on the model of Western prisons, either in the shape of a star or a cross'; he added that the Auburnian system was prevailing in terms of organization. Beijing Model Prison No. 1 therefore raises the question of how importation and dissemination occur. Apart from minor differences in interpretation, recent studies are unanimous in rejecting the idea of a simple transfer. They stress the importance of local configurations and the resulting effects of filtering, rearrangement, and hybridization. So it was a matter not of passive reception, but rather of appropriation through the prism of a national tradition.[6]

China's transformation was undoubtedly part of an international, even global, movement. Significantly, in 1910, the country sent delegates to the International Penal and Penitentiary Congress in Washington for the first time. Yet the Chinese system subsequently retained its own distinctive features, which is why it can be described as 'both radically modern and remarkably traditional', to borrow Frank Dikötter's words. As the historian points out, the penitentiary ideology of moral reform was not simply a Western import. It combined with national tradition, particularly (Neo-)Confucianism. Rather than speaking of a recycling of Western elements ranging from moral instruction to the progressive system, we could instead speak of 'translation'.[7]

The idea of educational confinement, for example, or that of coercive-corrective inculcation, has its own roots in Imperial China, as does the concept of the law as an instrument of moral education. The term *ganhua* expresses this idea of personal reform, moral change, and self-improvement in mental and behavioural terms. In China, the corrective prison system is conceived as a tool that uses modern means to attain a traditional aim: to organize the cohesion of the social body around virtue as its primary value. Only in this context can we appreciate the similarities between China and Western countries, both outside and inside the prison walls (in which there is a mixture of punishment and reward, such as an additional visit or a supplementary food ration, a constant assessment of 'merit' and 'progress', etc.). The creation of a knowledge/power nexus in China has also led to the development of a national form of criminology and penology (or 'penitentiary science'), which has shifted the focus from past criminal acts to the figure of the potential criminal individual.

There is one important peculiarity that needs to be mentioned: the principle of extraterritoriality. This principle, which was actually introduced during the two Opium Wars in the mid-nineteenth century, allowed foreign criminals arrested in China to be tried under the laws of their country of origin. The state of Chinese prisons was not the least of the Western justifications for maintaining this exception, which could have been called into question if China had undertaken to meet Western standards. 'Prisoners in Peking [Beijing] are being coddled at present,' Philadelphia's newspaper the *Public Ledger* reported in the mid-1920s.

> Mr Liu Chi, Mayor of the city, has issued orders that they must be fed twice a day; that the jailers should not inflict private punishment or extort money from them; that their cells should be kept clean; that they should be instructed in manual work, morality and Chinese reading; and that they should be helped to secure employment after being released. [. . .] All these innovations are the result of the extraterritoriality investigation now being conducted there. The Mayor has declared that the capital city of China should have model prisons; otherwise it may not seem feasible to the foreign jurists, who are studying legal procedure and prison conditions, to advise their governments to relinquish their treaty privileges of trying and punishing their own nationals according to their own western customs.

Moreover, meeting or exceeding Western (and Japanese) standards in this area was a way of ensuring the Republic's moral parity with Western nations. Symbolically as well as materially, national sovereignty in relation to external powers was therefore at stake. Inside and outside the prison, the disciplinary system that was supposed to produce loyal and productive citizens was also conceived as a means of accumulating 'moral capital' for the state, as Klaus Mühlhahn points out.[8]

This idea echoes Dikötter's interpretation that model prisons 'were the microcosm of an exemplary society in which the emulation of models – whether in the school, the factory, or the army – was seen simultaneously as a mission of educative transformation, a project for social discipline and a strategy for national power'. The new prisons, starting with Beijing Prison No. 1, were designed as the prototypes of an ideal society. They were intended to be 'cathedrals of modernity'. However, they were not alone in this role, but part of a whole range of model institutions, from schools to villages, factories to barracks, all designed to set standards and encourage emulation through inter-institutional indoctrination. The Chinese case once again echoes the disciplinary model, in that prisons were used alongside other institutions for poor and deviant people, from vagrants to prostitutes to drug addicts: workhouses, hospices, asylums, and so on. The development of the country's modern police force in the 1920s played a crucial role in this respect.[9]

There were issues relating to the expression of state authority that stemmed from a socioeconomic restructuring process. The coercion rationale meant a deeper penetration of penal institutions into social life, in a context of industrialization and commercialization. In this respect, the Republican era was also marked by profound inequalities in the penal confinement system. The penal system more generally, and the prison system in particular, targeted people at the bottom of the social ladder. In short, China had its own 'dangerous classes' that it had produced or only labelled as such. The social structure and the face of crime changed during this period: in the mid-1920s, the proportion of adult males involved in economic crime reached almost 85%. However, this change must be considered in light of corresponding social representations, especially among the elite, which saw poverty, ignorance, and idleness as breeding grounds for crime. The system reflects a social structure dominated by a small, highly educated elite who viewed ordinary people as backward and superstitious, and showed little or no concern for their own misdeeds, such as corruption. For commoners, some corporal punishments were openly reintroduced both outside and inside prisons a few years after their official abolition (such as bamboo caning).

As elsewhere, behind the metal gates and brick walls of Beijing's Prison No. 1, prison life had little to do with textbook prescriptions. This is not to say that nothing original was ever tried on the ground. For example, films were sometimes shown for educational purposes. Jan Kiely describes an attempt to develop an educational programme in the early 1920s, based on an in-house periodical that prisoners were involved in producing. The aim, however, was oral and written repentance rather than real rehabilitation. In any case, the experiment was short-lived, and even the prisoners' use of the library eventually dwindled to nothing. In practice, the system boiled down to work and moral education, based on an approach that was both religious and civic/patriotic. Misbehaviour was punished in various ways: prohibition of visits and correspondence, deprivation of personal belongings and food, or even temporary isolation in a dark cell.[10]

Behind the proclaimed ideal, management by fear prevailed. Given the role assigned to prisons as a tool of punishment, overcrowding and underfunding became chronic, and the establishments soon came to be reserved for long sentences. Corruption, abuse of power, the institutional production of apathy, direct or indirect forms of torture: the usual harms of the world of confinement were present, even if the situation was certainly worse in older prisons. Internal investigations soon revealed a failure that the number of deaths within the walls expressed better than any written report. It was a material failure, but also a symbolic one in terms of the institution's legitimacy. The public increasingly saw the model prison as a place of violence and arbitrariness, tarnishing not only its own reputation but also that of the Republic as a whole. In the 1920s and 1930s, several texts condemned the cruelty of the so-called 'model prisons'. Ching-Yueh Yen's account, published in 1931, is both atypical and instructive. In 1927, the author spent three months in one of them as a voluntary prisoner for academic purposes. He was involved in research that, in the late 1920s, resulted in a critical analysis of conditions in the new prisons, which were described as uncivilized and degrading. Pointing out that most of the reform movement had previously come from the West, he argued that China was only just beginning to chart its own course, and he dismissed the reforms of the early part of the century as a 'ridiculous joke'. Little did he know what the rest of the century had in store for his country's prison system.[11]

A century after it opened, Model Prison No. 1 was still standing. What is more, Chinese authorities continued to hold it up as an exemplary penal institution, staging it as a showcase for Western visitors. In October 2012, it even held an 'open day' so journalists could see for themselves how human rights had progressed behind bars. The prison interior certainly looked good: not only had it been cleaned up, but the inmates themselves had been moved elsewhere for this special occasion.[12]

Chapter 8

Model Jail Lucknow (India, 1949 [1867])

In official statistics compiled by India's northern state of Uttar Pradesh in the late 2000s, 'Model Jail Lucknow' generally appears at the top of tables ranging from 'Year of Construction of Prisons in Uttar Pradesh' to 'Prison Accommodation & Occupancy Rates'. The only prison with a name explicitly presenting it as a supposed 'model' is also counted separately. The 'Organizational Structure' of the 'Jail Administration and Correctional Services' places it in a category all its own, distinct from 'central jails' and more broadly from about fifty other Uttar Pradesh prisons, in a country where they are managed by the states.[1]

Not that this was the first prison in the region, or that it in any way influenced others that followed. In fact, it was one of the last of a succession of 'central jails' built or revamped from the 1840s to the 1870s. This period saw the final phase of a development that had slowly begun at the end of the previous century, finally establishing the colonial prison system as a cornerstone of imperial British rule. Although transportation and corporal punishment were still in use, imprisonment became the standard form of punishment throughout the country, and a Penal Code was enacted in 1860. The mid-nineteenth century was also a turning point because it marked the beginning of an equally long period of 'modernization', when prison authorities were emphasizing the virtues of discipline through captive labour. The facility that opened in 1867 was initially only known as 'Lucknow Central Jail' (and later 'Lucknow District Jail') but it did not stand out. No one was thinking of making it a 'model' anything, not even a model colonial prison. Another prison, Alipore, was regarded as a reference as early as the 1840s, based as it was on a 1838 report by the 'Committee on Prison Discipline' chaired by Lord Thomas Macaulay (several years before Pentonville Prison opened), recommending strict classification, solitary confinement, indoor hard labour, a strict diet (arguably a starvation diet in practice), and silence, leading to certain architectural changes in a few prisons. It was later in Agra near Kolkata, where a huge massive jail was built in 1846, that modest experiments with individual imprisonment took place in the 1850s. As Mira Rai Watts notes, after being transformed into a 'central jail' in the 1860s (renamed the Presidency Correctional Home), it 'became a model for other Bengal jails'. But in the 1870s, it was the Bhagalpur Central Jail that came to 'set the tone for prison architecture in Bengal and the rest of India', including Lucknow.[2]

There was no corrective purpose back then, much less any kind of humanitarian motive. The prison system was harsh, especially in central jails meant for 'hardened criminals':

> The colonial prison aspired not to teach morality but to contain and control the uncivilized. It also provided a forum in which the state could practice strategies of control that might be useful over the vast space of the colony as a whole. [. . .] Colonial officials were certainly familiar with the dominant and progressive penologies developing in Britain and its colonies, and in the United States. However, the prisons they constructed in India incorporated local resources and precolonial building practices and did not fully embrace imported Western models. British colonial prison officials determined that such imports were impractical in an Indian setting.

As we saw in chapter 2, there was nothing like a straightforward export of the British model to its colonies, even if the Panopticon or Pentonville Prison was likely to be mentioned in official texts. Entire sections of those inspirations were altered during the transfer process, and they were implemented belatedly, including architectural features like the radial plan. Watts adds:

> It was not until late in the century that prison models employed in Britain and the United States had any significant effect in India. And even then, when more permanent and generously spaced compounds employing imported concepts (such as the radial plan) were built, colonial officials remained disinterested in their moralizing potential, preferring instead to treat prisons as emblematic of a system of social classification, one that saw the Indian population as predisposed to crime.

So it was not a matter of moral reform, but rather close observation. As David Arnold has shown, the colonial prison was used 'not only as a place of confinement but also as a site of colonial knowledge, a means of acquiring insight into the material conditions of the population at large'.[3]

Lucknow became a 'model' in status and in name only in the mid-twentieth century. One thing that distinguishes this prison is that it has two birthdates (but not really two existences, considering there has been a continuum in terms of its actual prison practices): the first in 1867, and the second in 1949. Just under a century after it had first opened, in a sense it was reinaugurated in the wake of India's independence, in order to be converted into a 'model prison'. In any case, it received this distinctive 'honorary' name, which made it a benchmark for a postcolonial prison system that was meant to be thoroughly improved. However, India's prison reform drive began even before the official date of independence. In 1946, a special committee drew up a series of recommendations based on several guiding principles, particularly that prisoners should be separated by classification (a longstanding recommendation), and that they should be educated. After an initial trial elsewhere, in 1949 Lucknow Prison was chosen to be the touchstone of 'modern' prison reform. It was to house only adult male convicts (therefore excluding remand and juvenile prisoners), more particularly 'star class prisoners'.[4]

The post-independence reform agenda did not come out of nowhere. Most of the leaders of the Indian independence movement had spent considerable time behind bars, sometimes repeatedly, starting with Jawaharlal Nehru, who was imprisoned about ten times from the early 1920s. The future Prime Minister of India wrote a great deal about his experience, including his stay in Lucknow, where he was incarcerated the first time. In contact with 'ordinary criminals' (despite official efforts to split the prison population into separate groups), Nehru and other political prisoners gained first-hand experience of prison's specific contribution to a coercive system based on discrimination of class, caste, origin, colour, and religion. According to historian David Arnold, the colonial prison system was 'contested' because it was the scene of a struggle, not only between colonizers and 'natives', but also between prisoners and guards, inmates from upper and lower castes, and (especially from the 1890s onwards) political and common-law prisoners. This led Lucknow to be at least partly considered a political prison.[5]

Nehru's account of Lucknow Prison in the early 1920s

'Imprisonment for political offenses was not a new thing in the India of 1921. [. . .] But still in 1921 prison was an almost unknown place, and very few knew what happened behind the grim gates that swallowed the new convict. Vaguely we imagined that its inhabitants were desperate people and dangerous criminals. In our minds the place was associated with isolation, humiliation, and suffering, and, above all, the fear of the unknown. Frequent references to jail-going from 1920 onward, and the march of many of our comrades to prison, gradually accustomed us to the idea and took away the edge from that almost involuntary feeling of repugnance and reluctance. [. . .]

'My first term in jail, which ended rather suddenly after three months, was a hectic period both for us and the jail staff. The jail officials were half paralyzed by the influx of the new type of convict. The number itself of these newcomers, added to from day to day, was extraordinary and created an impression of a flood which might sweep away the old traditional landmarks. [. . .]

'In the jail every effort was made to keep us apart from the ordinary nonpolitical convicts, special jails being as a rule reserved for politicals. But complete segregation was impossible, and we often came into touch with those prisoners and learned from them, as well as directly, the realities of prison life in those days. It was a story of violence and widespread graft and corruption. [. . .]

'The general policy of the prison administration in the United Provinces (and probably in other provinces) had absolutely nothing to do with the reform of the prisoner or of teaching him good habits and useful trades. The object of prison labor was to harass the convict. He was to be frightened and broken into blind submission; the idea was that he should carry away from prison a fear and a horror of it, so that he might avoid crime and a return to prison in the future.

'There have been some changes in recent years for the better. Food has improved a little, so also clothing and other matters. This was largely due to the agitation carried on outside by political prisoners after their discharge. [. . .] A feeble effort is also made now to teach reading and writing to the boys and younger prisoners. But all these changes, welcome as they are, barely scratch the problem, and the old spirit remains much the same. [. . .]

'On the last day of January 1923 all of us politicals in the Lucknow Jail were discharged. There is always a feeling of relief and a sense of glad excitement in coming out of the prison gate.'

These are the words of Jawaharal Nehru, a man who had known barely anything about prisons before entering Lucknow for the first time in 1921. He wrote them in the 1930s, in a chapter entitled 'Lucknow District Jail'. While he mentions some relative advantages enjoyed by political prisoners during this period, he reports that conditions later became more restrictive, partly due to overcrowding.[6]

The prison reform project was therefore being spearheaded by former independence activists. As a means of putting an end to miserable confinement conditions, the aim was to raise Lucknow's standards to the same level as Western prisons, after which it could serve as a benchmark for the rest of India. It was in this context that the first staff training school was set up in Lucknow. An open-air prison yard was even created, marking the first step towards 'open prisons' in India. (According to official figures, there were eighty-eight of these minimal-security prisons in the early 2020s.) To a certain extent, the desired transformation of Lucknow was about making it part of an institutional archipelago. The prison was located close to other supervision or confinement institutions, including reformatory schools, local jails, the local headquarters of armed forces, and the prison administration office.

This sought conversion into a model prison anticipated and reflected a broader process that took place throughout the 1950s. After achieving independence, the new rulers asked the United Nations to help draw up a survey of the prison situation. One fruit of this collaboration was the codification of practical routines in an official handbook; an idea conceived at a meeting of Indian prison inspectors in 1952. After the UN published its own minimum rules for the treatment of prisoners in 1955, a domestic committee was set up in 1957, and the handbook was ready in 1959, unambiguously titled the *Model Jail Management Manual*.

The prison administration subsequently underwent a process of centralization and bureaucratization through the creation of the Central Bureau of Correctional Services in 1961. But developments in prisons were so slow that a new working group had to be set up by the government in 1972. It produced a report the following year, but this had no significant impact, as actual practices continued to bear little relation to written guidelines. This situation persisted to the point that yet another national committee – the All-India Committee on Jail Reforms – needed to be set up, meeting from 1980 to 1983 and making as many as 658 recommendations. . .

Committees of this kind were by no means a recent trend, being part of a long historical tradition rooted in the colonial era. There was a succession of reform committees in the nineteenth century and the first half of the twentieth century. As already mentioned, the first, best known, and most influential of these was established in 1836 under the direction of Lord Macaulay, whose report led to several central prisons being built, Lucknow included. A second prison commission was set up in 1864 to address the disproportionately high mortality and morbidity rates behind bars, and in 1877, a conference on prison discipline was held. Two quickly successive national committees in 1889 and 1892 led to the passing of the 1894 Prison Act. Replacing the 1870 Prisons Act, it was to remain the decisive legislation in the field for the next century. This law, which among other things was supposed to regulate the use of the whip and solitary confinement, provided a federal framework based on intimidation, coercion, and labour; anything but 'rehabilitation'. It was still in effect more than a century later, despite minor alterations and the enactment of local rules and regulations. Another national committee was created that met from 1919 to 1920, the last of the colonial era. It was unique in that it compared India's system with others in both East and West. The 1920 Report of the Indian Jails Committee was the first to assert prisoner rehabilitation as an objective to be pursued, based on a dual approach of prevention and reform. In addition to the usual principles (categorization of prisoners, importance of hygiene, role of coerced labour, etc.), it included considerations relating to medical assistance or sentence reduction. The state of Uttar Pradesh – the country's most populous state and one of its poorest, where Jails Reforms Committees were set up in 1938 and 1946 – claimed to be a leader in this respect.

As one might guess, the reform proposals were wishful thinking. They were rejected by colonial officers under the pretext that they were unenforceable and even inappropriate. In 1944, a follow-up report covering the previous two decades was published under the auspices of the Faculty of Law at the University of Cambridge, by a British lieutenant-colonel who had served as the Inspector General of Prisons for the Central Provinces and Punjab. The author mentioned 'a model Borstal Institution inaugurated at Tanjore, and a special jail set apart for mental defectives', but not yet anything like a model prison, in Lucknow or anywhere else. Reality was a far cry from the proclaimed intentions, and India's prison conditions were generally terrible. There as elsewhere, the history of prisons is one of ill treatment, poverty, overcrowding, corruption, lack of privacy, and violence, problems that could be expected from a prison system that never favoured rehabilitation but was organized around coercion and discipline, including in Foucault's sense of that concept. Within the division of coercive labour that was part of colonial domination, the role of the prison was twofold: on the one hand, political domination with overemphasis on order and discipline; and, on the other hand, economic exploitation through forced captive manufacturing (a 'prison-handicraft complex', as historian Anand Yang calls it in reference to the 'prison-industrial complex'). In this respect, the prison prefigured the factory rather than the other way around. And if there was some idea of 'remodelling' prisoners, this was mostly viewed through an industrial lens. There is nothing to suggest that Lucknow was somehow an exception to the rule.[7]

In a report prepared for the First United Nations Congress on the Prevention of Crime and the Treatment of Offenders in 1955, the principal of Lucknow's 'Jail Training School' wrote:

> In 1949 a Model Prison was set up in this State to which star class prisoners sentenced to long terms are committed. This institution is operating as a self-sufficient colony with working conditions as similar to the outside world as possible. The inmates choose their own occupation after observing other inmates at work and with the assistance of the prison staff. In this institution, persuasion and guidance are the methods of reform and rehabilitation and in the course of successive adjustments, the inmates gradually secure the privilege of working and earning their living outside the jail without any watch and ward.

The author further explains that in the 'Model Jail', 'self-discipline is inculcated among the inmates through gradually increasing freedom and responsibility', which 'helps to mould the character of prisoners for the better'. Truth be told, this official viewpoint seems unreasonably optimistic. However, it does appear that Lucknow Prison enjoyed a relatively favourable reputation among prisoners during the 1960s and 1970s. In 1979, the author of one of the few in-depth qualitative studies in the 1970s exploring prisons in India (if not the only one, inspired by the foundational sociological work on America's prisons) provided some clues in this direction, even describing Model Jail Lucknow as the prison 'Mecca' in Uttar Pradesh.[8]

Lucknow has kept the name 'model jail', but today its reputation and influence are uncertain at best. Significantly, this prison was not mentioned in the 1991 report by a visiting committee on prison conditions in India set up by Human Rights Watch. It is worth mentioning that this visiting committee was unable to visit anything. Under the police's suspicious gaze, it was not allowed access to any prison, and therefore had to rely on document analysis and interviews (with former prisoners, as well as doctors, lawyers, activists, researchers, and others). This illustrated the continuing opacity of the Indian prison system, despite decades of reform discussions and plans.[9]

It is therefore no surprise that the issue of prison reform came up once again in the late twentieth century and early twenty-first century, with the situation being described as more critical than ever. As a result of growing social pressure and a palpable spirit of national consensus, a revised version of the 1959 manual was produced in 2003. The *Model Prison Manual for the Superintendence and Management of Prisons in India*, a document of more than 300 pages and some thirty chapters, reviewed various aspects of the prison system, in terms similar to those of Western countries. It was the least they could do, considering that the Supreme Court, which was increasingly interventionist in this domain, had referred to 'subhuman' prison conditions.[10]

Even in a somewhat official publication, *The Indian Police Journal*, whose editorial board includes prison administration executives and members of the Bureau of Police Research and Development, one could read in 2012 that despite a renewed focus on prisons since the mid-2000s (evidenced by the revision of the reference manual), India was far from being an enlightened country in this domain. Not only is the legacy of colonial-era prison management still evident ('Carceral culture in contemporary India relies on the colonial discourse on prisons and its logic of a repressive state managing resistant, violent, and unruly subjects,' writes anthropologist Mahuya Bandyopadhyay, warning nonetheless that a genuine 'decolonial criminology' must go beyond 'revealing the colonial matrix of power'), but the gulf between principles and reality has even widened. The prison-based approach still dominates in the penal system. During the 2010s under the rule of Narendra Modi, the ratio of prisoners to convicts serving non-custodial sentences was 3 to 1, whereas in Western countries like France, the proportion is roughly the opposite. Scholars have highlighted a disconnect between theory and practice, as well as a new coercive arbitrariness in which 'reform' has become a power technique or control strategy based on an overly uniform representation of the prison population.[11]

However, old hopes have not been dashed. In 2008, not only was the Tihar Prisons complex still being touted as a model, but also the construction of the 'world's largest prison' (3,000 inmates) in Lucknow was announced as part of a general state reform. And in 2014, Indian Minister of Home Affairs Rajnath Singh – formerly Chief Minister of Uttar Pradesh, but also a former prisoner himself – announced a new phase of prison reform to address the miserable state that most of them were in. His slogan sounded a bit like a confession of amnesia: build more model prisons. There was an economic rationale behind it: lighter security infrastructure and fewer staff meant cheaper prisons. Even a 2018 report prepared for India's National Human Rights Commission stressed the importance of saving money. And in India as in other countries, now talk of 'models' increasingly refers to another, broader one: the 'public–private partnership model' that situates prisons within a commercial framework. The term 'model' proves especially enduring in this context. In 2023, a 'Model Prisons and Correctional Services Act' was devised, intended to serve as a foundation for all jurisdictions. Designed to replace the colonial-era legislation of 1894, it formally introduced objectives of reformation and rehabilitation. However, these aims appear all the more precarious given that the correctional framework is faltering worldwide.[12]

Counterpoint IV

The 'Nordic/Scandinavian' model

There is a unique case in which model status is granted not to just one particular prison, nor to an institutional type in general, nor even to a national penal tradition, but rather to an entire geographical region: the so-called 'Nordic' or 'Scandinavian' model. This reference carries so much symbolic power – both in Europe (because of geographical proximity) and in the Americas (due to a bewildering contrast with harsher punitive cultures) – that 'Scandinavia' is sometimes invoked as a kind of prison Eldorado, at least from a progressive perspective. It has generated numerous accounts from foreign observers expressing admiration and sometimes disbelief, largely because what distinguishes this model is often described as a difference not only in degree, but also in nature. Hence the question: how could an 'exception' be a 'model'?[1]

The appeal of the Scandinavian model finds its most visible (though somewhat misleading) expression in attempts to identify the 'world's best prisons', through various somewhat fanciful online rankings. Norway's Bastøy and Halden prisons never fail to appear on these lists. The facilities contrast so sharply with the conventional notion of a prison that they attract an unusual amount of media attention, even from entertainment outlets, providing rich material for journalists. For instance, a 2012 CNN report on Bastøy Prison was eloquently titled 'Welcome to the world's nicest prison'. As journalist John D. Sutter wrote, among other striking anecdotes about this unusual place: 'Founded in 1982, Bastøy Prison is located on a lush, 1-square-mile island of pine trees and rocky coasts, with views of the ocean that are postcard-worthy. It feels more like a resort than jail, and prisoners here enjoy freedoms that would be unthinkable elsewhere. It's the holiday version of Alcatraz.' His account detailed extraordinary features like the lack of fences, a nearby beach for prisoners, as well as fishing opportunities, a sauna, a tennis court, and well-paid work under minimal supervision. The article explains that despite holding around one hundred inmates convicted of serious, sometimes violent crimes, the facility operates so informally that it is difficult to distinguish officers from prisoners. While the article bordered on sensational with its jokey tone ('Plenty of people would pay to vacation in a place like this'), it concluded positively, noting low recidivism rates and giving concrete examples of prisoner rehabilitation. Other reports typically praise it as an ecological, open-air prison that is clean and without bars. John Pratt called it 'the shining jewel in the Scandinavian open prison system' in his widely discussed article on 'Scandinavian exceptionalism'.[2]

Similarly, a 2012 article in *The Guardian* described Halden as the 'most humane prison in the world', a designation that has been frequently applied to this facility, which opened in 2010 and reportedly 'smells of freshly brewed coffee'. Located in a forest and having a minimalist design, Halden maintains a quiet atmosphere in which fights are rare and escape attempts are even rarer. Despite being classified as high security (unlike Bastøy) and holding prisoners convicted of serious crimes, inmates are provided with amenities such as a grocery store, a modern gym, a recording studio, flat-screen TVs, and refrigerators in cells. With as many staff as inmates, it apparently offers greater comfort than many hotels or university campuses, though it remains the subject of controversy domestically, particularly surrounding mass murderer Anders Breivik's imprisonment on this site.[3]

Norway has long been a penal beacon. As early as 1965, Thomas Mathiesen, a future spearhead of the prison abolition movement, revealed the vast differences between Norwegian and American prisons in his first major empirical study – and this was during an era when the United States was widely considered one of the most progressive countries in the area of incarceration, long before its punitive excesses began.[4]

The famous examples of Bastøy and Halden tend to suggest that the Nordic or Scandinavian exception primarily lies in 'open prisons'. Although these did not originate in Northern Europe, they now serve as the region's distinctive 'trademark', and international attention has often focused on this aspect. This was the case in a 1976 study by John Snortum of three Swedish prisons: Studiegarden (a small 'educational facility' in operation since 1967), Gävle (a former maximum-security unit built in the 1840s, eventually becoming an internment centre, later transformed into a 'therapeutic community' in 1971), and Tillberga (a 'prison factory'). This comparative study revealed common characteristics that distinguished the Swedish model from the system in California. 'Compared to California prisons,' Snortum noted, 'Swedish prisons are smaller, more personal, more manageable, more heavily staffed, and more generously financed,' but the author also pointed out social and political tensions that could have undermined the legitimacy of the Swedish system. An article on Danish prisons in a 1977 issue of *Corrections Magazine* explained that American conservatives disparaged the Swedish facilities as 'country clubs'. Indeed, those odd prisons had neither watchtowers, nor perimeter walls, nor barbed wire, and sometimes there was barely any fencing to delimit inside and outside. Built as small-scale facilities with separate houses rather than the mammoth structures found elsewhere in Europe and America, they offered comfortable rooms instead of squalid cells, as well as modern workshops offering properly paid work, and ununiformed, unarmed guards who functioned more as support staff than supervisors. Other features included leave permits, freedom of movement, inmates' representatives, minimal censorship, and unrestricted visit arrangements.[5]

Prior to Norway's Bastøy and Halden, there were several emblematic institutions that epitomized this approach in neighbouring countries, particularly island-based prisons like Finland's Suomenlinna, which opened in 1971 off the coast of Helsinki. Located within a village, Suomenlinna's inmates contribute to the restoration of a UNESCO World Heritage Site and take their meals alongside guards. Proponents emphasize not only its rejection of punitive demagogy and its low recidivism rates, but also its reduced financial costs – painting a picture of an entirely advantageous system. Similarly, a 1977 legal article described Denmark's Ringe State Prison as an unprecedented endeavour in Scandinavia and Europe. Interestingly, even though it was then the most secure prison in Denmark, it barely met North America's minimum security standards. Opened on an island in 1976 with the goal of creating an environment resembling the outside world, it featured electronic surveillance, unbarred windows, and a perimeter wall, and was staffed by carefully selected ununiformed guards. Ringe's most unusual characteristic – remarkable then and now – was gender diversity among inmates. As this example illustrates, one of the most striking features of the Scandinavian model is that some prisons do not look like prisons.[6]

But this is not the only aspect that should be considered. What ensures inmate compliance in open facilities is that rule violations can result in transfer to 'normal' prisons. The latter differ significantly from international equivalents, further reinforcing the uniqueness of the Scandinavian system. As a volunteer teacher in American prisons explained in a 2013 article in *The Atlantic*, Scandinavian prisons are 'superior' because they treat prisoners as regular citizens. Although the article begins with the case of Suomenlinna, the author's statement did not solely apply to open prisons, since he had also visited high-security facilities throughout Scandinavia. Painting a picture that sharply contrasted with the United States both qualitatively and quantitatively, he described well-equipped prisons that allowed inmates to work outside and visit family despite serious convictions, and authority that did not mete out indiscriminate coercion. The difference in scale is crucial: Sweden's entire prison population (6,900) is less than half of the number of prisoners held on New York's Rikers Island at its peak (14,000), while several individual US prisons hold nearly twice Finland's prison population. But there is more to it: the contrast encompasses both outer prison design and inner organization, both vertical and horizontal relationships. In addition to lower incarceration rates, smaller facilities, and different rehabilitative principles, Nordic exceptionalism also stems from a model of 'official governance', according to David Skarbek's typology.[7]

The Scandinavian model reaches into every area, from penal philosophy to physical design to everyday management. Beyond prisons, the reputation enjoyed by Scandinavian countries is more broadly rooted in a criminal justice model based on limiting the use of prison, which is imposed only as a last resort. This limitation applies both to the decision whether or not to imprison, and to the length of custodial sentences, which means favouring alternative sentences (particularly for minors), making sentences shorter, avoiding the over-use of pre-trial detention, as well as emphasizing post-release support. This reflects not just architectural or organizational differences, but also fundamentally different ways of viewing crime and guilt. When two French lawyers published an op-ed piece in 2014 entitled 'Which model for our prisons: Scandinavia or the United States?', their question sounded merely rhetorical, if not comical. At that time, the United States was the epitome of punitive excess, the ultimate carceral repellent, whereas the Scandinavian countries represented a 'liberal', 'humanistic', sensible orientation.[8]

This may obscure the fact that regional 'penal cultures' are less clear-cut than commonly assumed. Despite its widespread use, the very concept of a Nordic or Scandinavian model remains debatable, especially when it is implicitly treated as stable and cohesive. There are a wide variety of arguments that seek to temper or even invalidate the theory of a Scandinavian exception, ranging from claims of excessive historical and geographical homogenization to the exposure of long-unnoticed or underestimated punitive practices. Without questioning the existence of non-standard prisons, they place the idea of a model in perspective.

First, to speak of a Nordic or Scandinavian model in general is to evoke exaggerated unity in a vast, differentiated area. Significant variations exist between Nordic countries. In the early 2010s, when Swedish prisons were emptying out, Norway considered renting prison spaces in the Netherlands due to waiting lists during prison renovation work. Conversely, over the past decade, Sweden's incarceration rate has risen sharply relative to neighbouring countries. A quantitative comparison between closed, secured prisons in Scandinavia and California, published in 1985 to counter excessive public attention to 'open prisons', found California to be inferior in almost every respect, and concluded that Finland's prison system was much less severe, while Norway's and Sweden's were the least severe of all. The study also highlighted significant inter-Scandinavian differences, and challenged common assumptions, particularly in arguing that Swedish prison policies were based more on 'damage control' than on therapeutic expectations.[9]

This leads to a second issue: the risk of oversimplifying historical trajectories that are complex and sometimes conflictual. When Sweden launched a prison construction programme in the 1950s, it drew inspiration from . . . the United States – this was before their paths diverged radically some twenty years later. Though Finland now has one of the world's lowest detention rates, it was the Nordic incarceration leader for a long time, with very high rates in the 1950s, as Nils Christie and other scholars have pointed out. The steady decline of its numbers since 1975 was not an uncontrolled evolution, but rather the result of pro-active prison reduction policies. Social unrest is not unheard of in Scandinavia. Its prisons experienced their own '1968' through strikes and revolts that had a significant impact on the direction they subsequently took. In 1970, a nationwide hunger strike involved 2,500 prisoners across thirty Swedish prisons – an event that spawned organizations like KRUM, an association advocating the humanization of prisons. In 1974, representatives of prisoners sent an 'open letter' to the French President, warning that contrary to what he had been claiming, Kumla Prison was far from being a model, and that its conditions were in fact physically and psychologically inhumane.[10]

History shows that the special reputation enjoyed by Scandinavian countries is relatively recent. The idea of corrective imprisonment reached Sweden in the early seventeenth century under the influence of Dutch, German, and then French correctional institutions, but few penitentiary facilities were built. Although John Howard's criticism was well known in Sweden in the nineteenth century, and the cell system seems to have been introduced around 1850, actual reforms remained weak, and achievements were late in coming, so that at that time, there was no Swedish prison serving as a model for the rest of Europe or the wider world.[11]

A third problem is one of comparison and transposition. As I have suggested, American progressives who visit Nordic prisons are particularly disoriented by what they observe, discovering a system that is so drastically different from their own that it would be unthinkable at home. One reason is that the nature of Nordic criminal justice systems stems from dominant values focused on combating socioeconomic inequalities and promoting assistance and rehabilitation, as well as national characteristics related to social structure and the nature of the state. And because of this, no matter how impressed they may be, many observers refuse to consider these countries as truly replicable models. The Scandinavian countries are considered to possess unique characteristics that their approach depends on (not only in terms of crime, but also in terms of demographics, political culture, etc.), and it is therefore deemed non-transferable. As two authors recently pointed out in an article discussing Tommie Shelby's book *The Idea of Prison Abolition*,

> Norway demonstrates the possibility that a system focused sharply on rehabilitation is consistent with humane treatment as well as low rates of incarceration and interpersonal violence. However, the Norwegian model evolved under conditions of low crime rates in an ethnically homogeneous society with a fiercely egalitarian culture. The possibility that it can be replicated elsewhere, especially outside the Scandinavian context, remains untested.[12]

In the 1960s and 1970s, some authors were already sceptical about the real possibility of importing this or that Scandinavian model. While it is tempting to say that this scepticism has only grown since then, several US states have in fact recently created Nordic-style units within their prisons. The most famous example is certainly the aptly named 'Little Scandinavia' project that opened in 2022 at SCI-Chester in Pennsylvania: a sixty-four-bed pilot unit designed to replicate a Nordic prison environment. Other notable examples include the Oregon State Penitentiary, which has an experimental unit inspired by the Scandinavian model (particularly Norway's), and San Quentin Prison (in neighbouring California), whose transformation into a 'rehabilitation centre' was also inspired by the Norwegian model.[13]

And there is yet a fourth issue, relating to the tensions and contradictions of 'Nordic exceptionalism'. The exact nature of Nordic penal cultures is the subject of debate, as research has revealed new complexities and questionable aspects that are not commonly acknowledged. In the 1960s and 1970s, some observers pointed out that in Northern Europe, prison was not reserved just for dangerous criminals or serious offenders, since relatively petty property offences or drunk driving could lead to imprisonment. An official French report published in 1977 highlighted Sweden's supposed dark side, citing high rates of suicide, divorce, and tranquillizer use as evidence that it was an intrusive welfare state with pervasive social control. Also controversial is its excessive resort to pre-trial detention and preventive solitary confinement – somewhat hidden punitive practices that have also characterized those countries in recent decades. Some authors have also pointed out that visible minorities are treated more harshly, suggesting that 'exceptionalism' may be a double standard, primarily applying to native-born offenders, but not so much to immigrants, marginalized groups, and more generally non-white people. Some field studies have more broadly highlighted the ambivalence of the prison experience, even in open prisons that hardly seem like prisons at all. This raises the question: if these prisons are so desirable, why are there not a greater number of eligible prisoners requesting to be transferred to them? Recalling the key elements of the debate on 'Nordic exceptionalism', a recent empirical study comparing Norway with England and Wales was clearly partial to Norway in the balance ('there is little doubt that the typical experience of imprisonment is more humane and less damaging in Norway than in England & Wales'), yet it was careful not to idealize Norway's example.[14]

In a 1976 lecture published posthumously in 1993, Michel Foucault, who had lived in Uppsala in the 1950s, invoked Sweden to maximize the effect of his argument (if a Swedish model prison had 'failed', what could possibly 'succeed'?), at a time when what one author called the 'discreet charm of Swedish prisons' was being widely celebrated:

> I will begin with the example of Sweden: in 1965, Sweden passed new penal legislation, and this legislation's first consequence,

> its first effect, was the creation – or at least a plan to create – seven large prisons, seven thoroughly perfected large prisons, applying all of the meticulousness necessary, and also all of the leniency that had been learned. Of these seven prisons, some were created: the first and largest was Kemela [*sic*], a kind of penal edifice, a pure realisation of Bentham's panoptic – in a word, the enchanted dream of classic penality.
>
> [Kumla] prison opened in '67 or '68 I believe. In 1971, what happened in this wonderful prison is what happens in all these prisons: first, a large group escaped and, second, the fugitives immediately resumed their lives of crime.
>
> If we assume that prison serves two purposes – first and foremost to ensure the detention of individuals in a definite and continuous way – then it is easy to see that the [Kumla] escape obviously proved that the apparatus was not up to scratch. Secondly, the fact that they reoffended after having just escaped from that wonderful model prison obviously proved that the aim of rehabilitation in detention had itself also failed. So what is the point of such a perfect prison, if there is neither security nor rehabilitation?

Setting aside transcription errors, translation oddities, and factual inaccuracies, the misspelled name refers to Kumla, a prison that opened in 1965 and can hardly be described as 'pure form of Bentham's Panopticon'. Foucault used this example to contextualize the creation of 'a programme that would be an alternative to classic prisons', leading to 'new model prisons, or rather alternatives to the prison, [in which] leave of absence was granted much more frequently, not simply as a reward for good conduct, but as a means towards reintegration into society'. In so doing, he framed the key terms of the lecture he had been invited to deliver: 'alternative to the prison' and 'failure of the prison'. Diffusion or decline of social control? It is still an open question, but from the perspective of the 2020s, the answer is quite clear. In any case, the trend towards tougher punitive measures in Northern Europe, where the far right is on the rise, suggests that Scandinavia is more likely to align itself with its southern neighbours than the other way round. This could result in the Nordic countries losing their model status in every sense of the word.[15]

Chapter 9

Stammheim, Stuttgart (Federal Republic of Germany, 1963)

Stammheim Prison (aerial view, 2024)
Source: Carsten Steger, via Wikipedia Commons (CC BY-SA 4.0)

Weiterstadt, State of Hesse, 1985. For the first time, the local information bulletin is looking a lot like a political leaflet. It calls for a street demonstration against the imminent construction of one of Europe's largest prisons. In this small town of about 20,000 inhabitants, the prison's disproportionate size is in itself likely to exacerbate the strong reluctance that usually greets plans to build prisons near people's homes, and generates local

'NIMBY' (not in my backyard) movements. But in this case, the reasons for rejection are more particular: it is specifically about avoiding a 'Stammheim II'. At that time, just mentioning this name was enough to stoke anxiety.[1]

'Stammheim would probably have remained a peaceful small town in northern Stuttgart had a new prison not opened there. . . . Meeting the highest security standards, it was chosen for the imprisonment of core members of the Red Army Faction (RAF) in the early 1970s.' This is how lawyer Frédéric Audren and sociologist Dominique Linhardt set the scene for their study of the RAF trial, the longest in the post-war Federal Republic of Germany (FRG). The elected officials of Weiterstadt were indeed concerned that it should remain a 'peaceful small town', but this hope was to be dashed, to say the least. . . Anyway, even though the 'German hysteria' surrounding armed struggle had dwindled a decade after the opening of that famous trial, the fear of seeing a new Stammheim spring up near one's home still served as a rallying point that motivated the rejection of new prisons. Stammheim had transformed from a model prison into a powder keg of conflict between state representatives and far-left 'urban guerrilla' activists. Its name alone revived the memory of the so-called 'Years of Lead', particularly the memory of the transformation of the prison arena into a realm of violent struggle. This expression, incidentally, was diverted from its original intention by filmmaker Margarethe von Trotta when she titled her film with the equivalent German term *Die bleierne Zeit* ('The Leaden Times'), to refer to the post-war atmosphere rather than to the revolutionary climate of the 1970s.[2]

Stammheim – a model prison? This characterization certainly sounds surprising given that the name is reviled even beyond the sphere of activists. And there are other names in German carceral history that might more readily come to mind first when this epithet is evoked. One might be more likely to think of Berlin's Moabit Prison, which we have encountered in previous chapters, since it was officially labelled a model institution

(*Musteranstalt*). Based on the principle of solitary confinement, this prison, which is still in operation, is historically associated with nineteenth-century Protestant clergyman Johann Wichern, one of the leading figures of the then-flourishing 'penitentiary science' (*Gefängniskunde*). Moabit was emblematic of the reforming period in Prussia, where the aim was to make prison a *Besserungsmaschine* (to use Thomas Nutz's expression), a 'machine' devoted to improvement, amendment, and moral reform, with labour playing a disciplinary rather than an economic role. That era soon came to an end, giving way to the advent of biomedical criminology in the final decades of the century. The epithet might also call to mind Fuhlsbüttel Prison (one of the county's most famous, nicknamed 'Santa Fu', located on the outskirts of Hamburg), where the influence of the panoptic model is most evident. Or one might think of other less well-known places like the Untermaßfeld Prison in Thuringia, under the Weimar Republic, or the forgotten earlier experiment of Munich Prison in the 1840s.[3]

A forgotten experiment: Georg Michael von Obermaier and Munich Prison in the 1840s

Although Georg Michael von Obermaier was a notable reform figure in his time, the Munich prison experiment under his tutelage is little known. An empathetic, even saintly portrait of Obermaier published in 1937 depicted him as a pioneer who was pragmatic above all, even when he tried to influence legislation.

A former prisoner of war in Russia, where he endured very harsh detention conditions, Obermaier entered the field of prison administration in 1825. He was appointed head of Munich Prison in 1842 on the back of his success at managing Kaiserslautern Prison. A proponent of reform, he was supported by the local government, but disliked by penologists of his time (particularly in Bavaria, a region known for the harshness of its Penal Code). Though Munich Prison was in poor condition and considered difficult to run, he worked to turn it into a 'model prison' during the rise of 'penitentiary science'. He advocated the abolition of the death penalty, opposed solitary confinement (which he intended to reserve for extreme cases), sought to avoid corporal punishments, and relaxed the rule of silence during work. Amendment, in his view, came by introducing rewards that encouraged good behaviour, in the spirit of the so-called 'progressive' system. Furthermore, Obermaier instituted 'superintendents', who took on intermediate surveillance tasks. This was an early form of power delegation to specially selected inmates who served as auxiliaries.

Munich Prison received foreign visitors, and its influence spread as far as Modena Prison in Italy, where Obermaier was enlisted as an adviser in the 1850s. He lost local support at the end of that decade after discipline problems were criticized, and he resigned in 1862. His departure coincided with the end of the reformist-philanthropic era of the 1830s to 1860s, driven by the liberal bourgeoisie. Obermaier's ideas and practices barely survived him, if at all: 'the reformatory spirit, the skillful approach to gain the will of the convict, the educational atmosphere, the more delicate psychological methods which gave real life to Obermaier's regime, were not recognized nor imitated'. Unlike the names retained by history, such as Carl Mittermaier and Nikolaus Julius, 'Obermaier was soon forgotten, so completely in Germany that even his necrology was not published until four years after his death'. With historical hindsight, this little-known experiment, predating what Thomas Nutz identifies as the first German model prison (that of Bruchsal in 1848), is all the more interesting given that, to this day, Bavaria remains a region emblematic of penal conservatism.[4]

Then why focus on Stammheim? One could answer that while the Moabit and Fuhlsbüttel institutions are arguably perfect examples of the tragic fate of model prisons, they belong to a historical period that has already been covered in this book. Moabit, in particular, was a spin-off of Pentonville (chapter 2). By contrast, Stammheim – often cited as Germany's most famous prison (and it is the only one profiled in the book *German History for Dummies*) – allows us to address not only another era, but also, more importantly, a different configuration: that of a prison caught up in exceptional circumstances. It raises the question of 'political detention' and high-security wings in peacetime, in contrast to Barcelona's Modelo during the Spanish Civil War (chapter 6).[5]

Another aspect is social amnesia with regard to the prison's early years, which are as if buried by subsequent events. The prison is so closely associated with the RAF (and 'far-left terrorist' groups more broadly) that there is a common but incorrect belief that it was built specifically for RAF members. It is nevertheless true that the 1970s were an exceptional time at Stammheim. When the trial of the RAF's figureheads began in 1975, the prison was subject to exceptional security measures: it was surrounded by police officers and surveillance cameras, topped with an anti-aircraft security net, and, more importantly, the airspace above it became a no-fly zone. Moreover, it was during this time that a special bunker-like structure was constructed specifically for the trial.

This leads to another question: was Stammheim not some kind of maximum-security prison? If so, it could hardly be said to have met the definition of a 'model prison' that emphasizes moral reform. A clarification is needed here to avoid retrospective distortion linked to the change brought about by this exceptional trial. For understandable reasons, in the collective memory, the prison is often associated with the death of Ulrike Meinhof in 1976, and Andreas Baader, Gudrun Ensslin, and Jan-Carl Raspe in 1977, under circumstances that were murky to say the least. (The official cause of death was suicide, reaffirmed by the courts in the 2000s, but this is still being challenged, if only marginally.) Due to the multiple hunger strikes that took place there, and the forced feeding that followed, it is also regularly associated with 'sensory deprivation' practices, in other words 'white torture' (total isolation bathed in permanent artificial light, which disrupts and then destroys elementary cognitive faculties). This sometimes causes it to be confused with the so-called 'dead wing' of Cologne-Ossendorf Prison, where Astrid Proll and, later, Ulrike Meinhof were to suffer their ordeals, hence the American qualifier 'supermax' occasionally attributed to it.

This, though, runs the risk of anachronism. Initially, the purpose of Stammheim Prison was far removed from any issue of 'terrorism'. It even predated the rise of social protest in the mid-1960s. While much ink has been spilled for the sake of what one historian called the 'Stammheim apparatus' – particularly when history belatedly caught up with former activists like Susanne Albrecht, who was arrested in 1990 and imprisoned in Stammheim the following year – the prison's original reputation has been erased. You have to go back in time to find traces of it.[6]

'Stammheim was designed as a model prison,' declared an October 1977 headline in *Le Monde*, after the suspicious deaths of those known as the 'Stammheim Three' (Baader, Ensslin, Raspe). The article began by highlighting a misunderstanding on both sides of the Rhine. If the detention system 'is usually described by the French side as particularly severe, inhumane, scandalous [. . .], from the West German point of view, it is rather its liberalism that, under certain circumstances, may have outraged some of the public'. Between two mocking remarks aimed at the 'urban guerrilla' protagonists, the journalist evokes the '"progressive" professions of faith' that had greeted the construction of a place of confinement then 'presented as a model prison'. Like many of his colleagues at the time, whose eyes were riveted to the seventh floor that housed RAF members, the journalist confines himself to the case of the Baader–Meinhof Gang, mentioning the facilities and equipment they would have benefited from, contrary to common-law inmates. A few decades later, speculation on this subject is still rife, fuelled by the account of a former prison official who reported that these privileges relative to ordinary inmates did exist.[7]

Suzanne Bergstermann's work not only tends to confirm these favourable confinement conditions, but it also more generally provides valuable clarification. Her book recalls that from the time when construction began in 1959 in a context of prison population growth, and then during the years after it opened in 1963, Stammheim was considered the most modern prison in the country. Surrounded by a certain prestige, it was the 'prison of superlatives'. The 'modernity' it was attributed in rhetoric had two facets from the outset: it was secure but also humane; strict but also healthy. It was primarily from this angle – that of a 'prison with comfort' (as one speaks of a room with a view) – that a journalist in *Die Zeit* presented this new penitentiary 'jewel' in September 1963. At the time, if discretion was on the agenda, this was because it was necessary to avoid letting 'honest citizens' know that Stammheim Prison was one of the most expensive buildings in the city, more costly than its cultural centres. The journalist wrote that when he visited the prison before it opened, he could only compare it to hotels, hospitals, or night shelters. These comparisons turn out to reflect a fairly favourable opinion of the new prison, even if he stops short of implying it is a jovial place: within those still-empty walls, the cameras and alarms were no doubt vigilant.[8]

Make no mistake: its so-called 'high-rise' architecture certainly broke with the panoptic or radial influence, with a view to visually normalizing the prison building, so it might somehow be forgotten. (From this perspective, it is difficult to imagine a more patent failure.) Nevertheless, the security aspect was clearly emphasized from the outset, both in public discourse and in its physical equipment. The prison was endowed with barbed wire, cameras, and motion detectors. And its architectural innovations included a sawtooth layout designed to prevent clandestine deliveries and messages, including verbal ones from window to window. Order and security were therefore at the forefront, but these were achieved by means of a more liberal system, at a time when the iron discipline of solitary confinement in old and filthy cells was nothing distant. This approach stems from the fact that Stammheim was mainly intended for remand prisoners who were theoretically innocent until proven guilty. It embodied the reformist ideals of the 1960s: architectural modernity, advanced security technologies, respect for human dignity, and the ideal of rehabilitation. But one should take its humanist proclamations with a grain of salt, since everything, including security itself, was linked to a higher principle of utility, and even subordinated to it. At that time, it was the most expensive prison in the country, and concern for hygiene was shown there, but its daily management was aimed at functionality above all, ensuring maximum efficiency and untroubled order.

Contrary to retrospective impressions, Stammheim was established during a quiet period. It opened just before the prison question returned to public visibility in Germany in 1965, when scandals were sparked by lethal violence in detention. So it was brought into service prior to the decade-long 'reformist' period in prison affairs (marked by a rehabilitative and even therapeutic creed), which started in 1967 and ended with the passing of the first federal prison law in March 1976. Moreover, if Stammheim continued to be regarded as a model prison in the first few years after it opened, it lost its reputation even before the RAF members were transferred, because by the end of the 1960s at the latest, the most modern German prison was struggling with well-known organizational problems: overcrowding, lack of employment opportunities, inadequate food, and poor medical care. Although largely devoted to the 1975–7 trial, an episode of a 2014 German TV series on 'places full of mysteries' briefly looked at this initial period, not without a few sensational staging effects. It pointed out that Stammheim was indeed a model institution, all the more regarded as a step forward for having replaced a dilapidated nineteenth-century prison whose overcrowded conditions had been appalling. It enjoyed this perception even though 'human rights' and 'rehabilitation' were not yet on the agenda: these watchwords would only enter the popular vocabulary with the watershed events of the late 1960s and early 1970s.[9]

In an effort to erase the stigma associated with Stammheim, in the 2000s the local Ministry of Justice invited journalists to visit the 'prison of all prisons', with a view to recalling its history and displaying its conformance with contemporary standards. After presenting the surrounding scenery as pastoral and almost idyllic, the authorities explained during an excursion onto the site that back when its name still resonated positively, the detention building was innocuously nicknamed the 'men's home'. It was only after it had been in operation for ten years that the introduction of a high-security zone for 'terrorist' leaders caused it to become widely known as the most secure prison in the country, if not in Europe and beyond (or the most oppressive, depending on one's perspective). This did not prevent it from being attacked by conservatives for exactly the opposite reason. The authorities were already engaged in this kind of communication work at that time, since the RAF's accusations that Stammheim was a 'torture chamber' forced officials to produce documentation intended to prove respect for human rights in detention, drawing attention to food, medical assistance, and visiting times, and even the volume of air available per prisoner. Although the Public Prosecutor's Office announced in 2003 that the investigation into the death of the 'Stammheim Three' would not be reopened, the prison has not entirely freed itself from controversy. In particular, there have been concerns about the possibility of hidden listening devices in cells.[10]

Stammheim's long-uncertain fate is a sign that it, too, is affected by the endlessly complicated memory problems encountered in other cases explored in this book. In 2007, the regional government announced that the prison would be demolished in

2012 to make way for a psychiatric hospital. But then the plan changed, and it was only the building holding RAF members that was supposed to be shut down. In the year when this closure was scheduled to take place, a quarter of a century after photographs of the deaths of the 'Stammheim Three' had inspired Gerhard Richter's 1988 series of paintings *October 18, 1977*, Andreas Magdanz exhibited his commemorative photo project *Stuttgart Stammheim* at the Stuttgart Museum.

The resulting destruction only ended up serving the dilapidated prison's reconstruction, including from a technological standpoint. Though one wing disappeared, a plan was made to expand the rest, which would even become what one journalist modestly called the most famous 'justice district' in Germany. After several twists and turns, new buildings were indeed erected, including a court of law. Today Stammheim is the largest prison in the region – supposedly meeting the highest standards of security and humanity.[11]

Chapter 10

Fleury-Mérogis (France, 1968)

Fleury-Mérogis Prison (1960s)
Source: Coll. École nationale d'administration pénitentiaire – Centre de ressources sur l'histoire des crimes et des peines

1968's model prison has died. Fleury-Mérogis is not even suitable for renovation. At least not all of it. So the idea is to do what is done with housing project buildings, and partially destroy it. [. . .] Described as a model prison when it opened in the spring of 1968, mainly because of its electronic surveillance system and its walls with large windows allowing light to pass through the bars, this penal institution [. . .] is now too dirty, too dilapidated and too overcrowded.

It took less than four decades for this French and even European flagship of modern prison design to become 'the prison you no longer visit', as the French conservative weekly *Le Point* called it in 2000. At the dawn of the twenty-first century, it was in a deplorable physical state, squalid throughout, with electricity, plumbing, heating, and even the security system all faulty.[1]

It is no coincidence that the article compared the 'mammoth prison' of Fleury-Mérogis to large suburban social housing estates. These were both born of the same era of 'urban gigantism'. As architect Augustin Rosenstiehl explains: 'It was a time of enormous, large-scale construction projects. Just when large 4,000-apartment housing estates were starting to appear, it seemed logical to design a gigantic prison with 3,200 cells.' At the time when the prison was built, this parallel with low-cost housing was frequently drawn to highlight either positive or negative aspects. In 1970, a volunteer visitor mentioned 'a few rare model prisons where the comfort level is comparable to that of social housing', and reported fairly positive comments made by an inmate. By contrast, a few years later, a theatrical play exploring the dehumanization of model prisons depicted them as 'a slightly worse version of council housing'. As one prison officer said: 'Anyone who visits Fleury-Mérogis is struck by how much it looks like the large modern apartment blocks.' One of the most striking elements of a field study by anthropologist Léonore Le Caisne on the prison's juvenile detention centre – which is often singled out as exemplary despite lacking any consistent educational project – is the way young prisoners link 'the prison' to 'the neighbourhood'. They are quick to present or represent the prison as a familiar 'annexe to the street' where they encounter friends or family.[2]

When it opened in 1968 after four years of construction (it was not fully operational until 1973), Fleury-Mérogis immediately stood out due to its size. Architect Dominique Rouillard writes that this scale is typical of an architectural era. He argues that 'megastructures are the dominant form of mid-twentieth-century urban utopia', and also claims that 'architecture lost its link to utopia in the late 1960s', precisely when Fleury-Mérogis opened. It is obviously a mega-structure. In the early 2000s, it had a theoretical capacity of nearly 3,500 places, but in practice it housed more than 4,300 beds in the men's section alone, adding up to a flow of around 12,000 inmates per year. This was at least double the capacity of Fresnes, which Fleury-Mérogis had superseded, just as Fresnes had supplanted La Santé in its time. References to Fleury-Mérogis rarely fail to mention that it is the largest prison in Europe. This gigantism stems from its original purported objective, which was to both relieve congestion at Fresnes and accommodate the inmates of La Santé, which was supposed to close (construction of Fleury-Mérogis was even accelerated for this purpose). But as often happens in these situations, instead of replacing existing prisons, it ended up supplementing them.[3]

Since its inception, Fleury-Mérogis has been a city within a city. Not only is it enormous, but it is also secluded: half a century after opening, it remains poorly served by public transport. Moreover, it seems as if the prison has absorbed the city, symbolically and materially. The common nickname 'Fleury' immediately evokes the prison, just as 'Orly' makes you think of the airport. Many local residents work for the prison administration. In 2010, the Contrôleur général des lieux de privation de liberté (an appointed inspector of France's detention sites) drafted a report with the help of a team of around twenty others. Once again drawing a parallel with large housing estates, the report described a 'profound reconception of prison architecture' due to the fact that this prison 'does not reveal itself from the outside through its superstructures (enclosure, watchtowers);

on the contrary, it hardly differs from the prevalent collective housing'.[4]

Aided by widespread access to television in the 1970s, Fleury-Mérogis established itself as the epitome of the French prison system. But this view is misleading, as journalist Pierre Tartakowsky explained in a 1995 book recounting his experience of working as a correctional officer to gain an understanding of the institution from the inside. With its famous '*tripales*' (three-pronged helix-shaped buildings), Fleury-Mérogis is indeed anything but ordinary. Significantly, it is often described as a 'monster' even within the prison administration. 'The Fleury-Mérogis complex is a monster that should not exist,' declared a union representative in 2000, when he appeared before a parliamentary commission investigating the situation in French prisons. Unlike La Santé and Fresnes, Fleury-Mérogis is a 'modern prison', but in some respects it is also 'an inhuman monster', as Albin Chalandon called it with a certain irony from a historical perspective. Chalandon is an unlikely critic, given his role as Minister of Justice from 1986 to 1988, during which time he tried to privatize the French prison system. The word 'monster' was also used by Jean-Louis Daumas, a former director of the juvenile correctional centre, who left an enduring impact on that facility.[5]

This 'monster' exemplifies the paradoxical pattern whereby model prisons sooner or later become counterexamples not to be followed. Criticism of Fleury-Mérogis is remarkably unanimous. It would be difficult to find a favourable account of the complex as a whole. The judgement expressed in a 2010 regional press article was by no means out of the ordinary:

> It is the biggest prison in Europe. When it opened in 1967–1968, it was touted as a 'model prison'. Nobody would say the same today. At best, it could be argued that this Fleury-Mérogis prison, which can hold more than 4,000 inmates, is – alas! – 'exemplary' of the situation in French prisons, described as scandalous by

> all authoritative voices, and condemned by European judicial institutions.

Several scandals have marred the prison's recent history, including a controversy in 2007 about disciplinary cells, where size and lighting standards were reportedly lower than those required for kennels and chicken coops.[6]

These criticisms come from various quarters. In the wake of the 2000 '*affaire Vasseur*' (mentioned in chapter 3), two books on incarcerated women unintentionally echoed each other, one written by a prison nurse and the other by a former female inmate. One mentioned the 'foul smell', the 'cold, methodical architecture', the 'sinister and shoddy construction', and an infirmary that is only 'slightly less dirty than the rest of the detention centre', not to mention a filthy disciplinary block. In short, it was anything but a 'three-star prison', despite the persistent cliché. The other author, who spent ten years there, evokes the 'anonymous gigantism' of a 'car-park prison'. Both of these accounts are testaments to violence, desolation, and filth, depicting inmates living in squalor. This did not prevent the authors from praising the dedication of some of the staff, arguing that this is what keeps the institution running. Surveillance officers remain underpaid and disrespected: in 2009, massive protests broke out, involving several hundred public sector employees. As *Le Monde* summed up the situation: 'They are protesting because Fleury, a model prison in 1968, has become a rubbish tip.'[7]

Fleury-Mérogis even bears the shameful stigma of panopticism. Foucault emphasized this historical persistence: 'As evidence of this strength and immobility, let us take a recent fact: the model prison opened at Fleury-Mérogis in 1969 [*sic*] simply took over in its overall plan the panoptic star-shape that made such a stir in 1836 at the Petite-Roquette.' Though not a follower of the author of *Discipline and Punish*, French sociologist Claude Faugeron confirmed his view:

> The Fleury-Mérogis prison complex, whose construction began in 1964 (the section for young prisoners opened early and provisionally the previous year), is a symbol of the prison technocracy of the time, which made de-urbanization and the consolidation of prisons its guiding principle. But the modernity of Fleury-Mérogis led to harsh incarceration methods, and its lack of social interaction made it difficult to bear, for both prisoners and guards. Fleury-Mérogis added gigantism to panopticism. [. . .] The experiment was so obviously unsuitable that it was not repeated.

Ironically, among its layout problems is the fact that, reversing the panoptic principle, some inmates can see the movements of guards entering the wings. Fleury-Mérogis is characterized by gigantism, panopticism, productivism; by standardization, automation, de-humanization; but not by adaptability or flexibility: the prefab reinforced-concrete elements have made the structure particularly unalterable, hastening its obsolescence.[8]

Yet at the time of its construction, Fleury-Mérogis epitomized modernity and even a pioneering spirit. France's new National Prison Administration School ('École nationale d'administration pénitentiaire', ENAP), responsible for training staff, was established there: a symbol in itself. Some professionals who visited had a positive, almost enthusiastic impression. They praised a facility that was well designed both functionally and aesthetically, seemingly capable of fulfilling an 'educational mission': 'It's hard to speak of a prison where life is good. . . Yet that's what you think when you visit Fleury-Mérogis.' The technical sophistication of the building initially earned it the nickname 'four-star' and even 'five-star' prison. But over time, only parts of the facility would inspire favourable opinions, some of them ambivalent. A working group that was part of a mid-1970s project on the 'Prisons of Tomorrow' (see chapter 11, box) expressed reservations after visiting the three-tiered D4 wing. They described a 'very cumbersome complex' with an imperfect layout that made it necessary to travel long distances. The women's wing drew this double-edged comment: 'The Fleury-Mérogis women's prison is a smaller, more humane facility. It is a building of the highest quality, even offering a certain luxury that, it seems, should not be exceeded.'[9]

Initially, some quite positive views were expressed even by the conservative press, including favourable comparisons with more attractive structures. Describing his visit to a 'different kind of prison' in March 1971, journalist Jean Ferniot wrote: 'Were it not for the presence of guards wearing the golden star of their administration on their uniforms, or for the existence of gates that look as if they were dreamed up by some contemporary "designer", Fleury-Mérogis could pass – let the leftists not use this as an argument – for a university: long, bright corridors, spacious rooms, large playing fields.' He concluded with a comment that would be considered radical today (this speaks volumes about the rightward ideological shift that has occurred since then): 'While I regret that not all prisons in France are like Fleury-Mérogis, I particularly deplore the fact that society has to make such efforts to restore to adolescents the dignity of which this same society has otherwise endeavoured to deprive them.'[10]

The mission of the prison's architect, Guillaume Gillet, was not a matter of re-socialization, but rather the optimization of space and security. However, it was his concern about prisoner rehabilitation that inspired his intention to recycle the radial layout. In 1975, Saudi Arabia enlisted him as a consultant for the design of a detention centre in Riyadh that was to be based on Fleury-Mérogis. Meanwhile, the Rebibbia Prison in Rome – whose construction began in the late 1930s but was only fully operational in 1971–2 – bears a certain resemblance to its French counterpart. Perhaps ironically, given his reputation as a prison architect, Gillet simultaneously worked for high-end coastal resorts on the French Riviera.

From Fleury-Mérogis to Saint-Tropez

The archives of the Atelier de Montrouge, a French architectural and urban planning collective active from the late 1950s to the early 1980s, reveal a surprising connection between two spaces that appear to stand in complete opposition: the prison and the beach. Within a series entitled 'Advisory mission and detailed urban planning of Pampelonne beach, Ramatuelle (Var), 1962–1963', one encounters the name of Fleury-Mérogis Prison's architect, Guillaume Gillet. Fleury-Mérogis is only the most famous of his achievements in the carceral field. Gillet – who had experienced captivity in Germany as a POW during the Second World War – designed approximately ten prisons built across France between 1959 and 1975. A major figure in the renewal of the prison estate during the 1960s, he served as principal architect for the Ministry of Justice for some fifteen years. He was also a leading figure in post-war French architecture, one of the architects most representative of *Les Trente Glorieuses*.

From the early 1960s, Gillet was also working far away from Fleury-Mérogis, in the Mediterranean region, on the Saint-Tropez peninsula. He contributed to a project entitled 'Conservation and development of the Saint-Tropez peninsula', and in 1962–3, as representative of the sites protection commission, he worked on a land-use planning study that aimed to define a no-build zone along Pampelonne beach. These projects occupied Gillet – who had previously served as consultant architect for the cities of Cannes and Antibes, as well as the Principality of Monaco – at the same time as his services were being solicited in the prison field, since construction of Fleury-Mérogis began in 1964–5. Quite a feat of architectural versatility. . .[11]

Criticism soon mounted, however, beginning with leftists. A few years after the facility opened, the 'Prison Information Group'

(Groupe d'information sur les prisons, GIP), founded by Daniel Defert and Michel Foucault, described Fleury-Mérogis's reality in less than glowing terms. They also published a second brochure on the prison as part of their *Intolérable* series.

> It's the model prison, the one that Pleven [the Minister of Justice] gives tours of. But it's the prison where there are the most suicides. The clean and silent prison. But this is because they hand out the most valium there, and if you do not agree to take some, they give you an injection. The prison without bars. But they put them back up every day. Electronically monitored. But they shout orders at you through a loudspeaker, and they listen in on you, even when you are asleep. It's the prison of the future.

A few years later, the 'Prisoners' Action Committee' (Comité d'action des prisonniers, CAP) took up the torch. In 1974, the *Journal des Prisonniers* stated:

> In 1968, Fleury-Mérogis was opened in the hope of closing Fresnes and La Santé. Unfortunately, it turned out that Fleury would not be enough, and the other two were retained. But this new prison is a total fiasco. [. . .] The prison is surrounded by workshops: more than half of them are unoccupied due to a lack of equipment. Then at Fleury, they said to themselves: the way forward is to make a prison where everything is automated; as a result, the prison has become 'robotized'. To open a cell door, the guard presses a button. To talk, an intercom is used. As a result, there is no human contact. Fleury has locked men in an electronic cage.

A collective book written by an action research group assembled by Félix Guattari had already warned that 'model prisons are the worst of all'. 'Everyone who leaves Fleury says it: "Being alone twenty-three hours out of twenty-four is unbearable."'[12]

This paradoxical situation affecting Fleury-Mérogis in particular and modern prisons in general was also noted by the press of the time. Journalist Marc Kunstlé covered this topic in the 1970s, co-writing a book in 1972 and publishing several articles, in which he reported on the extent of the criticism being heaped on Fleury-Mérogis. He quotes Edgar Faure's judgement: 'Fleury-Mérogis is an abominable world: imprisonment coupled with modernity is unbearable. The current system is completely absurd. The whole thing needs to be rethought.' Based on the account of a prison chaplain, Kunstlé concludes: 'Suicide is rarer in old prisons than in new ones, which are excessively modern and therefore inhumane. These push-button prisons like Fleury-Mérogis, where isolation is total, with one inmate per cell, create a situation that accentuates the prisoners' psychological fragility.' The journalist adds:

> In the view of this other magistrate, an investigating judge in the north, the Muret Prison [built by the same architect at the same time as Fleury-Mérogis], one of the world's most modern, is a 'magnificent submarine'. As in Fleury-Mérogis, everything is monitored from a central unit, a veritable electronic brain! Alas! It is in these prisons that boredom, anxiety, and phobias around homosexuality take the greatest toll, he says. Despite their relative comfort, they are more inhumane than the old ones, because they increase the prisoner's separation from the outside world.

Fleury became the symbol of a prison modernization paradox that can be found in other establishments. In late 1973, a prisoner in the dilapidated Eysses Prison said: 'I've stayed in Bonneville, Haute-Savoie, in an ultra-modern remand centre. In Muret, it was a model prison. But I prefer the discomfort of this old hovel.'[13]

The strongest evidence of Fleury-Mérogis's immediate failure, however, is that criticism came not only from left-wing activists and moderate journalists appalled by the state of the prison system, but also from official figures, albeit in slightly more measured terms. This is illustrated well by the words of Hélène Dorlhac de Borne, who was appointed Secretary of State for Prison Issues in 1974 – a unique portfolio in French history. In a book she wrote ten years after serving as minister, she devotes a passage to Fleury-Mérogis that addresses its dubious modernity from the outset. As she recalls, Fleury-Mérogis is the 'culmination of a whole series of research projects in the field of prison architecture' in order to 'meet modern standards of detention'. This 'gigantic, star-shaped concrete complex' has unbreakable glass instead of bars on the windows; however, 'security remains the dominant obsession'. This is how she describes it:

> The cells are bright, fairly spacious, with an isolated toilet area, and are equipped with a radio that can broadcast selected programmes and communicate instructions. Long white corridors: everything is almost as silent and sterile as in a hospital. The rational combining of modern gadgets with cells that were finally inhabitable could have given the impression that Fleury-Mérogis was the prototype of the ideal prison. It was not long before these illusions were dashed. In this prison that no one dares to call a 'model prison' anymore, people commit suicide more than anywhere else, take massive doses of tranquillizers, slash their own wrists, and climb onto the roofs.

The former Secretary of State cites other similar examples evincing despair and revolt. 'What do sociologists think about it?', she wonders.

> Automation is what causes dehumanization and creates the conditions for disorder and despair. [. . .] These modern prisons have been described as 'dehumanized'. The new prison conditions they offer have paradoxical consequences. They provide the inmate with decent living conditions and make his world less squalid. But in some cases, excessive modernity can be detrimental to

human contact, aggravating the isolation and sense of rupture that incarceration creates in the inmate. Their design therefore needs to be reconsidered.

In the year following the publication of Dorlhac de Borne's book, Fleury-Mérogis was rocked by a collective revolt. Since then, such movements have regularly occurred. Rare activist documents have preserved the memory of these little-known events.[14]

Fleury-Mérogis remains standing. In the late 1980s, French architect Jean-Denis Espinas explained that even though the harmfulness of the 'prison city' model had been proven, (with Fleury-Mérogis representing its apogee: 'overwhelming and brutal monumentality', 'hopeless monolithism and [. . .] uniformity'), the construction programme eventually known as 'Programme 13,000' still followed the same path. As for the prison itself, its planned demolition was temporarily postponed and then ultimately did not take place, due to massive prison overcrowding, an issue the Prison Information Group had re-characterized as over-imprisonment. In the early 2010s, a renovation programme set to span more than ten years was finally approved for Fleury-Mérogis, whose size is equivalent to at least four or five regular prisons. Europe's largest prison will most likely continue to make headlines.[15]

Counterpoint V

'Open prisons' (utopia/heterotopia)

Could there ever be an oxymoron more perfect than 'open prisons'? It is tempting to dismiss such a blatant contradiction as rhetorical hoodwinking. However, we should take the phrase seriously, if only as the expression of an ambivalent relationship with carceral ideals. It certainly reflects the failure of the classic prison utopia, which by definition is based on the supposed virtues of a closed space that is expected to encourage self-reflection and repentance. While prisons are typically classified as 'heterotopias of deviation', model prisons may better fit into another category that Foucault only briefly sketched in his 'heterotopology': 'heterotopias of compensation' (as opposed to 'heterotopias of illusion'). As he suggested, 'their role is to create a space that is other, another real space, as perfect, as meticulous, as well arranged as ours is messy, ill constructed, and jumbled'. In this sense, model prisons were conceived as harmonious environments intended to compensate for flaws and imperfections, not only those of conventional prisons, but also those of what the privileged classes perceived as 'disordered' working-class neighbourhoods. But the unrealistic desire to reconcile confinement with openness also marks the beginning of a new phase of utopianism. In this sense, the very notion of open prisons attests to the enduring and conflictual nature of the idea of a prison utopia.[1]

Given how confusing this contradiction can be, some clarification is probably in order. In principle, 'open prison' does not refer to a sentence served outside of prison as an alternative to incarceration, such as community service. And neither does it refer to a conventional prison in which cell doors are open for several hours a day to reduce the rigidities of traditional confinement – these are sometimes known as 'semi-open' prisons. Instead, an open prison must allow a certain freedom of movement both inside and outside the walls, by authorizing frequent visits and regular leave permits. It must also lack the typical security features of traditional prisons, such as watchtowers, barbed wire, and armed officers. Open prisons also provide for a wide range of cultural and educational activities, such as mounting theatrical plays or producing a newspaper, with the aim of fostering social reintegration. These special facilities typically house low-risk, rule-abiding offenders who are nearing the end of their sentences. They live in custody, but with reduced physical restraints. Depending on one's viewpoint, they could be seen as either a way of 'opening up prisons', or an extension of the prison system into the outside world.

When rural penal colonies were created in France in the 1830s, this was already in response to criticism of ordinary prisons. They were presented as a healthy and economical alternative to a cellular model that was considered too expensive and not conducive to the efficient organization of labour. Children were to be the first beneficiaries of a 'highly utopian project' that mobilized the elites 'to build a prison without the disadvantages of a prison', according to historian Jean-Jacques Yvorel, who points out that, contrary to this claim, children in France were punished more severely than adults in the nineteenth century. Yvorel even refers to a 'great confinement' of children under extremely harsh conditions in agricultural penal colonies like Mettray, which operated for a century (1839–1937). 'Mettray has been consistently praised and presented as the pinnacle of penal treatment for juvenile offenders,' writes the lawyer and former French Minister of Justice Robert Badinter. It was considered France's 'most venerated carceral institution', as the subtitle of Stephen Toth's book on Mettray makes clear. Yet it later became one of the most despised places in a punitive arena where competition was fierce. In his review of Toth's book, Jean-Lucien Sanchez sums up the general historical (and possibly logical) trend that Mettray represented: 'As Toth shows, what began as a resolutely utopian project that emerged from an optimistic representation of juvenile delinquents by reformers in the first half of the nineteenth century was marked by a slow drift towards a strictly authoritarian and punitive model.'[2]

Recent open prisons might share certain similarities with the penal colonies of yesteryear, but they break with the original utopian impulse, at least from an architectural point of view. As we have seen earlier in this book, the first model prisons were not concealed or buried in the landscape. They were designed to exhibit a certain monumentality, inspiring fearful respect through a strong visual manifestation to state authority. They were intended to be the proud, conspicuous, physical realization of an ambitious ideal of correction and rehabilitation. Just how much this ambition failed is shown by the very fact that attempts have been made to design open prisons that could blend into their surroundings, based on the new principle that acceptable prisons are those that resemble prisons as little as possible, somewhat undermining the logic at their foundation. The Massachusetts Norfolk Prison Colony exemplified this antinomy from 1927 to 1934. Its first superintendent, Howard Belding Gill, wanted to go against the grain of conventional architecture, as epitomized by Philadelphia's Eastern State Penitentiary, in order to create a 'model prison community'. One of the main principles of the 'new penology' that Gill envisioned was an 'open prison community', in which freedom of movement and contact with the 'outside' were possible. As Matthew DelSesto explains: 'With a program of records keeping, research, and documentation, Gill and other reformers involved in the prison had imagined that Norfolk would serve as a model for prisons around the country. However, the experiment was cut short when a 1934 public hearing determined that Gill was unfit to serve based on alleged mismanagement of Norfolk.' The facility came under fire for being too lax. Just a decade after this experiment began, an official report declared it a failure, especially regarding 'the potential value of increasing participation in justice systems'.[3]

It is unsurprising that the scale of the ambition to invent open prisons increased after the atrocities of the Second World War, culminating with the Hague Congress in 1950. It was in reference to that landmark meeting that five years later a French deputy prosecutor, Jacques-Bernard Herzog, wrote about 'the prison crisis and open prisons' in an academic legal journal. His article is typical of an era in which criticism of incarceration was by no means the preserve of radical fringe groups. 'There is no question that it is more relevant than ever,' he wrote about the prison crisis, going so far as to speak of an 'anti-prison trend in modern penology'. Herzog's text evoked the harm caused by both short and long sentences, which he characterizes as not only ineffective, but also damaging to the abilities of individuals. He further argues that punishment must be oriented towards 'treatment', a crucial watchword of the second half of the twentieth century. Hence open prisons, which appeared to be a 'satisfactory solution', even 'a well-developed and proven method of imprisonment'. The open prison 'is a prison without bars, that is to say, according to the simplest definition that can be given, an establishment whose security is not ensured by physical means', 'which has no walls, no fences, no locks, or special guards to replace these physical obstacles to escape'. The relaxation of surveillance needed to be matched and supplemented by prisoner empowerment. Herzog went even further, arguing that a form of self-government by inmates was the logical outcome of a renewed prison system. This was why an open prison could only work if prisoners were specially selected, something that necessitated the formulation of eligibility criteria. Incidentally, the text suggested that agricultural colonies had lost their appeal, Herzog criticizing the systematization of 'bucolic reformation' (*bucolisme pénitentiaire*).[4]

The jurist referred to a half-century of experience because the first open prison is widely considered to be the one that opened in Witzwil, Switzerland, in 1891. However, only part of the prison was 'open' at the time. In that special section, the emphasis was on socialization through agricultural work, which was believed to have educational and therapeutic benefits. The idea spread very slowly. In the United Kingdom, one can trace the origins of open prisons to borstals, particularly Lowdham Grange in Nottinghamshire, completed in 1931. Once borstals (for young offenders) are distinguished from adult open prisons, New Hall Camp (established in the mid-1930s as a remote annexe of Wakefield Prison in Yorkshire) is often identified as the first British open prison, characterized by the absence of surrounding walls or barbed wire. However, as one author noted as early as 1978, the term 'open prison' was not yet in use at the time. It would only later be applied to institutions like Leyhill in Gloucestershire, established in 1946 and still operational today. By the mid-1970s, there were some fifteen such facilities in the United Kingdom, housing just over 10% of the prison population. However, these prisons were not as distinct as people imagined. In 1977, an in-depth study that systematically compared three 'open' prisons with three 'closed' ones concluded that, overall, there appeared to be only 'slight' differences between the two categories, which were themselves not internally homogeneous. In fact, surveillance seemed tightest in some open prisons.[5]

As we have seen in the previous counterpoint, Scandinavia has been leading the open prison trend. In Denmark and Finland in the late 2000s, open prisons accounted for around a quarter or a third of the prison system (depending on the criteria used to determine this proportion). French lawyer Paul-Roger Gontard cited these figures in March 2010, when he presented the results of his 'feasibility study', commissioned by the Ministry of Justice. By no means a radical, Gontard is a self-described 'centrist' whose PhD dissertation examined open prisons. The title of his report is simply the question that prompted it: 'Can the open prison regime be extended to the French prison system?' In the name of humanistic values, and counter to a narrowly vindictive or repressive conception of penal detention, the author recommended developing several open prisons, since they had proved to be a 'real success in the search for minimum constraints and maximum security'. He listed numerous advantages, such as prisoner rehabilitation, reintegration preparation, recidivism prevention, and victim compensation (not to mention the environmental benefits), all at a below-average daily cost to the taxpayer. His report also identified four feasibility conditions, taking social acceptance into account: appropriate prisoner selection, coherent geographical distribution, easy access to public services, and location a reasonable distance from the transport infrastructure. Gontard pointed out that France was lagging behind in this area: while this model existed elsewhere in Europe (albeit on a generally modest scale), there was only one facility of this type in France, the Casabianda detention centre in Corsica.[6]

Casabianda is located in a rural seaside setting, housing around 200 male inmates who work on a farm, which is in fact one of the largest in Corsica, and was certified as organic by ECOCERT in 2004. So it is certainly a special case in the French prison system. But even favourable descriptions almost always include a reminder that it is actually a prison, and that although life there is healthy and productive, it is by no means pleasant. This is what journalist Frédéric Pottecher wrote in 1982, in an article looking back on making the first authorized TV report about French prisons in 1963. According to him, no one in the administration or the ministry seemed to know about this prison, which had been redesignated as an 'agricultural estate', with no disciplinary quarters or watchtowers, and mosquito nets instead of bars. He pointed out the striking differences that set it apart from the ordinary prisons to which its inmates could be transferred in the event of misconduct – a threat that helped enforce discipline. One of these differences was that the inmates did not reflect the overall composition of the prison population. Most of them (about three-quarters) had been convicted of sexual offences, and were considered relatively easy to manage. In Casabianda, 'there are few incidents, no violence, no gangs, no escapes', noted the National Assembly's June 2000 inquiry into French prisons. The facility 'does not resemble, according to the members of the commission who visited it, the idea one has of a prison'. It was not a panacea, but at least proof that things could be done differently.[7]

Although the Casabianda in question reopened in the late 1940s, its roots go back much further, to what Christian Carlier called 'the adventure of the Corsican "open prisons"' during the Second Empire. The original Casabianda was one of three agricultural prisons created around 1865 for forced labour sentences, located in an unsanitary and uninhabited area. Carlier continues: 'Prisoners of rural origin who had committed sexual offences were sent there. The experiment was a success in terms of prison management, but unfortunately malaria caused a true catastrophe, particularly in Casabianda,' which led to its closure in 1885. When its successor opened in the late 1940s, it was in a completely different context – a post-war time of reform that was a key moment in the establishment of model prisons. 'School-prisons', 'open prisons', and 'prisons in the fields' were on the agenda, as expressions of a progressive drive. As historian Hélène Bellanger explains in her study on the French post-war period, in the 1950s and 1960s, the scarce media reports on prison issues narrowly focused on a handful of model penal establishments. Casabianda was seen as a 'caricature' of these. Threats of closure hung over it in the early 1970s, but nothing came of them, and the prison still exists today. Another name associated with this period is Oermingen, the site of a prison school that operated from 1947 to 1987 in north-eastern France. In 1965, a police officer wrote an article in which he claimed that this so-called prison had 'absolutely nothing in common with the definition given in dictionaries'. Once the author's initial shock had passed, despite still having mixed feelings, he called it a bold venture, without daring to praise it any further.[8]

As for Casabianda, and other island-based prisons mentioned in this book, much could be said about the relationship between islands and prisons and, relatedly, between utopia and heterotopia. While the island may carry a sense of openness as a place of flight or escape, it can equally represent imposed isolation. Two configurations may be distinguished: one in which the island is reduced, wholly or nearly so, to the prison itself (carceral island), and one in which a prison occupies an island without wholly appropriating it (insular prison). Islands have historically served as privileged sites of relegation, housing penal colonies either before or alongside conventional enclosed prisons. Among the most notable examples of 'open' convict settlements are the Iwahig Penal Colony on the island of Palawan in the Philippines, established as early as 1904, and the İmralı penal settlement off the coast of Turkey, operational from the 1930s. Ian Brown described the former as a 'self-governing republic' on account of its being administered by the inmates themselves, while an English visitor evoked the latter in enchanted terms in the mid-1940s: 'I have no hesitation in saying that the Imrali penal settlement is the finest thing of its kind which I have seen in any country.'[9]

The idea of open or semi-open prisons has spread around the world, from Uruguay to Sri Lanka, although the rules and admission criteria vary. As suggested in chapter 8, one country that has sought to distinguish itself in this area is India, whose first notable experiment was a small annexe to the model prison in Lucknow, set up in 1949–50 for only a dozen inmates. Based on this experiment, the case of the Sampurnanand camp, named after an official representative of the state of Uttar Pradesh, was presented at the United Nations Congress in Geneva in 1955. Located in the middle of the countryside, the experiment was described as bold and unique, especially since it involved around 3,000 prisoners. There were barely any walls or barriers to prevent escape. It had unarmed guards, no corporal punishment in principle, and the ability to eat without an escort. The inmates were supposed to do paid public utility work and receive a salary equivalent to that of free workers. The report noted that the escape rate and operating costs were much lower than in ordinary prisons. This led to a growing trend: in the early 1980s, there were around twenty such facilities (variously described as 'prisons', 'camps', or 'colonies'). By the mid-2000s, the number had risen to around forty.[10]

The variations in terminology suggest that the definition of an open prison has sometimes undergone changes to become less narrowly circumscribed. In West Germany of the early 1970s, against a backdrop of growing dissatisfaction with the prison system after a series of scandals and protest movements, the idea of prisons 'without bars' began to be discussed. The resulting reforms included the introduction of so-called 'open' or 'semi-open' prisons. However, not only was the promised proportion of such establishments never reached, but their defining openness was limited, resulting in the more cautious addition of the prefix 'semi-'. In most cases, 'semi-open' essentially meant adjustments to sentences served outside, and greater flexibility in managing movements inside – but within a standard prison. There may have been no bars, but this was only because they had been replaced by translucent hard-plastic windows. Research has highlighted the ambivalence of the experience in these prisons offering a biased form of freedom. A significant proportion of prisoners find this situation as difficult as closed prisons, and so there are not many requests for transfer.[11]

In France, in the wake of the Gontard report, the State Secretariat for Justice announced in 2010 that open prisons would be built in 2015. They would be prisons without walls, bars, or watchtowers. Perhaps the fact that this announcement was made on April Fool's Day explains why nothing has happened since. Either way, the ambivalence remains: what has happened in recent decades is not so much that prisons have opened up towards society, but rather that quasi-carceral control has expanded into ordinary institutions and spaces. From this perspective, one might argue that model prisons function as a kind of 'heterotopic laboratory', where methods of social control based on the atomization of collective bodies are tested, turning a potential space of social resistance into one of individual subjection.

Chapter 11

Mauzac (France, 1986)

Mauzac Prison (2010s)
Source: © Contrôleur général des lieux de privation de liberté (CGLPL)

Mauzac: the model that was not a model? At least this is the view of Christian Demonchy, the architect who designed the prison in collaboration with Noëlle Janet: 'Mauzac is not a model prison, but a different kind of prison that benefited from a special programme.' Despite his disclaimer, the label 'model prison' is often applied to this unusual facility. Demonchy's reluctance to embrace this characterization stems from two considerations. First, Mauzac represented an experimental architectural approach, initially conceived as a special creation, with no intention of providing a general solution or institutional panacea for the whole prison system. Second, it has actually generated no comparable replicas or successors. Therefore, Mauzac has served as a model neither in theoretical conception nor in empirical application. It was rather a one-off that has occasionally been praised, but has not had any tangible influence on subsequent prison developments. Significantly, there has never been any systematic empirical assessment of Mauzac Prison, leading Demonchy to note that it had failed to 'serve as a model or even as an experiment'.[1]

Mauzac's reputation as a model prison persists nevertheless, for reasons that are partly contextual. Demonchy's architectural approach went against the tides of prison design and politics. Just after Mauzac Prison came into operation in 1986, France underwent a major political shift, with the return of a right-wing government that had explicitly criticized the left's supposedly lax approach to law and order. In this respect, ''86' was the reverse of ''68' politically as well as numerically. The newly elected neoconservative government launched a major prison construction drive that would become known as 'Programme 13,000', in reference to the number of new prison places to be created. Although Demonchy got involved in this programme in an attempt to make the most of the architectural specifications that had been decided, the guiding principles that had determined them essentially contradicted Mauzac's own underlying principles. They emphasized 'passive security' (achieving order by technological and physical means), whereas Mauzac was designed to promote human interaction and respectful relationships among all participants in the prison environment, both inmates and staff.[2]

To understand Mauzac's unique design philosophy, it helps to look back at its origins in 1970. The idea was to build a new prison in a remote location about thirty kilometres from Toulouse in the south-west of France. It had been the site of various buildings since the 1930s, including a disused gunpowder factory annexe and two workers' camps, one on either side of a canal. The north camp served as a military prison during the pro-fascist Vichy regime, later becoming a prison for Algerian nationalists during the Algerian War of Independence. The south camp held foreign workers in the early 1940s, especially Spanish Republicans, before becoming a women's prison after the Second World War, and then an ordinary detention centre in the 1950s. The site was considered large enough to accommodate a dual facility made up of two distinct parts. The first would contain a closed prison that, though conventional, would be oriented towards medical and psychological treatment, while the second 'would have all the features of an open facility'. According to an official report:

> The life of this community would revolve around shared activities – organized in a cultural and economic centre (chapel, cinema, lecture hall, mess hall, etc.), whose management prisoners could be called upon to participate in – and also around work. [. . .] The regime applied would be very liberal, and staff intervention would be limited to monitoring attendance at work and ensuring inmates are present in the centre at night and on rest days, except when leave permits are granted.[3]

But the turbulent 1970s decided otherwise, and the project did not materialize until fifteen years later, as the belated offspring of a 1974 commission that had produced a report on the 'Prisons of Tomorrow'. The new, dual-regime Mauzac Prison was designed and built between 1984 and 1986 on the initiative of the French Minister of Justice Robert Badinter, who presented it as a model for future prisons, both in France and abroad. The specifications called for 'a resolutely innovative regime' that would offer the possibility of entrusting prisoners with 'areas of controlled responsibility' and 'a living environment as close as possible to everyday life, in order to reduce the negative effects of imprisonment and better prepare prisoners for their release at the end of their sentence'. There was a focus on relaxed constraints, group activities, and sentence adjustments, such as work releases. With a capacity of around 250, Mauzac Prison was intended to be the opposite of the classic cellular model. It was not monolithic, but made up of some twenty small separate buildings known as 'pavilions', each only having two floors, and housing twelve inmates who were allowed to cultivate their own garden.[4]

'Prisons of Tomorrow'

In March 1974, a commission was set up under the aegis of a right-wing Minister of Justice to consider the question of 'Prisons of Tomorrow'. It consisted of around twenty members, including architects, magistrates, physicians, senior civil servants, a civil engineer, a social worker, and an educator. It was a critical moment: even though the protests would peak later during the summer of 1974, collective movements and full-blown uprisings had been punctuating prison life since at least 1971, a 'dark year for the prison administration', according to former Minister of Justice René Pleven.

Despite this extraordinary situation, the make-up of the commission revealed a certain conservatism. The most highly valued professions were over-represented, while lower-ranking positions were marginalized. Likewise, official representatives were present, but those who spoke on behalf of prisoners were absent, even though their voices had been central to the turmoil that had been shaking prisons in recent years. Nevertheless, a certain openness could be inferred from the presence of psychologist Simone Buffard, who had practised within Lyon's prison walls for some fifteen years after having been detained for acts of resistance during the Second World War. Her 1973 book, with its eloquent title and subtitle

('Prison Coldness: The Impossible Reform of Prisons'), was imbued with abolitionist fatalism.

In the end, the discussions did not make much progress. The work of the commission, whose members met five times between March and June 1974, was interrupted by a French presidential election and then by the crisis of the spectacular 1974 summer prison riots. The government essentially opted for legal parades. In any case, the tone of internal documents from September 1974, which attempt to take stock of this initiative – announcing the submission of a report but nothing more – betrayed a certain disappointment. Lamenting the lack of progress and the narrowness of the perspective adopted, the authors argued that the entire issue of prison space in all its complexity (architecture, geographical location, work organization, etc.) needed to be addressed. The initiative stopped there, and was largely forgotten. However, it is believed to have influenced a construction and renovation programme that led to the opening of a few prisons in the early 1980s, including Mauzac.[5]

Those features continued to exist in the decades that followed, within two distinct sections: known as the 'old camp' (which had to be rebuilt after a fire in 2003) and the 'new centre'. The latter has no high perimeter wall, only a wire fence, and has no prison yard, but rather a central common outdoor space known as the 'agora'. Nor are there cameras, electric locks, prison gangways, or double-entrance security doors. There are not even any 'cells', insofar as the living quarters were deliberately called 'rooms' to emphasize their more humane design. They are fairly spacious, with a shower and separate toilet, and inmates are provided with their own keys. But they are less distinctive than the rooms known as 'living units': the communal living spaces in each pavilion, centring on a shared kitchen, and fostering group activities. These are the hubs of the community life that is encouraged, which includes labour for some of the prisoners, on a nearby horticultural farm or in local workshops. Although Mauzac was not intended for any specific type of prisoner, most inmates are sex offenders who are reaching the end of their sentence. According to Demonchy, this is the main reason why the facility cannot be 'endlessly duplicated', even though its construction costs were lower than for a conventional prison.[6]

He also says that the idea behind his project was to depart from three characteristics that had defined the traditional cellular model that had dominated since the 1830s: the continuity of the prison structure as a whole; the management of all inner functional units as small prisons themselves; and the clear-cut spatial separation between guards and inmates. Consistent with this architectural deviation, at the heart of the compound lies a landscaped 'common' space intended as a meeting area. Demonchy explains that the classic design he was eager to improve upon was not the Panopticon, but the French *maison d'arrêt* – a 'detention house' only for remand, not for serving sentences, where there is no question of rehabilitation. In a way, Mauzac Prison even represents the opposite of the Panopticon, insofar as its design gives visibility not so much to the cells, but rather to the corridors, where correctional officers work. So it is only a 'Panopticon for public officials, docile and useful to the state', Demonchy says ironically, alluding to Foucault's definition of disciplinary power. The architect has also criticized what he calls the hospital model, which reduces people to passivity and idleness. From this standpoint, he considers Mauzac the antithesis of Fresnes (chapter 5) or Fleury-Mérogis (chapter 10). Not only does it break away from the individualization effect of the cell model, but by encouraging social activities, it also dispels the fear of inmate gatherings. Often likened to a 'village' or a 'farm school', Mauzac Prison is reminiscent of some of the Scandinavian experiments we encountered in counterpoint IV. In this regard, French philosopher Alain Brossat mocks 'men of goodwill' and their humanitarian scruples: 'What they want is not a society without prisons, but model prisons, clean Mauzac prisons or Scandinavian-style prison units, and a whole range of good alternative sentences.'[7]

The fact that Mauzac was a unique experiment did not give the architect free rein to do as he pleased in every area. This special prison drew even more criticism because Demonchy had previously designed holiday villages, including for Club Med. In at least one respect, the initial ambition was limited. Although visiting rooms known as 'studios' were set up (paving the way for 'family living units'), central government authorities would not allow them to be used until 2010. And despite its unique character, Mauzac shares features with some conventional prisons. According to a French specialist, it does not meet the definition of an 'open prison', mainly because of its closed double fence and the presence of watchtowers (but the author does not make much of a distinction between the compound's two sections). The number of reintegration counsellors and social workers within the facility remains very low. The prison also lacks government investment in certain areas, resulting in insufficient medical staff to cope with an ageing population. Not to mention it is remote and barely served by public transport.[8]

Official inspection reports reveal Mauzac's uneven trajectory. A report after a 2010 visit described the new section as having a 'calm' atmosphere and 'good' social climate, but when a surprise inspection took place in 2012 after numerous complaints, deteriorating conditions were found. New security measures had been implemented, including watchtowers, enhanced controls, and restrictive regulations, indicating that the focus of the prison's approach was shifting towards security. A 2022 report was more favourable, noting that several recommendations had been implemented, though problems remained in such areas as complaint handling. The inspection commission identified nine 'good practices' and made thirty-four new 'recommendations', but stopped short of calling the prison a model, noting that Mauzac's potential remained under-exploited, particularly regarding its agricultural estate. A 2024 report issued by an environmental association drew attention to the fact that Mauzac Prison is highly exposed to several major climate risks like heatwaves, fire, flooding, and storms.[9]

In the years that followed the Mauzac experiment, Christian Demonchy returned to designing more traditional prisons. But first he took the opportunity to correct a common misunderstanding. When he designed Mauzac, he did not have rehabilitation in mind. The prison promised nothing for the post-detention period, based as it was on two ideas: first, that despite all the talk about sentence individualization, imprisonment was in fact a collective punishment; and, second, that prisoners were normal people prior to being (labelled as) criminals or inmates. The design therefore focused on the present, not the past or the future, seeking the best way (or at least not the worst way) of organizing the enforced cohabitation of ordinary people in a confined space. These ideas guided the architectural choices that defined Mauzac's unique spatial arrangement and social environment. Regarding social pathologies and economic inequalities whose effects persist within prison walls, Demonchy admits that no architectural solution can ever solve them.

Chapter 12

Haren (Belgium, 2022)

Haren Prison (aerial view, 2022)
Source: © Inter-Environnement Bruxelles, 2022

At the end of September 2022, when Belgium's Haren Prison was finally inaugurated on the northern outskirts of Brussels, the authorities concerned must have been relieved. This uncertain opening of the country's largest prison was a hard-won victory after a particularly contentious process and several years of delays. Opposition had been so strong that there was a period when one could have wondered if the project would ever be completed.

Yet precautions had been taken to defuse any disagreement. When the plan to build a new prison was officially announced, this was done with a mixture of publicity and opacity. On the one hand, an intense public information campaign highlighted noble intentions: to stem prison overcrowding; to put an end to degrading detention conditions in archaic prisons; to make way for a 'more humane approach to detention' in a modern and even advanced penal establishment; and to create jobs in the process. On the other hand, the concrete unfolding of the operation was kept in the shadows, so as not to risk compromising it. It long remained unclear exactly how the profit-making private sector was used in the construction and management of the prison. The contract that the local authorities signed with a newly created private consortium called Cafasso – based on the DBFM delivery method ('Design, Build, Finance, Maintain') – was concealed for quite some time, even from federal legislators. Eventually the process stalled, the opposition became more organized, and the Haren construction project remained in suspension for a few years.[1]

This unusual situation was the result of an exceptional social protest in the mid-2010s. The movement was remarkable in several respects: its unusual scope and duration; the diversity of the 'repertoires of contention' deployed; the wide range of spaces targeted for occupation; and the multiplicity of arguments mobilized. The construction site became Belgium's first '*zone à défendre*' (ZAD), so it was far from being merely a matter of localist 'NIMBY' complaints. Nearby residents and outsider activists joined forces to protest against the project from standpoints both local and general, theoretical and practical, social and ecological. They ranged from principled opposition to the increasing recourse to imprisonment (when, legally, the custodial sentence should be a measure of last resort), to the protection of the Keelbeek site, a territory historically marked by peasant struggles, still semi-rural and rich in arable land. In September 2015, activists occupying the Keelbeek site were brutally evicted by police, who tricked them by timing the operation to take place when many of them were away at the law courts to hear a decision relating to an appeal filed against the project.[2]

Beyond this occupation, a broader opposition developed in the 2010s, uniting experts with ordinary citizens. Its battle assumed various forms, including physical occupation, legal action, and civil disobedience: petitions, letters to officials, public debates, leaflet distribution, and so on. Federated under the name 'Platform to End the Prison Disaster' (later 'Haren Observatory'), a dozen trade unions and associations joined with academics to organize public events alerting citizens to the human rights violations and environmental injustice that the project would entail. It was also opposed by legal professionals, particularly because of the practical difficulty of travelling between the prison and the law courts. Caught in a cycle of alternating phases of acceleration and interruption, in late 2015 the project was blocked by the city of Brussels, which turned down the planning application. Some weeks later, a judicial investigation was opened, looking into 'invisible' conditions in the contract-awarding process. Despite the failure to address any of these issues, and opponents' resulting condemnation of multiple violations of the rule of law, the project was eventually approved. In 2018, the remaining occupiers were driven out by authorities so that construction could finally begin, bringing an end to the opposition movement, which was chronicled in a collective book published in 2019.[3]

This unusual mobilization is explained by a central characteristic of the Haren project, one that contradicted the initial announcements of the 'Masterplan' (as the vast three-phase construction and renovation project was known when officially approved in 2008): the very large scale of the planned facility, which opponents were quick to brand as a 'mega-prison' or '*maxi-prison*'. Though the prison would be large by European standards, the authorities believed it was justified by the need to reduce overcrowding and modernize incarceration conditions. The stated aim was to replace three old jails in downtown Brussels (Saint-Gilles, Forest, and Berkendael) with a penitentiary complex offering nearly 1,200 places – the largest prison ever built in Belgium. In a context of rising prison numbers, this approach might have seemed logical, yet it was surprising in many respects. During the planning phase, a working group consisting of researchers and corrections professionals was set up to discuss the pros and cons of several prison projects, including Haren. One of its conclusions was that massive prisons should be avoided. Modest size was a core feature of an alternative proposal based on the opposite approach, called *De Huizen* ('The Houses'). This 'new paradigm', which formed the basis for the European 'RESCALED' movement founded in Belgium in 2019, advocates urban detention facilities in buildings housing a maximum of thirty detainees, integrated into the heart of cities rather than located on the periphery. Yet it was Haren, which was poorly served by public transport, that ended up prevailing. Although 'detention houses' were not ruled out by the 'Masterplan', they supplemented conventional prisons instead of replacing them.[4]

Economic motives were decisive, but ultimately the taxpayer did not reap any savings. The public expenditure was spread over time, but not reduced – quite the contrary. The total cost of the 'public–private partnership' (PPP) was exorbitant, adding up to more than one billion euros over a quarter-century, with some estimates predicting the total could double, or even reach three billion, given the hidden costs and cost overruns that are common in this field. While PPP contracts increased long-term costs for taxpayers, they also served the cause of capital accumulation via immediate profit extraction for the construction consortium and steady revenue streams through maintenance contracts. Yet the prison project still aimed to achieve an economy of scale, at both the prison and city level. The official line was that the old prisons Haren would replace needed to close because they were emblematic of an archaic prison system. But unofficially, their closure was intended to free up real estate that had socioeconomic potential and could be transferred to the market sphere. From this perspective, the eviction of prisons from the city centre – which is actually just an optical illusion, since some of the old buildings remain operational – is an integral part of the accelerated gentrification of the Belgian capital. Through privatization, marketization, and appropriation, some aspects of the overall process meet the definition of what David Harvey terms 'accumulation by dispossession', where public assets become sources of private profit. At the same time, Haren also illustrates the historical transition leading to the construction of prisons-as-cities instead of the integration of prisons into cities: significantly, the core building is called 'The City Hall'.[5]

From prisons in the city to the prison-as-city

By presenting itself alternately as a city, a town, or a village, Haren Prison illustrates a broader historical transformation in penal architecture. Following the political unrest of the late 1960s and early 1970s, the notion of the prison as a city has supplanted the waning ambition – both theoretically and practically – to integrate prisons into the urban fabric. This shift tends to resolve the strained relationship between prison and city by embedding urban logic within the prison, rather than the other way around. Prisons are now increasingly framed as quasi-urban microcosms, employing urban or residential terminology: squares, streets, alleys, neighbourhoods, patios, and the like. This evolution reflects a penal rationale that officially prioritizes facilitating reintegration into ordinary social life.

This trend is not confined to Belgium; it is observable across Europe. For obvious reasons, prisons located on islands are at the forefront of this change, especially in Scandinavia.

Aside from Norway's Bastøy Prison (counterpoint IV), one can cite Storstrøm Prison, on the Danish island of Falster, south of Copenhagen. In France, the analogy is evident in the successive construction plans of the late twentieth century, with the prison layout increasingly mirroring ordinary urban life. For instance, a plan called 'Architecture and Prisons' (1984–5) was based on this premise: 'thinking about the city in the prison first, and the prison in the city afterwards'. In Spain, the analogy materializes in so-called '*centros tipos penitenciarios*'. Often located on the periphery of urban areas for economic and logistical reasons, these institutions are designed as 'self-sufficient small towns'. Traditional carceral features are minimized or obscured, both linguistically and spatially. As Valérie Icard contends, this organizational shift is not merely an attempt to 'humanize' imprisonment. Instead, it primarily serves to optimize the management of inmate flows and maintain internal order. The fragmentation and atomization of spaces mitigate the risks of escape and the spread of unrest, while the new architectural configuration reinforces spatial differentiation within the institution. This design effectively hinders mutinies and escapes, functioning as a potent disciplinary tool to preserve carceral order.[6]

To legitimize this widely opposed initiative, it was necessary to present Haren as a model prison. Several arguments were advanced for this purpose, some of them paradoxical. First, even though the prison was to be oversized by ordinary standards, from the outset it was presented not as a city but as a 'prison-village' or a 'penitentiary village', playing on this image's reassuring community connotation. Haren's central open space and its twenty or so buildings (with names like 'Ocean House', 'Mountain House', and 'Lake House') caused it also to be compared to a university campus, designed to be as green as it was secure. The fact was, its architecture marked a drastic break with the famous traditional 'star-shaped' layout (sometimes called 'panoptic'), which in Belgium is associated with nineteenth-century reformer Édouard Ducpétiaux. And its proponents claimed that its design was environmentally sustainable in the spirit of 'green prisons', since it would have features like solar panels, rainwater recovery, and vegetated roofs. The prison's multidimensional character was also cited as justification for its size. It was designed to incarcerate men and women, adults and minors, and include an arrangement of 'closed' and 'open' areas, so that coercion and care could live side-by-side, and there was also to be a medical-psychiatric centre. Finally, as in Mauzac (chapter 11) – but in a very different context – the project boasted a structure consisting of 'living units' that were supposed to favour human contact, despite a framework steeped in technical innovation. Behind its apparent gigantism, the prison would in fact favour small infrastructures intended to foster both individual autonomy and community life.

It is worth giving some attention to the paradox of 'autonomy' granted to captive persons, which is typical of the dominant twenty-first-century conception of model prisons in Europe. In this sense, the prison's specifications echo a concept developed by Madeleine Akrich and Michel Callon based on France's 'Programme 13,000'. In place of the 'disciplinary diagram' identified by Michel Foucault, the two authors signalled the emergence of an 'interactive diagram'. They argued that this new model is imbued with a liberal, individualistic, contractualist view of human nature that sees the inmate as an autonomous and responsible individual, capable of controlling their own activities and engaging in 'projects'. In this 'technology of power' (Foucault), the transformation supposedly inculcated by imprisonment proceeds not so much through introspection (as was typical of the religiously inspired ideas of the nineteenth century), but rather through prisoners' visible ability to 'manage' themselves. Interpreting a subtle mixture of discipline and control in this model, Guillermo Kozlowski and David Scheer noted that it partially redefined the idea of autonomy. Prisoners are reconceptualized as entrepreneurial individuals responsible for their own 'rehabilitation' through market-oriented skill acquisition. This particular autonomy does not encourage independence of mind, but rather self-management as an economic agent in a world that is competitive in terms of jobs and wages in low-income sectors.[7]

Kozlowski and Sheer further suggested that what risked becoming autonomous above all, given the level of computerization, was the technology itself. Because although there is still an architecture shaping a framework that constrains power relations, it is now a computerized and digitalized architecture ('prison cloud' included), which is just as imperceptibly intrusive as the panoptic model was supposed to be, but in a decentralized and automated way. The magnetic badge that replaces traditional keys, and provides access to 'rooms' rather than 'cells', is typical of this ambivalence between autonomy and control. On another level, this ambivalence is found in two new professional roles, 'detention companions' and 'security assistants', the former oriented towards assistance, the latter towards coercion, both providing 'dynamic security'.

The inauguration of Haren Prison was a turning point, but it did not silence critical voices, which had plenty of issues to condemn, since the prison immediately encountered several problems. The prison needed to economize on labour and so was serviced by an insufficient number of staff, who were also inexperienced and poorly trained. Working conditions for prison officers quickly proved to be more challenging than anticipated, revealing a number of professional splits. The level of staff absenteeism quickly became a major problem, especially as the prison's maximum capacity was soon reached and exceeded, at least in the men's section. In 2023, a quelled mutiny hit the headlines, as did a major police operation linked to drug trafficking within the prison. Reports also highlighted equipment malfunctions, which were considered particularly problematic in view of the technical refinement promised by the for-profit private company responsible for building a structure that, before opening, had been awarded two prizes for its architectural design. The company responsible for maintenance, meanwhile, had every interest in cutting corners to maximize profitability, taking advantage of a favourable balance of power that translated into low accountability, contrary to the recommendations of the Belgian government and the European Courts of Auditors.[8]

Recent events have confirmed that the situation was tense. In a January 2023 press release, associations spoke out against the 'predictable fiasco' of a would-be model prison that was in fact dysfunctional and oppressive. A few months after its inauguration, the prison had already seen a worrying string of incidents, including assaults on staff, suicide attempts, and suspicious deaths. Overcrowding was already setting in with the installation of additional bunks in certain cells. The opening of a 'social defence' section – which human rights organizations criticized as contrary to European standards – illustrated the tendency towards deterioration rather than improvement. Just as opponents warned, Haren's impact on the judicial system has been particularly problematic: every day, the distance between the prison and the Brussels courts causes 'blank hearings', where defendants do not arrive on time. This problem is exacerbated by internal organizational dysfunction such as understaffing in the prison registry office and confusion in prisoner lists – issues that worsen the judicial backlog and concretely illustrate the harmful effects of moving prisons out of city centres to distant areas. The 2023 annual report of the Prison Supervisory Committee painted a mixed picture. Mirroring the many external criticisms of the prison and of the processes behind its creation, it mentions overworked staff, questionable disciplinary practices, and inadequate communication, not to mention numerous grievances lodged by both guards and inmates. Since then, warnings and complaints have multiplied from various bodies such as medical associations and public sector unions. In March 2025, staff went on a short strike, mainly because of repeated assaults against correctional officers and social workers.[9]

These operational failures are not mere implementation issues, but rather structural contradictions inherent in the half-privatized mega-prison model. The focus on profit maximization necessarily conflicts with adequate staffing, maintenance, and activities. And although the geographical isolation might facilitate urban gentrification, it also undermines the operation of the institution, revealing how carceral geography is influenced more by economic imperatives than by the needs of the courts.

Historically, some model prisons have succeeded in maintaining a good reputation for several years after opening, but in Haren's case, its characterization as a model was challenged from the outset. The contradictions surrounding this institution reflect penal orientations – extension, distancing, diversification, and privatization – that heavily rely on technological sophistication, combined with humanitarian claims that poorly mask economic motives and security considerations. This case is typical of a headlong rush that, under the pretext of curbing prison overcrowding, only spurs on the detention rate.

Haren is not just the name of a local controversy. It encapsulates the contradictions of contemporary punishment: humanitarian rhetoric masking economic exploitation; technological innovation producing bureaucratic dysfunction; and modernization generating regression. These contradictions are reflected in many inmates' attachment to old prisons that are sometimes dilapidated or unsanitary, but at least not as oppressive. These are not paradoxes to be resolved, but structural features of the neoliberal government of social insecurity. The resistance to Haren, though ultimately unsuccessful, revealed other possibilities and demonstrated that current trends are neither natural nor inevitable.[10]

Counterpoint VI

Counter-models (utopia/dystopia)

In the 1980s, Norbert Elias observed that utopias had been increasingly taking on a disturbing character. At a time when the word 'dystopia' was not yet in widespread use, the author of *The Court Society* raised the question: why have dark, nightmarish utopias taken precedence over dream-like utopias? It is hard not to think of Elias's words when reflecting on the American 'supermax' prisons that were flourishing during the period when he was writing. I began this book with the historical, correctional definition of model prisons, whose stated purpose was to render imprisonment productive by reforming the presumed moral deficiencies and criminal tendencies of lower-class deviants. But a reversed idea of utopia could be applied to prisons that focus merely on detention and incapacitation. These represent 'models' of sorts, or counter-models, insofar as they are not just prisons of evil repute, but also facilities that can be regarded as paradigms in their own right: cohesive creations epitomizing a doctrine or ideology, some of them having actually spawned imitations.[1]

This paradigm was termed 'the warehouse prison' in a study of Solano State Prison (California) by John Irwin, a former convict turned criminologist. Writing in the early 2000s, he described the emergence of these punitive institutions stripped of any rehabilitative or transformative pretensions, designed purely for the disposal of the 'new dangerous class'. Irwin argued that these facilities represented a fundamental departure from the correctional ideal. They were built quickly and cheaply, prioritizing maximum-security features. Irwin noted that they were more like industrial warehouses than traditional correctional facilities, with their stark concrete structures, minimal social activities, and containment emphasized over correction. Generally speaking, California stands out in this respect. Not only did the massive expansion of California's prison system turn the Golden State into a 'Golden Gulag' (as Ruth Wilson Gilmore called it), but it was also the birthplace of the harshest experiments in terms of technologically advanced (but conceptually regressive) punitive confinement.[2]

A few years before Irwin's book, Zygmunt Bauman similarly studied Pelican Bay State Prison, about 400 miles north of Solano. He rejected the idea that it was nothing but a sophisticated update of Bentham's Panopticon and its obsession for permanent control. He considered it a model in its own right, as a paradigm of exclusion. There is no rehabilitation objective at Pelican Bay, not even in theory, only a technique of pure neutralization and expulsion. It hardly even matters how the prisoners spend their time. In any case, they cannot do much, confined as they are, almost constantly, to their tiny cells, without work, diversions, or even a window, their only light source being a fluorescent tube that is permanently on. Operating according to a principle of extreme automation, Pelican Bay was conceived by Bauman as a repository for globalization's 'scum' – that is, people who had been designated as 'surplus' in an increasingly unequal society. This is particularly the case in the United States, where prison plays a decisive role in both reflecting and reinforcing class and race divisions, with street crime targeted much more than white-collar crime. In her ethnographic study of Pelican Bay, Keramet Reiter confirmed that the twenty-three-hour-a-day lockdown was the defining characteristic of this new form of carceral dystopia. She identified only three ways out: parole, snitch, or die. Yet this prison was publicly praised by officials when it opened in 1989. At Pelican Bay's inauguration, the state governor proudly declared: 'California now possesses a state-of-the-art prison that will serve as a model for the rest of the nation.' A few years later, 3,000 inmates incarcerated there filed a class-action lawsuit against the Department of Corrections. And in 2013, nearly 30,000 prisoners across the state stood in solidarity with the Pelican Bay inmates, in what was arguably the largest coordinated hunger strike in history.[3]

Beyond Pelican Bay, this type of penal establishment constitutes a paradigm. However repulsive the notion may be, one could speak of an American supermax (counter-)model: a high-security prison that, like the one in Lewisburg at the beginning of this book, claims to neutralize inmates, with no pretention to rehabilitation, nor any respect for human rights. This is what Loïc Wacquant calls the 'meta-prison', dedicated in all its aspects (including architecture, technology, activities, schedules, and social relations) to redoubling what incarceration inflicts on those most resistant to a harsh prison regime. Pushing the principle of exclusion to the extreme (even to the point of dispensing a kind of social death), the aim is to neutralize dangerousness through punishment. In sharp contrast to the 'open prisons' mentioned in the previous counterpoint, carceral logic is pushed to its absolute limit in order to deal with those who are (or are supposed to be) the 'worst of the worst' (terrorists, mass murderers, gang leaders, unruly prisoners, etc.), in line with the principles of maximum harshness for all and complete individual isolation. It could be seen as a modern version of the Philadelphia tradition of solitary confinement, one that absorbs the entire prison through the addition of electronics, and dispenses with the charitable rhetoric. Human rights advocates have repeatedly condemned the torturous sensory deprivation that takes place in this type of institution, making it a factory of madness producing apathy or violence.[4]

The supermax's date of birth is somewhat uncertain. It could be situated in a variety of times and places. Its origins are sometimes traced back to Alcatraz because of the place that this facility occupies in the popular cultural imagination. Commissioned in the mid-1930s to confine unruly prisoners and gangsters, it closed in 1963. But recent studies have rejected this idea, because although Alcatraz was harsh, life there was not reduced to the near-total isolation characteristic of supermaxes. Marion Prison in Illinois, which was intended to replace Alcatraz, is often cited as the first supermax because of the harsh conditions imposed there after the murder of two wardens in late 1983. However, other authors think that the first of its kind came later (1986) in another state (Arizona), in the form of Florence State Prison, which served as a prototype for Pelican Bay. In any case, supermax prisons housed around 2% of inmates in the United States at the turn of the twenty-first century. This might sound like a small proportion, but it is significant in a country whose prison population was passing the two million milestone at that time. At a local level, dystopias can extend to an entire city or county. The documentary film *Prison Valley* brought attention to the case of Cañon City, Colorado, a 'prison-like city where even those who live on the outside live inside'.[5]

Supermax prisons epitomize the 'new penology' identified by Malcolm Feeley and Jonathan Simon in 1992. This approach focuses on group management through the prisms of risk and dangerousness, rather than the treatment of individual offenders, with all that this implies in terms of diagnosis, assessment, and classification. Probabilistic and preventive, it is based on so-called 'actuarial' methods, covering much more prosaic policing practices, which are subject to professional routines and cultural representations. As usual, architecture plays a central role. Architect Guillaume Abel Blouet, a leading French figure in nineteenth-century prison design, was already arguing that 'an architect can, by means of well-understood combinations, foster acceptance of this or that system of imprisonment which theory may have classified as utopian'. Commenting on this view, Jacques-Guy Petit evokes 'geometry in the service of utopia'. As we have seen throughout this book, it is widely believed that an effective system of prisoner moralization, isolation, and surveillance will be achieved through advances in architecture and technology.[6]

Technological fetishism applies just as much to dystopian systems, but in reverse. This is starkly manifested in facilities like California's overcrowded, high-security Calipatria State Prison, where human surveillance is backed up by an electrified high-voltage 'escape-proof' fence. Designed to cause instant death to anyone attempting escape, it delivers more than 5,000 volts of lethal current. Following complaints from ornithologists about bird deaths, it was modified to be 'ecologically correct', becoming 'the world's only birdproof, ecologically responsible death fence' (as Mike Davis ironically described it). It is an episode that reflects the staggering priorities of this dystopian system. Calipatria State Prison represented a recycling of the fortress model, as opposed to the 'campus' model of the 'New Generation Prisons' built in the United States in the 1960s and 1970s.[7]

The supermax 'model' is typical of a wide-ranging historical trend: the end of correctional utopia and the growing acceptance of a purely retributive, harsh regime that could be seen as dystopian. Yet one might argue that, rather than being a mere contrast or reversal, it represents the logical extension of the utopian prison's core contradictions. As Michael Gordin, Helen Tilley, and Gyan Prakash have asserted,

> Despite the name, dystopia is not simply the opposite of utopia. A true opposite of utopia would be a society that is either completely unplanned or is planned to be deliberately terrifying and awful. Dystopia, typically invoked, is neither of these things; rather, it is a utopia that has gone wrong, or a utopia that functions only for a particular segment of society.

In this respect, the promise to shape human behaviour through environmental and institutional control would find extreme expression in a technological structure of total domination. Supermax prisons represent what could be termed a 'negative utopia': not the absence of utopian thinking, but rather a perversion of its fulfilment. The original philanthropic vision of making prison time profitable and conducive to obedience has been abandoned, leaving only the core belief in the utility and convenience of custody. The result is a perfected control machine that achieves its utopian dream of absolute order through the systematic production of physical and psychological harm.[8]

To put it differently, I would argue that in comparison with the traditional correctional prison, rather than representing a shift from utopia to dystopia, the supermax illustrates the distinction between two different concepts of discipline. Instead of Foucault's understanding of discipline as 'a relation of docility-utility', aimed at producing 'normalized', tractable yet productive subjects, supermax facilities are closer to what Max Weber conceptualized as 'the chance that, because of a practised disposition, a command will find prompt, automatic, and schematic obedience among a definite number of persons'. Weber's definition emphasized the '"habituation" characteristic of uncritical and unresisting mass obedience', which fundamentally differs from the productive disciplinary mechanisms Foucault analysed in the penitentiary system. And what can produce this 'habituation' better than a carceral structure?[9]

This is not to imply that a more appealing architecture guarantees any progress. As Sara Benson's book on Kansas's Leavenworth Prison has shown, the most 'model' architecture can mask oppressive functions. Leavenworth's design was modelled on the Capitol, and yet it was a symbol of state violence under the guise of democratic legitimacy. It would be tempting to think that truth is stranger than fiction, had science fiction not shown such considerable imagination in its depiction of prison dystopias, starting with Giovanni Battista Piranesi's *Carceri d'invenzione*. This sub-genre could be divided into three groups. The first describes prisons as places of terror. The second depicts not so much prisons themselves, but rather carceral societies. The third group, probably the smallest, imagines a prison-free society. However apt this distinction may be, the American TV series *Oz*, which was broadcast at the turn of the twenty-first century, stands out among recent fictional depictions of prison life, though not without blurring the lines between retribution and rehabilitation. Although this drama, which was like an ancient tragedy in the modern world, became known for the harshness it depicted, its main setting was a pilot facility, or rather an experimental unit, operating an open-door regime under the aegis of a progressive warden who, though he was more of a social worker than a guard, constantly struggled with disillusionment.[10]

The influence of the supermax prison is pervasive worldwide. France had nothing to contribute to Jeffrey Ross's 2013 book *The Globalization of Supermax Prisons*, but it might soon join the ranks of the countries the author studied. Although the dark history of the French *quartiers de haute sécurité* (QHS) in the 1970s should stand as a grim warning, in May 2025, right-wing French Justice Minister Gérald Darmanin announced plans to create new high-security prisons. More broadly, this global expansion reveals how the supermax functions not merely as a penal institution, but also as what anthropologist Lorna Rhodes calls a 'technology of punishment': a systematized approach to human control that extends beyond the prison walls. The model's appeal lies precisely in its promise to solve the 'problem' of unruly prisoners through technological and architectural innovation, as the physical realisation of what could be called a techno-carceral utopia/dystopia.[11]

This proliferation is occurring within the broader historical context that Samuel Moyn has charted. He argues that the human rights discourse that emerged in the 1970s was the final idealistic project to rise from the ruins of earlier failed utopian dreams of revolution and decolonization. The irony is profound: at the very moment when human rights were being established as the ultimate moral framework for international justice, the United States was perfecting the supermax model as the ultimate technology of strict confinement. The emergence of supermaxes thus represents a counter-movement to human rights conceived as what Moyn calls the 'last utopia', revealing how carceral dystopia has developed alongside, and in conflict with, the humanitarian, universal utopianism of the human rights movement. This partly explains the revival of the idea of prison abolition, with a momentum that might be as strong as it was in the early 1970s, but in a very different, opposite context. Does this mean that being sceptical or critical of the very possibility of long-lasting 'model prisons' automatically leads to embracing the idea of prison abolition? This and related aspects will be discussed by way of conclusion.[12]

This overview admittedly suffers from all the characteristic flaws of the genre. Complex, extensive histories have been overly compressed, with emphasis placed on beginnings and aspirations rather than actual practices, and even these were rendered in a highly summary form. Aspects that could provide enough material for entire volumes have been reduced to a couple of sentences, sometimes only a few words. The focus has remained on whole institutions, with minimal attention to the specific practices or programmes that have been regarded – whether justifiably or not – as 'models'. Still less attention has been devoted to actual prison conditions and everyday life. In short, descriptive precision has been sacrificed for breadth of coverage. For something more detailed, readers are encouraged to seek out the many specialized, meticulous studies now available.

The panoramic approach adopted here has deliberately served a different purpose: to provide historical perspective on contemporary developments. This historical examination eventually brings us back to our present time, when so-called 'model prisons' are still being designed and built. Half a century ago, prison systems had undergone such a profound legitimacy crisis that it seemed plausible to claim that the era of carceral punishment would soon end, even if that meant the unfortunate advent of a 'control society' pervaded by subtle repressive mechanisms. In many respects, one could say that this control society has indeed emerged, with non-custodial sentences, on the one hand, and, on the other, surveillance technologies, electronic monitoring, and algorithmic governmentality now pervading everyday life. But this transition remains incomplete and ambivalent. The prison endures as a central institution of punishment. Or, rather, as the centrepiece of the differential control of illegalisms.

Conclusion: The meaning of model prisons

'Has the prison a future?' Sandra Bucerius and Michael Tonry wondered in the early 2020s, suggesting that the meaning of that question had changed dramatically over a few decades. 'Half a century ago, it appeared to be in terminal decline. [. . .] From the 1940s through the mid-1970s, leading practitioners and scholars believed the prison's days were numbered, except possibly residually for the most serious crimes and most troubled offenders. [. . .] The prison era seemed to be passing, even in the United States.' Yet the prison persists on a larger scale than ever before. 'It is easy to see why, especially for people who came of age in the 1970s or later, the prison's end or near end appears to be an impossible dream.' Although imprisonment was widely considered an obsolete institution that would soon be overtaken by other – albeit probably more insidious – systems of control and coercion, it actually underwent an unexpected revival in the late twentieth century. The history of punishment reached a turning point with the development of so-called 'alternative' sentences. However, these did not replace prison, but only supplemented it. Moreover, these sentences now operate not in opposition to incarceration, but in tandem with it. The 'punitive turn' is not *post*-carceral; it is simultaneously carceral, *para*-carceral, and, one might even say, *meta*-carceral. And it has reached such a massive scale that scholars persuasively argue that the late twentieth century marks a third historical stage in the expansion of penal prison, following its emergence in the late sixteenth century and its development in the early nineteenth century.[1]

Admittedly, the fact that a few prisons are touted as 'models' plays only a minor role in this general expansion. The unexpected resurgence of imprisonment in advanced capitalist societies is essentially the result of far-reaching trends related to the 'neoliberal government of social insecurity': as Loïc Wacquant shows, along with other aspects like neighbourhood targeting, police profiling, and the extension of probation, the return of the prison forms an integral part of the advent of a penal state that exerts material and symbolic violence against dispossessed and dishonoured populations, doubly marginalized on the grounds of class and status. Nevertheless, the focus on so-called 'model prisons' provides an insightful vantage point: that of the progressive-looking or well-meaning façade of this process, assuming that the promotion of certain prisons as exemplars still stems from humanitarian, charitable, or curative motives rather than strictly punitive ones. The persistent pursuit of model prisons in times of mass incarceration is contributing to legitimizing a prison system that was widely held to be thoroughly discredited not so long ago.[2]

The paradox of carceral modernization

However, by looking back, we can reduce the risk of amnesia with regard to the plausibility of model prisons worthy of the name. As this book has hopefully shown, history provides plenty of examples across the globe to refute the belief that nothing truly ambitious has ever been attempted in the prison field. Only one conclusion seems obvious at the end of this historical overview: so-called 'model prisons' are unable to resist the ravages of time, and incapable of retaining their model status durably and consistently. This is even an understatement, given the clear pattern of systematic failure that has emerged. In many ways, the fate of model prisons reveals what could be called the paradox of carceral modernization. From the outside, modern prisons in general, and model prisons in particular, appear to represent indisputable progress in every respect when compared with old jails notorious for dereliction and overcrowding. From the inside, however, they are criticized by many of those who live or work there (including inmates, correctional officers, social workers, and visiting lawyers), to the point where they seem inferior to former establishments that, though dilapidated or crumbling, were still regarded as more 'human' and 'liveable'. In these new, more advanced prisons, architectural compartmentalization and technological sophistication are problematic, as they disrupt human relationships to space and time. The reduction of direct human contact generates an atmosphere often described as cold and sanitized, reinforcing feelings of isolation and oppression. This is evidenced by numerous indicators, from inmate suicides to staff requests for transfer to other facilities. The history of model prisons is arguably less repetitive and more startling than the history of prisons overall, yet it presents a predictable series of unsuccessful attempts, if not disasters. All variations and nuances aside, there would appear to be only one sensible interpretation: that model prisons have failed perpetually, and perhaps definitively, in a way that is neither accidental nor contingent, but structural.[3]

In the case of such unusual experiments, it is irrelevant to deplore the lack of ambition, efforts, and resources. The same goes for factors that are contextual (unfavourable circumstances that derail the intended project), conceptual (the lack of any audacious penal theory), or material (architectural flaws). These reasons may be partially valid in some cases, but they cannot account for perpetual failure. Two types of structural explanation are more plausible. The first concerns prison itself, the very logic of confinement, reinforced by the social characteristics of a deprived prison population. This explanation is sometimes approached as a critique of 'spatialism' or 'spatial utopianism': the illusory belief in the ability of a circumscribed space – cleverly designed and deftly managed as it may be – to serve disparate purposes (to deter, intimidate, confine, subdue, discipline, control, moralize, reform, rehabilitate, cure, etc.), let alone overcome social contradictions. The second type of explanation is external to prison itself, situating the problem within the larger institutional set on which this heteronomous institution depends, namely the penal system. Wondering 'what becomes of "model" prisons?', French sociologist Philippe Combessie answers:

> The long-term failure of attempts at 'model' prisons seems to suggest that, even with substantial financial resources, the prison apparatus itself has no possibility of radically changing its operating logic, as long as the entire penal system, of which it is only a part, remains unchanged, and especially so long as prisons are obliged to accommodate everyone sent to them, however many.

Taken together, these explanations discredit the idea of any genuine 'model prison'.[4]

This means that any new attempt is doomed to fail, unless there is a shift in connotation. The term 'model prison' is flexible enough to lend itself to different uses. In its theoretical sense, it can even be taken as narrowly retributive or castigating. Thus, El Salvador's Terrorism Confinement Centre (CECOT, opened in 2023) is presented by autocrat Nayib Bukele as a 'model prison' of sorts; and this sinister institution, where torture is commonplace, has indeed inspired political leaders in Costa Rica, Ecuador, Colombia, and Chile. However, the dominant conception in the early twenty-first century is rather tinged with managerial ideology. In the United States, a good example is FCI McKean, a federal prison located in north-western Pennsylvania. In the article 'A Model Prison', published in *The Atlantic* in 1995,

Robert Worth characterized it as probably the best-managed medium-security prison in the country. Describing an environment reminiscent of a university campus (in contrast to the growing brutality of the country's penal system), Worth noted that since opening six years earlier, there had been no record of any escape, suicide, murder, or rape at the prison. The director's credo was neither humanitarian liberalism, nor any conservative conception of reformation, but rather efficient management, in line with neoliberal thinking, which hardly gives serious consideration to the idea that prison could produce virtuous citizens. All that matters is the effective imposition of obedience during the period of detention. This has significant implications: while it considerably lowers the bar for defining a model prison, it also defuses common objections that highlight the disparity between claims and practices.[5]

In Europe, too, including Nordic countries, prison's prevailing uses reflect reduced ambition. In Norway, 'Model 2015' refers to a standardized prison structure that, while purportedly aimed at mitigating the harms of imprisonment, ultimately prioritizes cost reduction and operational efficiency. Increasingly widespread is the idea that a model prison is simply one that ensures acceptable confinement conditions, meaning only that it complies with current normative human rights standards. The notion that prison could be a place of reformation has not exactly vanished, but it has been practically stripped of any substance. The lack of reliable official statistics on the paths that prisoners follow after release speaks volumes about how seriously the rehabilitative ideal is taken. Some prisons are likely to be labelled 'models' only because they demonstrate efficiency in maintaining order, defined as keeping disturbances and collective movements to a minimum. This was what Victor Serge suggested in the passage already partially quoted in chapter 6:

> I know of only one perfect and irreproachable work of architecture in the modern city: prison. Its perfection lies in the total

> subordination of its design to its function. [. . .] The chance of escape is reduced to infinitesimal proportions. They used to escape from the Bastille. They used to escape from Noumea, despite the ocean fraught with squalls. They still escape from Guiana, across the virgin forest. No one escapes from the model jail.[6]

The French case is telling in this regard. The spectacular revolts of the first half of the 1970s remain deeply etched in the memory of the prison authorities. Over the past two decades, the prison population record has been broken over and over again, leading French prisons to be commonly described as 'powder kegs' just waiting to 'explode'. Yet they do not. There certainly are disturbances, but nothing comparable to the turmoil of the 1970s. From this perspective, new prisons represent a success of sorts: they succeeded in making collective protest movements particularly difficult within their walls. Guy Autran, architect of Seysses Prison in France, made this point clear in the early 2000s, when he was quoted as saying 'the prison of the twenty-first century' was built explicitly 'to bring the inmate to accept his condition without revolt'. Empirically, despite architectural attempts to ease carceral pressure, modern prisons have generally provided means of tightening control. Inmates' movements are supervised more closely, and they are given less room for adaptation or negotiation that might lighten institutional constraints. Based on the primacy of so-called 'passive security', these prisons still pursue the utilitarian aim that has always guided the history of penal imprisonment: to achieve efficiency at a lower cost.[7]

Yet the rehabilitative ideal has not been extinguished entirely. Despite numerous setbacks, prisons that are operational and others merely planned are still being characterized as supposedly exemplary of a special type, sustaining the idea that imprisonment could be constructive, even beneficial. Against all odds, they persist in the quest for a virtuous prison, promising to revive a moribund 'carceral utopia'. It is as if the unwinnable nature of the challenge (on historical if not on logical grounds) were fuelling the desire to tackle it. Furthermore, the notion of 'model' has been reactivated by the international transfer of prison standards to countries in the Global South, a process through which countries in the Global North can regain – by comparison – a relatively favourable position. New 'model' prisons partly financed by the United States and the European Union are even being built across the Caribbean, which reflects a 'growing obsession with prison construction as the only perceived solution to crime', as two scholars have recently pointed out. They continue: 'We are often asked by policymakers around the world to point to a "model prison", and we tell them the same thing: there are no "model prisons"; there are humane, holistic, decolonized *systems*.'[8]

These attempts indeed play a role in legitimizing the wider prison system while leaving the foundational structures of the social order intact. By continuing to sustain the possibility of a prison that is virtuous, beneficial, or at least conforms to the supposed values of a respectable political regime, by establishing a goal that is certainly distant and challenging but possibly attainable, so-called 'model prisons' contribute to the reproduction of a system that is otherwise disparaged. The repetition of history is not without surprises: there are now 'green prisons' designed to minimize environmental harm while sensitizing inmates to ecological issues. As Yvonne Jewkes and Dominique Moran have shown, under cover of irreproachable intentions, these prisons do more for the preservation of the prison system than for that of the environment. Similarly, model prisons assume a legitimation role that extends beyond their own existence. By keeping the fiction of perfectible punishment alive, they contribute to the perpetuation of mass incarceration masked as perpetual reform. The promise of better punishment acts as a temporal displacement mechanism: current failures are attributed to imperfect implementation rather than structural impracticality, while true success can always be postponed until the next architectural innovation or organizational refinement. This approach has a crucial ideological effect. It maintains the legitimacy of 'better' incarceration by perpetually delaying its realization to a future when a suitably improved institution will have been achieved. In so doing, it obscures the structural impossibility of this improvement, especially within existing social relations.[9]

This legitimizing role is even more obvious in the case of notoriously appalling prison systems, especially (though not exclusively) those of authoritarian or despotic regimes, where the term 'model prisons' is mere window dressing or political duplicity. In those cases, it is easy to understand why this idea continues to exert a strong appeal, even in highly unrealistic forms, as exemplified by Wadi el-Natrun Prison, north of Cairo, which the Egyptian regime promoted heavily in the early 2020s. Promoting particular prisons as models is mainly a sign of growing public scrutiny in this domain, compelling prison authorities to maintain appearances, even when the backstage reality bears little resemblance to the official narrative. One could easily dwell on the gap between abstract principles and lived experience. The most common critical gesture is to point out the disconnect between pretensions and reality, between prison rules 'by the book' and prison life 'on the ground'. Necessary though this may be, it is perhaps insufficient. At the end of this journey through time and space, it is not enough to merely highlight the disjunction between plans and reality, or even to dispel the illusion that such models could live up to their claims. What is needed is a shift in perspective similar to that applied to the prison system in general to understand why the idea of the model prison endures despite all the evidence that undermines it.

To this end, one crucial aspect must be emphasized, by moving the focus from the carceral space itself to its broader social functions. Doing so revives a critical legacy that, beyond its variants, shares the basic premise of considering prison by reference to something other than itself: the labour market, state power, class relations, social inequality, racial domination, uneven law enforcement, conventional yet debatable definitions of crime, and so on. An essential element can then be reintroduced, namely what Michel Foucault called the 'differential management of illegalisms'. This conception reversed the common view of prison failure, making it an ingredient of its success. It is the only way to fully explain why prison continues to be reproduced despite its chronic, even congenital, failure; a reasoning that also applies to model prisons.

A successful failure

Numerous criticisms have been directed at Foucault's conception of 'the birth of the prison'. In particular, they have pointed out how poorly disciplinary regimens were actually enforced in penitentiaries. However, what remains relevant in Foucault's perspective is the way he situated prison's specific role within a broader system of power relations. He argued that: 'A penal system must be conceived as a mechanism intended to administer illegalities differentially, not to eliminate them all. [. . .] Legal punishments are to be resituated in an overall strategy of illegalities. The "failure" of the prison may be understood on this basis.' His general theory, which places prison at the heart of the differential control of illegalisms, can still be seen as valid, provided it is supplemented by complementary perspectives formulated by scholars in critical and radical criminology.[10]

In this respect, Foucault's approach undoubtedly requires updating and adjustment. For example, the objective of gaining knowledge of prisoners was pursued erratically throughout the twentieth century. Likewise, the containment of a somewhat professionalized 'delinquent milieu, closed in upon itself, but easily supervised', which he emphasized (while nevertheless predicting its decline at the end of *Discipline and Punish*), is now certainly less important than the warehousing of a population whose status is increasingly stigmatized as 'incorrigible'. The role of what Marx called the 'relative surplus population' has changed significantly, as have relations between capital and labour. Under neoliberal capitalism, which prizes mobility as a core value, immobilization and containment play a more crucial role than ever. The relevant question is not so much: in what ways and to what extent are prisons becoming neoliberal? Rather, it is this: in the context of neoliberalism, what is the role granted to an institution that operates according to a fundamentally different logic, that of sovereign state power? This is not to describe prison as a 'pocket of resistance' to the prevailing neoliberal logic, but to argue that its embeddedness in a social order that overvalues mobility explains why the power to confine remains a decisive one. It is the power to supervise and immobilize populations that are drifting, unstable, and disconnected from ordinary circuits of social integration, while marking them with the stigma of incarceration.[11]

From this perspective, one could argue that however credible and sincere it may be, the enduring quest to realize a model prison helps channel attention and criticism towards the *internal* operation of prisons at the expense of the *external* operation of the prison system. It frames the debate in terms of managerial efficiency (and perhaps respect for human rights, depending on the country) rather than in terms of power relations, inequality, and domination, even within the systems of law and justice. In doing so, it diverts attention away from the pivotal role that the prison system plays in the social construction of crime, intellectually as well as institutionally. A few days spent observing ordinary hearings in a criminal court are enough to grasp the profoundly unjust character of the administration of justice (in other words, of the rule of law *in practice*), so starkly unequal is the distribution of resources and constraints. As it primarily targets those who are materially deprived and symbolically stigmatized, placed in a position of inferiority that undermines their very capacity to assert their own sense of what is fair, the judicial verdict is inextricably a social judgement – a reassertion of the social order. This is something that speculation about the best means of improving the prison is prone to overlook.

In Europe in the early twenty-first century, the progressive view of prisons is that individuals should be confined in decent material and moral conditions: free from overcrowding, housed in premises that respect their bodily integrity, provided with a daily schedule that includes useful activities, and enabled to maintain ties with relatives on the outside. In other words, if one ends overcrowding, idleness, dilapidation, unsanitary conditions, harassment, sexual deprivation, and exploitative labour; if one reduces the rupture between inside and outside as much as possible (commonly called the 'normalization' of detention conditions); and if one provides those released from prison with enough resources to begin 'rehabilitation' or 'social reintegration', then the problem will be resolved.

It will not – far from it. Even in the very unlikely event that practices in detention were to approximately conform to legal norms and align with the rules of 'normal' life on the outside, the prison problem would not be resolved at all. At most, one might be tempted to say this would only be the beginning. And even taken together, detention conditions (the objective side) and prison experiences (the subjective side) represent only a fraction of the problem. To limit the carceral question to what happens within prison walls, evading the institution's social and political functions, is to offer a partial, if not misleading, representation of it.

In this sense, whether willingly or not, the notion of model prisons plays a diversionary role. While the criteria of acceptable prison management continue to be discussed, and the gap between announcements and concrete action is measured, and the possibility or impossibility of tolerable prisons is debated, essential questions get lost from sight: who is being imprisoned (and by extension who is not) and on what grounds? What are the characteristic social backgrounds and life trajectories of those who judge and those who are judged? How are legal and especially penal norms delimited, defined, and hierarchized? How are they determined and applied? On what explicit or implicit assumptions are they based, particularly concerning what constitutes social harms and legal offences? What are the prevailing representations of white-collar crime, environmental crime, and street crime? In short, who benefits from the penal system? The issue of the social construction of crime is the subject of insightful reflections in academic scholarship, but it barely features in public debate. To examine model prisons from a strictly functional or managerial perspective (considering, for example, the extent to which they operate properly, respect human rights, and are truly dedicated to rehabilitation) contributes to steering this debate in the wrong direction, circumventing questions about how the social order is defined and how the penal state defends it. The focus on perfectible spaces can throw a veil over the power relations and 'politics of crime policy' that determine 'who are the criminals' in the first place.[12]

Rejecting the utopia of the model prison does not necessarily entail embracing that of prison abolition; an ideal that, it is worth remembering, is far from new. It is part of a longstanding tradition stretching back to William Morris, Leo Tolstoy, and Peter Kropotkin in the nineteenth century and even earlier thinkers. Nonetheless, its renewed momentum in the early twenty-first century can be seen as a shift in utopian thinking. Whereas the notion of 'model prisons' once represented the utopian pole of penal reform (the belief that imprisonment could be made productive or constructive), prison abolition may now constitute a compelling political utopia, one that aims to surpass rather than merely reform the carceral framework, particularly given the exhaustion of carceral utopianism. The enduring fantasy of 'good' prisons may be symptomatic of a broader crisis: the eclipse of any cohesive and compelling vision of emancipatory transformation in an era that desperately needs one. As Mike Davis observed towards the end of his life, 'only a return to explicitly utopian thinking can clarify the minimal conditions for the preservation of human solidarity in the face of convergent planetary crises'. From this perspective, it is important that the idea of prison abolition gain credibility, if only to widen the range of conceivable possibilities.[13]

More cautiously, and admittedly more sceptically given the current state of affairs, I would suggest that challenging the notion of 'model prisons' decisively strengthens the argument for reframing the problem as that of over-incarceration rather than prison overcrowding, with a view to promoting a drastic reduction of imprisonment rates in a spirit of radical penal minimalism. This may sound less ambitious than wholesale abolition, but it is not antithetical to it. It would represent a crucial first step in establishing a genuinely transformative vision, while acknowledging the deep-rooted nature of the problem. As French economist turned philosopher Frédéric Lordon noted, 'It is perhaps the most unmentionable paradox of neoliberalism that, in fact, delinquent behaviours, stigmatized as aberrations to be eradicated, largely derive from a set of values that neoliberalism itself ceaselessly promotes.' This observation acknowledges that the problem extends far beyond questions of human rights or even prison abolition, though it has crucial implications for both. More broadly, it suggests that our entire sociopolitical system is at issue. Inspired by famous authors as varied as Fyodor Dostoevsky, Victor Hugo, and Winston Churchill, people often assume that prisons should be seen as a touchstone of the whole social order, rather than an anomaly within it. But there is still a long way to go before the idea is really taken seriously.[14]

In the closing exchange of a 1972 interview, Foucault was asked point blank: 'Do you know of a model prison?' 'No,' he answered.

> But there *do exist* better prisons than those in France. In Sweden, fifteen years ago, on the road from Uppsala to Stockholm, I saw an institution that resembled a very comfortable French school building. The problem is not a model prison or the abolition of

prisons. Currently, in our system, marginalization is effected by prisons. This marginalization will not automatically disappear by abolishing the prison. Society would quite simply institute another means. The problem is the following: to offer a critique of the system that explains the process by which contemporary society pushes a portion of the population to the margins. Voilà.[15]

Notes

Introduction: A history within the history

1 Justin Peters, 'How America's model prison became the most horrific facility in the federal system', *Slate*, 20 November 2013; Karen Morin, '"Security here is not safe": Violence, punishment, and space in the contemporary US penitentiary', *Environment and Planning D: Society and Space*, 31, 2013, pp. 381–99 (quote p. 383). To avoid cluttering the text with an excessive number of endnote markers, multiple references cited within a given paragraph are grouped into a single endnote at its end.

2 Morin, '"Security here is not safe"', p. 392. Lewisburg is even compared to the 'camp' paradigm elucidated by philosopher Giorgio Agamben: a concrete, spatial-architectural expression of a normalized quasi-state of exception (see *Homo Sacer: Sovereign Power and Bare Life*, trans. Daniel Heller-Roazen, Stanford University Press, 1998; *State of Exception*, trans. Kevin Attell, University of Chicago Press, 2005).

3 Austria (Leoben): Jim Lewis, 'Behind bars . . . sort of', *The New York Times*, 14 June 2009. Japan: Paul Leighton, '"A model prison for the next 50 years": The high-tech, public–private Shimane Asahi Rehabilitation Center', *Justice Policy Journal*, 11 (1), 2014, pp. 1–16. United Kingdom: Kevin Lockyer, with Max Chambers, *Future Prisons: A radical plan to reform the prison estate*, Policy Exchange, 2013. (See further Laura Mark, 'Thinktank moots "Hub prison" proposals', *Architects' Journal*, 17 June 2013; 'Thinktank calls for

new model of "cutting-edge" prisons', *Building Design*, 21 June 2013.)

4 Loïc Wacquant, *Punishing the Poor: The Neoliberal Government of Social Insecurity*, Duke University Press, 2009, p. 6; Michael Tonry, 'Punishments, politics, and prisons in Western countries', *Crime and Justice*, 51, 2022, pp. 7–57. According to the Institute for Crime & Justice Policy Research's 2024 World Prison Brief, the world prison population has increased by more than a quarter (27%) since the beginning of the century, which is not much less than the population increase in general. The upward trend is particularly strong in Oceania and Africa, but it is also evident in Asia and the Americas. Perhaps unexpectedly, the data reveal that Russia has recently experienced the sharpest decline in prison population, a (somewhat deceptive) reduction that has played a decisive role in the overall European decrease (Helen Fair and Roy Walmsley, 'World Prison Population List', 14th edition, May 2024, p. 2).

5 My own translation of Foucault's expression here. Alan Sheridan's phrasing 'differential administration of illegalities' (in Michel Foucault, *Discipline and Punish: The Birth of the Prison*, trans. Alan Sheridan, Vintage, 1991 [1977], p. 272) is somewhat misleading, as 'illegalism' is an antonym of 'legalism', not 'legality'. See also on this topic, Alex J. Feldman, 'Foucault's concept of illegalism', *European Journal of Philosophy*, 28 (2), pp. 445–62.

6 See Tom Crook, 'Model institutions and the geography of social reform in early Victorian Britain', *The Historical Journal*, 62 (3), 2019, pp. 789–812, whose reflection goes beyond the studied case.

7 It is worth nothing that the implausible description regarding Guantanamo came from the rear admiral in charge as 'Commander, Joint Task Force Guantanamo' in 2007–8: Mark H. Buzby, 'Guantanamo is a model prison (really)', *The Wall Street Journal*, 4 June 2008. For an example of sharply opposing views on the same new prison, namely New Zealand's Paremoremo Prison (later renamed Auckland Prison), see Ian Templeton, 'Model prison – or just a merciless monster?', *The Guardian*, 4 February 1969.

8 Unofficial title: in the mid-1970s, a prison located in Arras, northern France, was depicted as 'a truly model prison, although to our knowledge the prison administration has not given it this label' (Anne Guérin, *Prisonniers en révolte. Quotidien carcéral, mutineries et politique pénitentiaire en France (1970–1980)*, Agone, 2013, p. 190). In a different vein, there is an 'exceptional prison' in Brazil that is

even 'widely celebrated', but it is of a very special kind: this 'model' place is for police officers only, especially those who 'deviated from "acceptable" killing' (Samira Bueno and Graham Denyer Willis, 'The exceptional prison', *Public Culture*, 31 (3), 2019, pp. 645–63).

9 'Let us defend ourselves, if we can, against a further generalization of the panoptic system imitated by the English from the prison of Ghent; and let us protect ourselves against the theory of model prisons' (Louis-Pierre Baltard, *Architectonographie des prisons*, self-published, 1829, p. 18). Officials would later also warn of the inherent risks of these imports, arguing that foreign templates might prove incompatible with national specificities. This was an argument advanced by the Deputy Inspector General of French Prisons in a report written following his travels through Prussia, England, and Spain in the early 1840s (Léonce Hallez-Claparède, *Rapports sur les prisons de la Prusse. . .*, Imprimerie administrative de Paul Dupont, 1843, p. 72).

10 The earliest instances that can be found through the Gallica portal of the Bibliothèque Nationale de France (http://gallica.bnf.fr) date back to the early 1820s. Some of the uses mentioned in this box come from this source.

11 Clare Anderson, *Convicts: A Global History*, Cambridge University Press, 2022, p. 390; Timothy J. Coates, 'The Portuguese Empire, 1100–1932', in Clare Anderson (ed.), *A Global History of Convicts and Penal Colonies*, Bloomsbury, 2020 [2018], pp. 37–64 (p. 54). In France, two distinctions were made between 'deportation' and 'transportation'. The former was a (political) punishment, whereas the latter was an enforcement measure (implying forced labour) that applied to ordinary convicts. Introduced later (1885) and in force until 1970, 'relegation' was an additional penalty whose recipients were henceforth stigmatized as 'repeat offenders'.

12 Christian Carlier, *Histoire de Fresnes, prison 'moderne'. De la genèse aux premières années*, La Découverte/Syros, 1998, pp. 28–55; Foucault, *Discipline and Punish*, p. 231. 'Besides providing a wealth of information on matters of architectural design and management, particular institutions were compared and contrasted; and in a handful of instances, Howard even paused to consider whether or not they might be considered "models", fit for promotion and emulation' (Crook, 'Model institutions', p. 795). Note that citing John Howard as the sole author of *The State of the Prisons* is misleading: it was actually a collective work (R. W. England, 'Who wrote John Howard's

text? The state of the prisons as a dissenting enterprise', *The British Journal of Criminology*, 33 (2), 1993, pp. 203–15).

13 On Amsterdam's Rasphuis: Foucault, *Discipline and Punish*, p. 120; Pieter Spierenburg, 'From Amsterdam to Auburn: An explanation for the rise of the prison in seventeenth-century Holland and nineteenth-century America', *Journal of Social History*, 20 (3), 1987, pp. 439–61 (quote p. 445). On recent historiographical developments: Falk Bretschneider and Natalia Muchnik, 'Pour une vision globale de la prison', *Socio*, 14, 2020, pp. 7–18. The medieval period continues to be the subject of historiographical disagreement. For example, Guy Geltner attempted to demonstrate that the formation of the penal prison began earlier (at the turn of the fourteenth century) and further south than is generally accepted (in Italy rather than the Netherlands). The debate persists regarding the ancient period as well. For instance, French historian Yann Rivière has revisited the issue of prisons in ancient Rome, disputing the established theory that they were not, strictly speaking, used as punishment. See Guy Geltner, *The Medieval Prison: A Social History*, Princeton University Press, 2014 [2008]; Yann Rivière, *Le Cachot et les fers. Détention et coercition à Rome*, Belin, 2004.

14 Massimo Pavarini did elaborate on 'The penitentiary as a model of the ideal society', in Dario Melossi and Massimo Pavarini, *The Prison and the Factory: Origins of the Penitentiary System*, trans. Glynis Cousin, Palgrave Macmillan, 2018 [1977], pp. 203–46.

15 Didier Bigo, 'Ngaragba, "l'impossible prison"', *Revue française de science politique*, 39 (6), 1989, pp. 867–86; Christophe Châtelot, 'Makala, prison modèle', *Le Monde*, 30 November 2012; Foucault, *Discipline and Punish*, pp. 296–7. The case of Mettray, which Foucault considered to be 'the disciplinary form at its most extreme, the model in which are concentrated all the coercive technologies of behaviour' (p. 293), will nonetheless be mentioned in a section devoted to 'open prisons' (counterpoint V).

16 On Ventas Prison, see the website (https://carceldeventas.org/) and Sarah Leggott, 'Gendered repression and sexual violence in Francoist Spain: The testimonies of Mercedes Núñez Targa', *CAUCE. Revista Internacional de Filología, Comunicación y sus Didácticas*, 42, 2019, pp. 61–74, who writes that 'up to 14,000 women were crowded into a prison that was built to house only 500' (p. 67). On French examples: Jacques Bourquin, 'La Rochefoucauld-Liancourt et le projet de prison d'essai pour jeunes détenus', *Revue d'histoire de l'enfance 'irrégulière'*,

special issue, 2007, pp. 195–206 (quote p. 206); Élise Yvorel, 'À la marge des prisons pour mineurs. Les prisons-écoles, des structures carcérales à vocation éducative et professionnalisante', *Revue d'histoire de l'enfance 'irrégulière'*, 7, 2005, pp. 17–40. Neighbouring countries: Geneviève Heller, *Ceci n'est pas une prison. La Maison d'éducation de Vennes. Histoire d'une institution pour garçons délinquants en Suisse romande (1805–1846–1987)*, Antipodes, 2012; Marie-Sylvie Dupont-Bouchat, 'Le procès d'un système. La fermeture du pénitencier de Saint-Hubert (1954–1956)', *Revue d'histoire de l'enfance 'irrégulière'*, 13, 2011, pp. 61–79.

17 Jeremy Bentham, *The Panopticon Writings* (ed. Miran Božovic), Verso, 2011. *Contra* Foucault: Janet Semple, 'Foucault and Bentham: A defence of panopticism', *Utilitas*, 4 (1), 1992, pp. 105–20. Here I mostly rely on Michelle Perrot, *Les Ombres de l'histoire. Crime et châtiment au XIXe siècle*, Flammarion, 2001, pp. 65–100; Emmanuelle de Champs, 'La prison panoptique de Jeremy Bentham. Les paradoxes de la captivité', *Les Cahiers du CEIMA*, 6, 2010, pp. 15–29; François Boullant, 'Retour sur le concept de panoptisme', in François Dieu and Paul Mbanzoulou (eds), *L'Architecture carcérale. Des mots et des murs*, Privat/ÉNAP, 2011, pp. 21–3; Christian Laval, 'Ce que Foucault a appris de Bentham', *Revue d'études benthamiennes*, 8, 2011, and his afterword in Jeremy Bentham, *Panoptique*, Mille et une nuits, 2002 [1791], pp. 59–65.

18 Foucault, *Discipline and Punish*, pp. 224–5; Augustin Rosenstiehl and Pierre Sartoux, *Construire l'abolition*, École d'architecture Paris-Malaquais/Urbsédition, 2005; Perrot, *Les Ombres de l'histoire*, p. 87; Chantal Callais, 'La première prison panoptique demi-circulaire en France. Une aventure humaine et technique', in Dieu and Mbanzoulou (eds), *L'Architecture carcérale*, pp. 75–92; Agathe Mathiaut-Legros, 'Une prison modèle? La prison circulaire d'Autun, un projet idéal à l'épreuve de la réalité', *In Situ*, 46, 2022; K. H. Hamilton, 'Model prison to be built in Illinois', *Scientific American*, 116 (2), 1917, p. 65. Faced with critics who argued that it was impossible to restore a model that was irretrievably out of date (the prison was due to close at the end of the 1950s), Koolhaas replied that the Panopticon had proved more flexible than later architecture. The late twentieth century, he added, was like a film in fast motion: 'It has become impossible to build a prison that is not out of fashion by the time it is finished' (Rem Koolhaas, 'Project for the renovation of a Panopticon prison', in Thomas Y. Levin, Ursula Frohne, and Peter

Weibel (eds), *CTRL[SPACE]: Rhetorics of Surveillance from Bentham to Big Brother*, ZKM Centre for Art and Media, 2002 [1981], pp. 120–7). Examples of prisons inspired by Bentham's Panopticon, including Presidio Modelo, are documented on a dedicated webpage hosted by University College London's Bentham Project (Faculty of Laws).

19 Among classic contributions, see Georg Rusche and Otto Kirchheimer, *Punishment and Social Structure*, Transaction, 2003 [1939], pp. 127f.; David Rothman, *The Discovery of the Asylum: Social Order and Disorder in the New Republic*, De Gruyter, 2002 [1971], pp. 79f.; Foucault, *Discipline and Punish*, pp. 123f. and 238f. See also Negley K. Teeters, 'The passing of Cherry Hill: Most famous prison in the world', *The Prison Journal*, 50 (1), 1970, pp. 3–12; Norman Johnston, 'The world's most influential prison: Success or failure?', *The Prison Journal*, 4 (4) (Suppl.), 2004, pp. 20–40.

20 'Model prisons of a former day had become antiques over the decades, unfit for habitation', wrote the Secretary of the Pennsylvania Committee on Penal Affairs of the Public Charities Association (Leon T. Stern, 'Jails: Yesterday and today', *The Prison Journal*, 25 (3), 1945, p. 98). On Walnut Street: Michael Meranze, *Laboratories of Virtue: Punishment, Revolution and Authority in Philadelphia, 1760–1835*, University of North Carolina Press, 1996. On Eastern Penitentiary: Ashley T. Rubin, *The Deviant Prison: Philadelphia's Eastern State Penitentiary and the Origins of America's Modern Penal System, 1829–1913*, Cambridge University Press, 2021. For an overview from 'proto-prisons' to modern prisons to 'warehouse prisons': Ashley T. Rubin, 'Prison history', *Oxford Research Encyclopedia of Criminology*, 26 April 2018.

21 See Jacques-Guy Petit: 'L'amendement ou l'entreprise de réforme morale des prisonniers en France au XIXe siècle', *Déviance et société*, 6 (4), 1982, pp. 331–51; 'Aspects de l'espace carcéral en France au XIXe siècle', in Jacques-Guy Petit (ed.), *La prison, le bagne et l'histoire*, Librairie des Méridiens, 1984, pp. 157–67; *Ces peines obscures. La prison pénale en France, 1780–1875*, Fayard, 1990, pp. 61 7 and 229–48. A rich collection of primary sources on nineteenth-century prison reform, including materials related to the Auburn Prison System, is available online as part of the '19th Century Prison Reform Collection', selected by Katherine Thorsteinson and hosted by Cornell University's Digital Library. As with other facilities, Auburn's reported opening date fluctuates, in this case in the range of 1816 to

1823, and sometimes even beyond, depending on the source. This uncertainty is due to the fact that it opened before it was fully completed and functional (new sections opened in the early 1820s), and to organizational changes that took place within the penitentiary at that time, which complicates efforts to pinpoint a single inauguration date.

22 Albert Ten Eyck Gardner, 'A Philadelphia masterpiece: Haviland's prison', *The Metropolitan Museum of Art Bulletin*, 14 (4), 1955, pp. 103–8; Norman Johnston, 'John Haviland, jailor to the world', *Journal of the Society of Architectural Historians*, 23 (2), 1964, pp. 101–5 and *Forms of Constraint: A History of Prison Architecture*, University of Illinois Press, 2007, pp. 134–5; Nir Shafir, 'The international congress as scientific and diplomatic technology: Global intellectual exchange in the International Prison Congress, 1860–90', *Journal of Global History*, 9 (1), 2014, p. 78. Through international congresses, 'the prison and the treatment of prisoners became an early international benchmark for the standard of government and civilization attained by a nation-state or even colony' (Mark Finnane, 'Introduction: Crime and justice in the Age of Empire', in Mark Finnane (ed.), *A Global History of Crime and Punishment in the Age of Empire*, Bloomsbury, 2023, p. 15).

23 Stephan Scheuzger, 'Contre une vision diffusionniste de la "naissance de la prison". Perspectives sur les débuts de l'histoire mondiale des régimes pénitentiaires modernes', *Socio*, 14, 2020, pp. 55–75; Frank Dikötter and Ian Brown (eds), *Cultures of Confinement: A History of the Prison in Africa, Asia, and Latin America*, Cornell University Press, 2007, especially pp. 5–6 (Frank Dikötter, 'Introduction', pp. 1–13), pp. 19–20 (Carlos Aguirre, 'Prisons and prisoners in modernising Latin America (1800–1940)', pp. 14–54), p. 68 (Florence Bernault, 'The shadow of rule: Colonial power and modern punishment in Africa', pp. 55–94), p. 123 (Anthony Gorman, 'Regulation, reform and resistance in the Middle Eastern prison', pp. 95–146), p. 310 (Clare Anderson and David Arnold, 'Envisioning the colonial prison', pp. 304–31); Florence Bernault, 'The politics of enclosure in colonial and postcolonial Africa', in Florence Bernault (ed.), *A History of Prison and Confinement in Africa*, Heinemann, 2003, pp. 1–53 (pp. 38–9); Marie Morelle, Frédéric Le Marcis, and Julia Hornberger (eds), *Confinement, Punishment and Prisons in Africa*, Routledge, 2021; Lalel Khalili and Jillian Schwedler, 'Introduction', in Laleh Khalili and Jillian Schwedler (eds), *Policing and Prisons in the*

Middle East: Formations of Coercion, Hurst, 2010 [2008], pp. 1–39 (pp. 20–1); Ervand Abrahamian, *Tortured Confessions: Prisons and Public Recantations in Modern Iran*, University of California Press, 1999, pp. 27–8 and 44–5; Kent F. Schull, *Prisons in the Late Ottoman Empire: Microcosms of Modernity*, Edinburgh University Press, 2014, pp. 45–8 and 132.

24 Robert Waite, 'The "model prison of the world": The Albany County Penitentiary and 19th-century prison reform', *New York History Review*, 21 August 2011. Later, another US facility, Michigan State Prison, would be described as 'the world's model penitentiary'. According to an early twentieth-century account, it was 'governed, practically speaking, by kindness' ('The world's model prison', *New Zealand Graphic*, XXXVIII [7], 16 February 1907, p. 28).

25 Foucault, *Discipline and Punish*, p. 271. Unlike Fourier's Phalanstère, which remained theoretical as all attempts to implement it failed, Godin's Familistère was actually built in northern France between 1859 and 1880. Like its predecessor, it was a bold social experiment designed to establish an idealized and perfectly organized way of life. Yet the two projects diverged in critical respects: where Fourier's model was agricultural, Godin's was grounded in the principles of 'industrial democracy' (see Michel Lallement, 'An experiment inspired by Fourier: J. B. Godin's Familistere in Guise', *Journal of Historical Sociology*, 25 (1), 2012, pp. 31–49). The title of this section is a nod to Colin Crouch's *The Strange Non-Death of Neoliberalism*, Polity, 2011 (which itself was a nod to George Dangerfield's *The Strange Death of Liberal England*, Constable, 1936).

26 See Petit, 'L'amendement ou l'entreprise de réforme morale', p. 334; Michael Ignatieff, 'Historiographie critique du système pénitentiaire', in Petit (ed.), *La prison, le bagne et l'histoire*, pp. 9–17 (pp. 14–16); Norbert Elias, *L'Utopie*, La Découverte, 2014, especially pp. 107–8 and 279. I also rely on the preface by Quentin Deluermoz (quotes pp. 11–12 and 27). For a perspective that rules out any utopian ambition while still holding out for a 'successful' prison, see Joycelyn M. Pollock et al., 'A utopian prison: Contradiction in terms?', *Journal of Contemporary Criminal Justice*, 28 (1), pp. 60–76.

27 Patricia O'Brien, *The Promise of Punishment: Prisons in Nineteenth-Century France*, Princeton University Press, 1982, p. 13; Catherine Duprat, 'Punir et guérir. En 1819, la prison des philanthropes', *Annales historiques de la Révolution française*, 228, 1977, pp. 204–46 (pp. 217 and 240); updated version in Michelle Perrot (ed.),

L'Impossible prison. Recherches sur le système pénitentiaire au XIXe siècle, Seuil, 1980, pp. 64–122 (quote p. 101).

28 Foucault, *Discipline and Punish*, p. 236; O'Brien, *The Promise of Punishment*, p. 304; John Pratt, 'Birth of prison revisited', in Finnane (ed.), *A Global History of Crime and Punishment*, pp. 139–62 (pp. 161–2; 'carefully calibrated regimes of suffering', p. 155).

29 Foucault: *Discipline and Punish*, pp. 264–5; 'Truth and juridical forms', in *Power: Essential Works of Foucault*, ed. James D. Faubion, trans. Robert Hurley et al., New Press, 2000, pp. 1–89; 'Prison talk: An interview with Michel Foucault', trans. Colin Gordon, *Radical Philosophy*, 16, 1977, pp. 10–15; 'La prison vue par un philosophe français', in *Dits et écrits I (1954–1975)*, ed. François Ewald and Daniel Defert, Gallimard, 2001, pp. 1593–9 (especially pp. 1593–4). Also Perrot, *Les Ombres de l'histoire*, pp. 183–4; Dominique Kalifa, 'Imaginaires carcéraux', in *L'Impossible photographie. Prisons parisiennes 1851–2010*, Musée Carnavalet, 2010, pp. 143–7 (quote p. 145); Olivier Faure and Bernard Delpal, 'Retour sur les enfermements', in Olivier Faure and Bernard Delpal (eds), *Religion et enfermement, XVII*[e]*–XX*[e] *siècles*, Presses universitaires de Rennes, 2005, pp. 13–27; Martine Kaluszynski, 'Réformer la société. Les hommes de la société générale des prisons, 1877–1900', *Genèses*, 28, 1997, pp. 76–94 and 'La prison en débats sous la IIIe République', *Parlement[s]. Revue d'histoire politique*, 36 (2), 2022, pp. 39–55.

30 Alain Brossat, *Pour en finir avec la prison*, La fabrique, 2001, p. 7. In her study on 1970s Italy, historian Élise Santalena uses the expression 'prison utopias' to describe a short-lived prisoner-led attempt to radically reform prisons from within ('Utopies carcérales dans l'Italie du deuxième *biennio rosso*', *Italies*, 25, 2021, pp. 107–21).

Chapter 1 La Tour-Maîtresse, Geneva (Switzerland, 1825)

1 Alexis de Tocqueville, *Écrits sur le système pénitentiaire en France et à l'étranger*, in *Œuvres complètes*, IV (2), Gallimard, 1984, p. 65. The new prisons in Geneva and Lausanne were the 'darlings of philanthropists', writes Michelle Perrot in her introduction to the first volume (*Œuvres complètes*, IV (1), Gallimard, 1984, p. 21). See also Perrot, *Les Ombres de l'histoire*, pp. 109–58 (p. 128 about the '*bonbonnière*').

2 Alexis de Tocqueville, *Écrits sur le système pénitentiaire*, IV (1), p. 65 and IV (2), pp. 69–70; Petit, 'L'amendement ou l'entreprise de réforme morale', pp. 335f.; Jean-Louis Benoît, *Tocqueville. Un destin paradoxal*, Tempus, 2013 [2005], p. 181. I am also referring to Louis Chevalier's

classic book on Paris during the same period, *Laboring Classes and Dangerous Classes in Paris During the First Half of the Nineteenth Century*, trans. Frank Jellinek, Howard Fertig, 1973 [1958].

3 See Robert Roth, 'Prison modèle et prison symbole. L'exemple de Genève au XIXe siècle', *Déviance et société*, 1 (4), 1977, pp. 389–410; 'La réalisation pénitentiaire du rêve pénal à Genève', in Petit (ed.), *La prison, le bagne et l'histoire*, pp. 189–200; *Pratiques pénitentiaires et théorie sociale. L'exemple de la prison de Genève (1825–1862)*, Droz, 1981.

4 Roth, 'Prison modèle et prison symbole', p. 399; *Pratiques pénitentiaires et théorie sociale*, pp. 161–71; Perrot, *Les Ombres de l'histoire*, p. 237; Caroline Cuénod, 'La Prison de Jeremy Bentham à Genève', 2014. This fifteen-minute documentary supplements a book chapter: 'L'ombre de la discipline, la prison de Bentham à Genève', in Pierre Bergel and Vincent Milliot (eds), *La Ville en ébullition. Sociétés urbaines à l'épreuve*, Presses universitaires de Rennes, 2014, pp. 361–5.

5 Roth, 'La réalisation pénitentiaire du rêve pénal', p. 189; Johnston, *Forms of Constraint*, p. 112.

6 Tocqueville, *Écrits sur le système pénitentiaire*, IV (1), p. 292; Roth, *Pratiques pénitentiaires et théorie sociale*, p. 223. In January 1837, Christophe Aubanel sent a memorandum to the French Minister of the Interior praising the merits of the prison under his supervision. Asserting that the Geneva prison was the only institution truly based on 'Bentham's pure model', he championed the panoptic layout's advantages for maintaining internal order and organizing labour, while challenging the notion that such a design proved too expensive. More generally, Aubanel conceived of the prison system as a 'corrective school' that combined rehabilitative and deterrent functions (Christophe Aubanel, *Mémoire sur le système pénitentiaire. . .*, Bonnant, 1837, especially pp. 5 and 86).

7 Assemblée nationale, *Enquête parlementaire sur le régime des établissements pénitentiaires*, vol. 4, *Rapports des cours d'appel de France*, Imprimerie nationale, 1873–5, pp. 502–3.

8 Roth, *Pratiques pénitentiaires et théorie sociale*, pp. 305–6.

Chapter 2 Pentonville, London (England, 1842)

1 Robin Evans, *The Fabrication of Virtue: English Prison Architecture, 1750–1840*, Cambridge University Press, 2010 [1982], pp. 363–7; Johnston, *Forms of Constraint*, p. 90f.; Carlier, *Histoire de Fresnes*, p. 68; Jean-Claude Vimont, *La Prison. À l'ombre des hauts murs*, Gallimard, 2004, p. 36; Michael Ignatieff, *A Just Measure of Pain:*

The Penitentiary in the Industrial Revolution, 1750–1850, Macmillan, 1978, pp. 3–14.

2 John Pratt, '"This is not a prison": Foucault, the Panopticon and Pentonville', *Social & Legal Studies*, 2, 1993, pp. 373–95; Evans, *The Fabrication of Virtue*, pp. 1, 7 and 366–7; Petit, 'Aspects de l'espace carcéral', p. 161; Clive Emsley, *Crime, Police, and Penal Policy: European Experiences 1750–1940*, Oxford University Press, 2007, pp. 171–4 (quote p. 171); Ignatieff, *A Just Measure of Pain*, p. 5.

3 Alyson Brown, *English Society and the Prison: Time, Culture, and Politics in the Development of the Modern Prison, 1850–1920*, The Boydell Press, 2003, pp. 66–7; Evans, *The Fabrication of Virtue*, pp. 367–8; Crook, 'Model institutions and the geography of social reform', p. 794.

4 Sandra Scicluna and Paul Knepper, 'Prisoners of the sun: The British Empire and imprisonment in Malta in the early nineteenth century', *British Journal of Criminology*, 48 (4), 2008, pp. 502–21; Mira Rai Watts, 'Imperial vision, colonial prisons: British jails in Bengal, 1823–73', *Journal of the Society of Architectural Historians*, 77 (2), 2018, pp. 146–67 (quote p. 167).

5 Thomas Nutz, 'Global networks and local prison reforms: Monarchs, bureaucrats and penological experts in early nineteenth-century Prussia', *German History*, 23 (4), 2005, pp. 431–59 (pp. 452–6); Johnston, *Forms of Constraint*, pp. 102–3. As Rubin points out, 'Pentonville is often described as following the Pennsylvania System, but it was more a hybrid of the Pennsylvania and Auburn approaches' ('Prison history', p. 11). It 'was an amalgam of existing ideas and regimes', argues Pratt ('Birth of prison revisited', p. 147).

6 Dikötter, 'Introduction', pp. 6–7; Ricardo D. Salvatore and Carlos Aguirre, 'The birth of the penitentiary in Latin America: Toward an interpretive social history of prisons', in Ricardo D. Salvatore and Carlos Aguirre (eds), *The Birth of the Penitentiary in Latin America: Essays on Criminology, Prison Reform, and Social Control, 1830–1940*, University of Texas Press, 1996, pp. 1–43 (p. 11).

7 Ernest Teagarden, 'A Victorian prison experiment', *Journal of Social History*, 2 (4), 1969, pp. 357–65; J. M. Moore, 'Behind Victorian bars', *History Today*, 69 (1), 2019, pp. 60–7; Julius Van Daal, *Beau comme une prison qui brûle. Une émotion populaire en 1780*, L'Esprit frappeur, 1998 [1994], p. 62; Keith Soothill, 'Prison histories and competing audiences, 1776–1966', in Yvonne Jewkes (ed.), *Handbook on Prisons*, Willan, 2007, pp. 27–48 (pp. 37–8); Yvonne Jewkes and

Helen Johnston, 'The evolution of prison architecture', in Jewkes (ed.), *Handbook on Prisons*, pp. 174–96 (pp. 182–6). On Millbank (and related issues), see Fran Cottell and Marianne Mueller, 'From pain to pleasure: Panopticon dreams and Pentagon Petal', in Anthony Julius, Malcolm Quinn, and Philip Schofield (eds), *Bentham and the Arts*, UCL Press, 2020, pp. 244–69.

8 Pratt, 'Birth of prison revisited', p. 149; Evans, *The Fabrication of Virtue*, p. 360.

9 'Extraordinary escape from the Pentonville (model) prison', *The Bradford Observer*, 5 December 1850, p. 8.

10 Erving Goffman, *Asylums: Essays on the Social Situation of Mental Patients and Other Inmates*, Penguin, 2022 [1961]; Evans, *The Fabrication of Virtue*, p. 419; Ignatieff, *A Just Measure of Pain*, p. 4; Ursula R. Q. Henriques, 'The rise and decline of the separate system of prison discipline', *Past & Present*, 54, 1972, p. 83.

11 Ignatieff, *A Just Measure of Pain*, p. 3.

12 Thomas Carlyle, 'Model Prisons' (1850), in *The Works of Thomas Carlyle*, vol. 20, *Latter-Day Pamphlets*, ed. Henry Duff Traill, Cambridge University Press, 2010, pp. 48–86; Jules Seigel, 'Carlyle's model prison and prisoners identified', *Victorian Periodicals Newsletter*, 9 (3), 1976, pp. 81–3. See also John Morrow, *Thomas Carlyle*, Hambledon Continuum, 2006, pp. 145–7. Marx and Engels's review: *Neue Rheinische Zeitung: Politisch-ökonomische Revue*, no. 4, April 1850, in *Marx and Engels Collected Works* (MECW), vol. 10, *Marx and Engels 1849–1851*, Lawrence & Wishart, 1978, pp. 301–10.

13 The warehouse analogy (which we will encounter again in counterpoint VI) was used by John Irwin in *The Warehouse Prison: Disposal of the New Dangerous Class*, Oxford University Press, 2004. Evans, *The Fabrication of Virtue*, p. 7; Catherine Cox and Hilary Marland, '"He must die or go mad in this place": Prisoners, insanity, and the Pentonville model prison experiment, 1842–52', *Bulletin of the History of Medicine*, 92 (1), 2018, pp. 107–8; Terence Morris and Pauline Morris, *Pentonville: A Sociological Study of an English Prison*, Routledge, 2001 [1963], p. 12 on Pentonville and Millbank.

14 Evans, *The Fabrication of Virtue*, p. 2 and ch. 9.

15 Carl Cattermole, 'I've been in Britain's grimmest prisons, but Pentonville's the worst', *The Guardian*, 6 July 2015; Robert Wright, 'London's Pentonville prison lambasted by inspectors', *The Financial Times*, 12 March 2020; Sarah Wigglesworth, *Unlocking Pentonville*, London, 2017, pp. 40–7.

Counterpoint I Models of (re)conversion

1 Felix Ackermann, 'The spirit of Lukiškės: A prison as microcosm of modern Vilna', *Journal of Belarusian Studies*, 7 (3), 2015, pp. 42–69, and 'Prisons in memoriam', *Eurozine*, 17 May 2021; Nicolas Offenstadt, 'Faire d'une prison une fête?', *L'Humanité*, 17 November 2023.

2 Isabelle Heullant-Donat and Élisabeth Lusset, 'Les enjeux patrimoniaux d'une abbaye-prison en reconversion. Le cas de Clairvaux', *In Situ*, 48, 2022 (quote § 14).

3 La prison Sainte Marguerite, École nationale d'administration, Strasbourg, July 2014; Franck Delorme, 'L'École nationale de la magistrature: une architecture nouvelle pour une justice rénovée (1960–1972)', *In Situ*, 46, 2022.

4 Stephan Degenhardt, 'Zu Hause in der Zelle', *Der Spiegel*, 49, December 2013, p. 50.

5 See, for example, Sarah Gilbert, 'Prisons converted into hotels – in pictures', *The Guardian*, 17 June 2013; Sophie-Claire Hoeller, 'Slammers with style: 7 former prisons that are now hotels', *Thrillist*, 29 April 2014; Jean-Claude Vimont, 'Irlande du Nord: visites de la prison d'Armagh avant sa transformation en hôtel', *Criminocorpus*, 30 May 2015; Mark Johanson, '9 former jails with surprising second lives', CNN, 24 August 2015; Leila Miller, 'The prison that helped build "the city at the end of the world"', *Los Angeles Times*, 12 February 2024. In the mid-2000s, more than eighty 'prison museums' could be identified worldwide, based on a broad definition that included all places of detention (Mitchel P. Roth, *Prisons and Prison Systems: A Global Encyclopedia*, Greenwood, 2006, pp. 303–5, appendix A).

6 Frank Dikötter, '"A paradise for rascals": Colonialism, punishment and the prison in Hong Kong (1841–1898)', *Crime, Histoire & Sociétés/Crime, History & Societies*, 8 (1), 2004, pp. 49–63; Camila van Diest, 'Citizen participation, associations and conflict: The transformation of Valparaíso's former prison', *Latin American Research Review*, 55 (4), 2020, pp. 790–803; Victoria Ruetalo, 'From penal institution to shopping mecca: The economics of memory and the case of Punta Carretas', *Cultural Critique*, 68, 2008, pp. 38–65.

7 Frédérique Berthet and Rémy Dal Molin, 'La prison Sainte-Anne d'Avignon. D'ouvertures en fermetures', *Vacarme*, 72, 2015, pp. 112–29; Caroline Soppelsa, 'La conservation des traces écrites dans les prisons. Entre conflits de mémoire, *dark tourism* et contraintes de la reconversion architecturale', *Siècles*, 56, 2024, § 17.

8 Closed in 1952, Guingamp Prison became an administrative building used for tax archive storage. It was listed as a historic monument in 1997. See Emmanuel Laot, 'La prison de Guingamp, de l'ombre à la lumière', *Criminocorpus*, 31 January 2024.

9 Michael Welch, *Escape to Prison: Penal Tourism and the Pull of Punishment*, University of California Press, 2015, especially pp. 1–25, 34–6 and 136–9. In a subsequent study, Welch has focused on former sites of political imprisonment in post-conflict societies (*The Bastille effect: Transforming Sites of Political Imprisonment*, University of California Press, 2022). See also Jacqueline Z. Wilson et al. (eds), *The Palgrave Handbook of Prison Tourism*, Palgrave Macmillan, 2017.

10 Alana Barton and Alyson Brown, 'Dark tourism and the modern prison', *Prison Journal*, 199, 2012, pp. 44–9; Justin Piché and Kevin Walby, 'Les musées de prison au Canada: une réflexion abolitionniste', *Déviance et société*, 42 (4), 2018, pp. 643–62 (quote p. 656); Philippe Artières, *La prison en héritage? Pour une patrimonialisation critique du pénitentiaire*, Éditions de la Sorbonne, 2024.

Chapter 3 La Santé, Paris (France, 1867)

1 Simon Piel, 'La mythique prison de la Santé vidée de ses détenus avant une large rénovation', *Le Monde*, 4 August 2014; Véronique Vasseur, *Médecin-chef* à *la prison de la Santé*, Le Cherche Midi/ Le Livre de poche, 2000, p. 62. On the first stage of the '*affaire Vasseur*', see Suzanne Daley, 'Expose of brutal prison jolts France's self-image', *The New York Times*, 28 January 2000. On the '*affaire*' as a 'social form', see Luc Boltanski, *Distant Suffering: Morality, Media and Politics*, trans. Graham D. Burchell, Cambridge University Press, 1999, pp. 57–76.

2 Michel Fize, 'Histoire de la "prison modèle" de la Santé, 1867–1914', *Revue de science criminelle et de droit pénal comparé*, 404, 1983, p. 707, and *Une prison dans la ville. . . : Histoire de la 'prison modèle' de la Santé*, CNERP/Ministère de la Justice, 1983, 2 vols (*1867–1914*, *1914–1983*).

3 Michel Fize, *Une prison dans la ville. Histoire de la 'prison modèle' de la Santé (1867–2014)*, Buchet-Chastel, 2015, pp. 20 and 22; Caroline Soppelsa, *Maison d'arrêt de Paris La Santé. Synthèse de l'essai historique commandé par l'Agence publique pour l'immobilier de la Justice*, APIJ/Ministère de la Justice, 2014, p. 10. See also her 'La maison d'arrêt de la Santé: une prison dans Paris', *Criminocorpus*, 28 July 2014, which offers a 'virtual tour'.

4 Fize, *Une prison dans la ville* (2015), pp. 70–80.
5 Ibid., pp. 70–4; Alain Corbin, 'Purifier l'air des prisons', in Petit (ed.), *La prison, le bagne et l'histoire*, pp. 151–6 (pp. 153–4).
6 Norbert Finzsch and Robert Jütte (eds), *Institutions of Confinement: Hospitals, Asylums, and Prisons in Western Europe and North America, 1500–1950*, Cambridge University Press, 1996; Michel Foucault et al., *Les Machines à guérir (Aux origines de l'hôpital moderne)*, Mardaga, 1979; Marc Renneville, 'Psychiatrie et prison: une histoire parallèle', *Annales Médico-Psychologiques*, 162, 2004, pp. 653–6 (quote from Cabanis, p. 653); Petit, 'Aspects de l'espace carcéral', p. 157; Pierre-Louis Laget and Françoise Salaün, 'Aux origines de l'hôpital moderne, une évolution européenne', *Les Tribunes de la santé*, 2 (3), 2004, pp. 19–28; Michel Foucault, *Abnormal. Lectures at the Collège de France, 1974–1975*, ed. Valerio Marchetti and Antonella Salomoni, Verso, 2003, p. 23; Prince Kopotkine [Pyotr Kropotkin], *In Russian and French Prisons*, Ward and Downey, 1887, pp. 349–50.
7 Fize, *Une prison dans la ville* (2015), p. 114.
8 Jean-Claude Vimont, *La prison politique en France. Genèse d'un mode d'incarcération spécifique, XVIIIe–XXe siècle*, Anthropos/Economica, 1993, p. 455.
9 Robert Badinter, 'Préface', in Fize, *Une prison dans la ville* (2015), pp. 9–10 (quote p. 10); Jean-Baptiste Jacquin, 'À la Santé, la difficile montée en puissance d'une prison modèle', *Le Monde*, 25 February 2020.

Chapter 4 Kresty, Saint Petersburg (Russia, 1892–3)

1 See 'Russia to launch Europe's largest prison', *AFP World News*, 17 October 2014; Will Stewart and Damien Gayle, 'Russia prepares to open Europe's biggest prison with 4,000 inmates, a sauna and even a museum', *Daily Mail*, 20 October 2014; Marina Starodoubtseva, 'Destin d'une célèbre prison à Saint-Pétersbourg', *Russia Beyond*, 2 November 2014. On the 'disappearence of prison' – that is, the trend to remove the prison from public view – see John Pratt, *Punishment and Civilization: Penal Tolerance and Intolerance in Modern Society*, Sage, 2002, ch. 3.
2 Roger Bartlett, *The Bentham Brothers and Russia: The Imperial Russian Constitution and the St Petersburg Panopticon*, UCL Press, 2022, pp. 177–204.
3 Johnston, 'John Haviland, jailor to the world', p. 102; *Forms of Constraint*, pp. 126–8.

4 Vladimir Chernavin, 'Prison life in USSR (1930–31)', *The Slavonic and East European Review*, 12 (34), 1933, pp. 63–78; Aleksandr I. Solzhenitsyn, *The Gulag Archipelago, 1918–1956: An Experiment in Literary Investigation*, trans. Thomas P. Whitney, Harper & Row, 1974, p. 437.

5 V. I. Lenin, 'Our foreign and domestic position and party tasks: Speech delivered to the Moscow Gubernia Conference of the RCP(B)', 21 November 1920, trans. Julius Katzer, online at the Marxists Internet Archive; Olga Strelkova, 'The "Kresty" prison and tourism: The past, the present, and the future', in Wilson et al. (eds), *The Palgrave Handbook of Prison Tourism*, pp. 261–76 (p. 265).

6 Philippe Artières, 'Une prison tsariste. Le cas de la forteresse de Schlüsselbourg: de la prison d'exception à la prison modèle, aller-retour (1880–1917)', in Philippe Artières and Pierre Lascoumes (eds), *Gouverner, enfermer. La prison, un modèle indépassable?*, Presses de Sciences Po, 2004, pp. 257–67; Philippe Artières and Denis Dabbadie, 'Résister à la prison par l'autobiographie. Vera Figner et les prisons tsaristes', *Cultures & Conflits*, 55, 2004, pp. 15–37; Emma Goldman, *My Disillusionment in Russia*, Dover, 2003 [1923–4], pp. 81–3.

7 Bruce Adams, *The Politics of Punishment: Prison Reform in Russia, 1863–1917*, Northern Illinois University Press, 1996, especially pp. 9–10, 132–3, 142–3, 169–70, 198–9. Adams incidentally recalls that according to Kropotkin, whom we encountered in chapter 3, 'conditions in France were worse than in Russia' (p. 5). He further argues: 'By the end of the nineteenth century, certainly by 1917, Russia was running its prison system for the same purposes and according to the same standards in use in European nations and the United States' (p. 9).

8 Jules Boullaire, 'Étude historique sur le régime pénitentiaire en Russie', *Bulletin de la Société Générale des Prisons*, 3, 1886, pp. 355–67; Ackermann, 'The spirit of Lukiškės', pp. 42–69. The proceedings of the Saint Petersburg Prison Congress (as well as other historical prison congresses) and additional documents are available (in French) on the website of the École nationale d'administration pénitentiaire (ENAP). In English, see C. D. Randall, *The Fourth International Prison Congress*, Government Printing Office, 1891.

9 Adams, *The Politics of Punishment*, pp. 196–9.

10 Stuart William, 'Kresty: Historic and notorious jail for Arctic activists', *AFP*, 12 November 2013; 'Mayor appalled by conditions in historic Russian prison', *Associated Press Newswires*, 8 July 1997; Roy

King, 'Russian prisons after Perestroika: End of the Gulag?', *British Journal of Criminology*, 34, 1994, pp. 72–3; Nils Christie, *Crime Control as Industry: Towards GULAGS, Western Style*, 3rd edition, Routledge, 2000, ch. 6 ('The Russian case'); *A Suitable Amount of Crime*, Routledge, 2004, p. 40; Gilles Favarel-Garrigues, 'Priorités et limites de la politique pénitentiaire en Russie', in Artières and Lascoumes (eds), *Gouverner, enfermer*, pp. 111–33 (p. 126, n. 1).

11 Stephanie Simon, 'Russian prison has lock on history', *Los Angeles Times*, 27 March 1996; Anna Badkhen, 'Prison gates open for business', *The Moscow Times*, 11 August 1999; Carol Perehudoff, 'Russian visitors find prison visit can be arresting', *Toronto Star*, 9 April 2005; Ian Bucknell, 'Penal dustbins', *The Guardian*, 20 February 2001.

12 Maria Antonova, 'Prison hospitality', *Russian Life*, 53 (5), 2010, p. 14; Galina Stolyarova, 'Kresty Prison could soon house hotel or gallery', *The St Petersburg Times*, 25 July 2012; Olga Strelkova, 'The "Kresty" Prison and tourism', p. 271; Holly Alsop, 'Kresty Prison: A forgotten site of memory?', *William & Mary in St Petersburg*, 3 October 2010; Felix Ackermann, 'Prisons in memoriam', *Eurozine*, 17 May 2021.

Counterpoint II Envisioned model prisons

1 Hilary Cottam, 'In the nick of time', *The Guardian*, 17 July 2002; Robert Martinson, 'What works? – Questions and answers about prison reform', *The Public Interest*, 35, 1974, pp. 22–54; Simon Henley, *The 21st Century Model Prison*, Proceedings – 4th International Space Syntax Symposium, London, 2003, and 'A model prison', *Building Material*, 12, 2004, pp. 32–5. See further Jewkes and Johnston, 'The evolution of prison architecture'.

2 Cottam, 'In the nick of time'.

3 Caroline Charpentier, 'Projet pour une prison alternative – Le *Kanopticon*', École d'architecture de Versailles, 2003, especially pp. 63–7.

4 Factual information is taken from French newspapers, both print and online, especially: 'Prison "modèle": le ministre de la Justice a choisi Saint-Julien', *Le Progrès*, 14 December 2011; Jean-Michel Dejenne, Boris Targe, and Antoine Danel, 'Prisons: gare à la privatisation du service public pénitentiaire', *Libération*, 31 January 2012; Angela Bolis, 'Dans le Jura, la prison modèle de Pierre Botton sème la zizanie', *Le Monde*, 14 March 2012; Catherine Coroller, 'Pierre Botton récidive dans son projet de prison', *Libération*, 2 August 2012; Hélène Leclerc, 'Le projet de prison Botton est abandonné à Saint-Julien-sur-

Suran', *Le Progrès*, 15 November 2012; Laurent Valdiguié, 'Pierre Botton. L'emmerdeur', *Journal du dimanche*, 8 September 2013; Valérie de Senneville, 'Pierre Botton, l'homme qui voulait changer la prison', *Les Échos*, 20 February 2014.

5 Olivier Milhaud, 'L'enfermement ou la tentation spatialiste. De "l'action aveugle, mais sûre" des murs des prisons', *Annales de géographie*, 2 (702–3), 2015, pp. 140–62.

Chapter 5 Fresnes (France, 1898)

1 Catherine Herszberg, *Fresnes, histoires de fous*, Seuil, 2006, pp. 14–15.

2 Vimont, *La Prison*, p. 58 (Humbert); Carine Trévisan, 'Ce qu'ont dit les murs de Fresnes', *Le Temps des médias*, 1 (4), 2005, pp. 91–2 (Calet); Denis Langlois, *Le Cachot*, Maspero, 1982 [1967]; Louis Beretti, *Même à mon pire ennemi. . . Souvenirs d'une parenthèse: prison de Fresnes, 1980–1985*, L'Insomniaque, 2010; Bénédicte Vergez-Chaignon, *Vichy en prison. Les épurés à Fresnes après la Libération*, Gallimard, 2006, pp. 131 and 397 (pp. 119–22 on Fresnes as a 'model prison'); Hélène Bellanger, *Vivre en prison*, Hachette, 2007, p. 84.

3 Christian Carlier, Catherine Prade, and Marc Renneville, 'Brève histoire des prisons de Paris, de la prise de la Bastille à l'ouverture de Fresnes', *Criminocorpus*, 9 June 2010. See Carlier, *Histoire de Fresnes*, on which this chapter is heavily based. I also draw on Christian Carlier, Juliette Spire, and Françoise Wasserman, *Fresnes, la prison. Les établissements pénitentiaires de Fresnes, 1895–1990*, Écomusée, 1993, which contains numerous photos.

4 Carlier, *Histoire de Fresnes*, pp. 100 and 143.

5 Ibid., pp. 72, 116, 132, 176; Vimont, *La Prison*, p. 35.

6 Petit, 'Aspects de l'espace carcéral', p. 163; Vimont, *La Prison*, p. 54; Carlier, *Histoire de Fresnes*, p. 122; Alix Héricord and Serge Lastennet, 'Une réconfortante hygiène. L'hôpital carcéral de Fresnes', *Vacarme*, 10, 1999, pp. 23–5 (p. 24).

7 Petit, 'Aspects de l'espace carcéral', p. 165; Carlier et al., *Fresnes, la prison*, pp. 11 and 55; Carlier, *Histoire de Fresnes*, p. 182; Paul Mimande, *Criminopolis*, Calmann Lévy, 1897.

8 Carlier, *Histoire de Fresnes*, pp. 154–6; Johnston, *Forms of Constraint*, pp. 117–19 (quote p. 117); Jayne Mooney, 'Rikers Island: The failure of a "model" penitentiary', *The Prison Journal*, 100 (6), 2020, pp. 687–708; Ruetalo, 'From penal institution to shopping mecca', pp. 48 and 59 (n. 20).

9 Carlier, *Histoire de Fresnes*, p. 176.

10 Héricord and Lastennet, 'Une réconfortante hygiène'; Nicolas Derasse and Jean-Claude Vimont, 'Observer pour orienter et évaluer. Le CNO-CNE de Fresnes de 1950 à 2010', *Criminocorpus*, 26 September 2014; Jean-Lucien Sanchez, 'Les débuts du fonctionnement du centre national d'orientation de Fresnes', *Criminocorpus*, 2 March 2022.

11 Carlier et al., *Fresnes, la prison*, p. 9; Carlier, *Histoire de Fresnes*, p. 105; Jacques-Guy Petit, Claude Faugeron, and Michel Pierre, *Histoire des prisons en France, 1789–2000*, Privat, 2002, p. 138; Petit, 'Aspects de l'espace carcéral', p. 167.

12 Hervé Guénot, 'Fresnes, jadis prison modèle', *Le Figaro*, 8 November 1998; Olivier Faye, 'Plongée dans l'enfer de la prison de Fresnes: "On est encore dans les années 1800"', *Le Monde*, 13 June 2025. In English, see, for example, Eleanore Beardsley, 'Inside French prisons, a struggle to combat radicalization', NPR, 25 June 2017. For a broader perspective: Gilles Chantraine, 'French prisons of yesteryear and today: Two conflicting modernities – a socio-historical view', *Punishment & Society*, 12 (1), 2009, pp. 27–46.

Chapter 6 Cárcel Modelo, Barcelona (Spain, 1904)

1 Victor Serge, *Men in Prison*, trans. Richard Greeman, PM Press, 2014 [1930], p. 56. I will elaborate on *modelos* in the Spanish-speaking world in counterpoint III. Note that the development of Spain's modern prison system in the second half of the nineteenth century did not entail the demise of alternative (or, rather, complementary) methods of punishment. The Spanish Penal Code of 1870 retained the death penalty and provided for sentences based on territorial expulsion: transportation, banishment, and exile. With a view to expand convict transportation, Spanish authorities conducted a broad review of foreign penal systems, examining not only neighbouring European powers like France and Portugal, but also distant models such as Russia's Siberian exile and Chile's Pacific penal settlements. In 1875, a few years after penal colonies were introduced in 1869, the Spanish Royal Academy of Moral and Political Sciences organized an essay competition to address proposals to systematize transportation to the colonies, following the example of England, which had transported convicts to Australia from 1788 to 1864. Social reformer Concepción Arenal – who had an influence on the designers of Barcelona's Modelo – was awarded first prize for her essay strongly opposing this method of punishment (Élodie Richard, 'La déportation comme alternative à la prison, un concours de l'Académie royale

espagnole des sciences morales et politiques (1875)', *Hypothèses*, 1 (6), 2003, pp. 99–109). Penal colonies were nevertheless established by royal decrees in 1889, some twenty years after the 1870 Penal Code. Among other projects, including a penal colony for Isla de Culebra, in the Caribbean, an agricultural penal colony based on hard labour was planned for the island of Mindoro in the Philippines, but it was never realized. However, the cohabitation of prison confinement and penal expulsion illustrates the importance of the 'punitive mobility' highlighted by Clare Anderson in her 'global history from below' (*Convicts*, especially ch. 7 on prisons).

2 For an illustrated historical overview, see Isabel Margarit Pelaz, 'La Modelo: crónica en blanco y negro', *Historia y vida*, 596, 2017, pp. 64–70 (shorter version in '10 cosas que tal vez no sabías sobre la Modelo de Barcelona', *La Vanguardia/Historia y Vida*, 4 November 2017). See also Paul Gibbins, 'La Model: The brutal story of Franco's notorious torture prison', *Vice*, 10 February 2019. For an architectural overview: Johnston, *Forms of Constraint*, pp. 106–7. Reference works in Catalan include: Josep M. Solé i Sabaté (ed.), *Història de la presó Model de Barcelona*, Pagès, 2000, and Rosario Fontova, *La Model de Barcelona. Històries de la presó*, Generalitat de Catalunya/ Departament de Justícia, 2010, which is richly illustrated.

3 See Pelai Pagès I Blanch, *La presó Model de Barcelona. Història d'un penitenciari en temps de guerra (1936–1939)*, Abadia de Montserrat, 1996 (the author draws on Pedro Fraile's *Un espacio para castigar. La cárcel y la ciencia penitenciaria en España (siglos XVIII–XIX)*, Ediciones del Serbal, 1987); Pedro Fraile, 'Discursos penitenciarios, encierros y celdas: Las cárceles modelo de Madrid y Barcelona', *Scripta Nova. Revista Electrónica de Geografía y Ciencias Sociales*, XXIV (642), 2020, pp. 1–39. On the patronage system: Òscar Montero-Pich, 'La obra de los patronatos de presos en la Cárcel Modelo de Barcelona', *Revista de Historia de las Prisiones*, 2, 2016, pp. 166–84. Silone's account: Ignazio Silone, 'A first encounter with Dostoevsky', trans. Francis Steegmuller, *Dissent*, Spring 1959, pp. 200–1.

4 Ricardo Bofill (with Jean-Louis André), *Espaces d'une vie*, Odile Jacob, 1989, p. 18; Òscar Montero-Pich, 'Las investigaciones de Joaquim Fuster sobre la moral del delincuente (y su sexualidad) en la prisión modelo de Barcelona (1929–1935)', *Revista de Historia de la Psicología*, 37 (4), 2016, pp. 19–26; Pedro Fraile and Quim Monastra, 'Surveillances, social management, and architectural morphologies: An approach to the prison and the hospital in 19th-century

Spain', *Journal of Historical Sociology*, 32, 2019, pp. 206–7. The prison 'ambivalence' is stressed by François Godicheau, 'Répression politique, mobilisation politique et violence dans une institution pénale. La *Cárcel Modelo* de Barcelone pendant la guerre civile espagnole', *Crime, Histoire & Sociétés/Crime, History & Societies*, 8 (1), 2004, pp. 7–26.

5 Rubin, 'Prison history', pp. 14–15; 'A model prison', *The Hospital*, 2 April 1892, pp. 4–5; Jorge Alberto Núñez, *Fernando Cadalso y la reforma penitenciaria en España (1883–1939)*, Universidad Carlos III de Madrid, 2014, pp. 185f.

6 See François Godicheau, 'Militer pour survivre. Lettres d'anarchistes français emprisonnés à Barcelone (1937–1938)', *Sociétés & représentations*, 13, 2002, pp. 137–50.

7 Godicheau, 'Répression politique, mobilisation politique et violence', p. 15. After a visit in November 1937, Scottish MP John McGovern, a member of the Independent Labour Party (ILP), published an account that depicted the situation in the Modelo as less dreadful than in other institutions where torture was commonplace. 'On Sunday, November 28, we went to Carcel Modelo (prison in Barcelona) and presented our credentials to the Director of the men's prison. [. . .] We were informed that there were fifteen hundred prisoners in the Modelo – five hundred anti-Fascists, five hundred Fascists, and five hundred criminals. [. . .] It was a real Prisoners' International in the Modelo. They came from France, Greece, Germany, Italy, Austria, Belgium, Holland, Switzerland and America, as well as Spain' ('Terror in Spain', ILP, 1937, pp. 8–9). This document is available thanks to the Warwick Digital Collections.

8 Godicheau, 'Répression politique, mobilisation politique et violence', pp. 25–6.

9 Ricard Vinyes, 'L'univers carcéral sous le franquisme', *Cultures & Conflits*, 55, 2004, pp. 39–65 (quote p. 58).

10 George Orwell, 'Spanish prison', *The Observer*, 24 December 1944.

11 Amélie Nuq, *Péchés de jeunesse. Déviance, marginalité et rééducation dans l'Espagne franquiste*, Presses universitaires de Rennes, 2024, pp. 95–138.

12 Joanna Weschler and Alejandro Garro, *Prison Conditions in Spain: A Helsinki Watch Report*, Human Rights Watch, 1992–4.

13 CPT, *Report to the Spanish Government on the Visit to Spain Carried out by the CPT from 19 to 22 June 2012*, Strasbourg, April 2013 (quote p. 5); Obra colectiva, *La Cárcel Modelo de Barcelona, 1904–2004.*

Cien años bastan, derribemos la Modelo para no levantar otra, Etcétera, October 2014.

14 On this process, typical of the issue of conversion (counterpoint I), and more broadly on the prison as a (counter-)cultural space, see Pilar Cruz Ramón, 'La Modelo. De lugar de represión y cultura a lugar de cultura y participación', *Artigrama*, 38, 2023, pp. 149–65.

Counterpoint III *Modelos*

1 Accounts from that era include D. Manuel Silvela, 'La prison de Madrid' (1876), *Bulletin de la Société générale des prisons*, 7–8, 1885, pp. 929–47; Francisco Lastrès, 'L'ancienne et la nouvelle prison', *Bulletin de la société générale des prisons*, 3, 1886 [1884], pp. 318–42; Y. Beaury Saurelle, 'La prison modèle de Madrid', *Bulletin de la société générale des prisons*, 1, 1888, pp. 97–8. Comparison between Madrid and Barcelona in Fraile, 'Discursos penitenciarios, encierros y celdas'. On the depiction of the *modelo* in Galdós's novel: Michael Schnepf, 'Scandal and *La Cárcel Modelo*: More intertextual "bouncing" in Galdós's *La desheredada*', *Romance Quarterly*, 49 (1), 2002, pp. 36–49 (quote p. 47, n. 15); Liana Ewald, 'Confinement, consolation, and confession in Galdós's *La desheredada*', *Hispanic Review*, 76 (4), 2008, pp. 361–86. 'The construction of the new model prison was symbolically associated with the destruction of the old one,' Alfredo González-Ruibal and Carmen Ortiz write about Carabanchel ('The prison of Carabanchel (Madrid, Spain): A life story', in Marie Louise Stig Sørensen and Dacia Viejo-Rose (eds), *War and Cultural Heritage: Biographies of Place*, Cambridge University Press, 2015, pp. 128–55 (quote p. 131)).

2 Fraile and Monastra, 'Surveillances, social management, and architectural morphologies', pp. 198–207; Núñez, *Fernando Cadalso y la reforma penitenciaria*, especially pp. 111–20.

3 Léon Lallemand, 'La "Carcel modelo" de Vitoria, province d'Alava', *Revue pénitentiaire*, 6, 1891, pp. 803–8; Scheuzger, 'Contre une vision diffusionniste', p. 66. The prison in Bordeaux, France, should not be confused with the prison of the same name in Montreal, Canada. Built between 1908 and 1912, the latter was one of the only prisons in the country with a design based on the Pennsylvania model, and probably including some Belgian inspiration. See Pierre Landreville and Ghislaine Julien, 'Les origines de la prison de Bordeaux', *Criminologie*, 9 (1–2), 1976, pp. 5–22.

4 José María Pérez Fernández, 'Un paseo por el reformismo penitenciario del S. XIX a través de la cárcel modelo de Valencia', *Ars Longa*,

9–10, 2000, pp. 179–89. The former prison has been renovated to make way for what is now an administrative complex. For a critical view on 'penitentiary reform' (and on the idea of the model prison as illustrated by Madrid's case) in Spain after 1868, see Pedro Oliver Olmo and Luís Gargallo Vaamonde, 'La noción de "reforma penitenciaria" española en el desarrollo del sistema liberal de prisiones: cuestión de enfoques y aportes historiográficos', *Revista de Historia de las Prisiones*, 3, 2016, pp. 104–29.

5 Salvatore and Aguirre, 'The birth of the penitentiary in Latin America', pp. 14 and 32. For recent accounts, see, for example, Nora Gamez Torres, 'Uncovering a dark secret at "Model Prison"', *Miami Herald*, 29 October 2014; Luis Rondon Paz, 'Cuba's model prison and its history', *Havana Times*, 4 April 2016; Tony Perrottet, 'A Cuban island that has played both paradise and prison', *The New York Times*, 2 January 2018.

6 Alessandro Monteverde Sánchez, Hugo Jose Castro Valdebenito, and Juan Saavedra Ávila, 'Modelos, tendencias y cotidianidades en los inicios de la cárcel penitenciaria de Santiago de Chile. 1843–1860', *Diálogos. Revista Electrónica de Historia*, 19 (1), 2018, pp. 69–101.

7 Salvatore and Aguirre, 'The birth of the penitentiary in Latin America', pp. ix–x and 9; Johnston, *Forms of Constraint*, pp. 61–2; Scheuzger, 'Contre une vision diffusionniste', p. 65.

8 Fédération Internationale des Ligues des Droits de l'Homme, *20 années d'activité de la FIDH en Colombie*, February 2004, p. 47; Jesús Antonio Muñoz Gómez, 'Notes toward a historical understanding of the Colombian penal system', *Crime and Social Justice*, 30, 1987, pp. 77–93 (p. 88 on Bogotá). For a personal account by a former political prisoner who 'got to know the National Model as a judicial inspector', see William Carrillo Leal, 'From my prison cell: Time and space in prison in Colombia, an ethnographic approach', *Latin American Perspectives*, 28 (1), 2001, pp. 149–64 (quote p. 151).

9 Ricardo Salvatore, 'Criminology, prison reform, and the Buenos Aires working class', *The Journal of Interdisciplinary History*, 23 (2), 1992, pp. 279–99; Salvatore and Aguirre, 'The birth of the penitentiary in Latin America', pp. 10–11 and 28.

10 Ruetalo, 'From penal institution to shopping mecca', pp. 48–50. Similar patterns emerged elsewhere, such as in Buenos Aires, at the prison known as 'Villa Devoto' (officially the Federal Correctional Complex of the Autonomous City of Buenos Aires), built in the 1920s and 'considered to be the country's "model" prison' half a

century later in a 1978 article in a feminist journal (Jan Braumuller, 'Argentine women: Abduction and torture', *Off Our Backs. A Women's Newsjournal*, 8 (8), 1978, p. 10). Based on Amnesty International information, this article described appalling prison conditions, far below United Nations minimum standards: 'Villa Devoto is no "model" of respect for human rights; it is a model of repression and torture which physically and psychologically destroys Argentine women' (p. 11).

11 Juan Silva Riestra, 'La cárcel modelo de São Paulo', *Archivos de Medicina Legal e Identificação*, 6 (13), 1936, quoted in Salvatore and Aguirre, 'The birth of the penitentiary in Latin America', p. 38; Ryan C. Edwards, 'Post-colonial Latin America, since 1800', in Anderson (ed.), *A Global History of Convicts*, pp. 245–70 (pp. 247–8); Scheuzger, 'Contre une vision diffusionniste', p. 65.

12 Carlos Aguirre, 'The Lima penitentiary and the modernization of criminal justice in nineteenth-century Peru', in Salvatore and Aguirre (eds), *The Birth of the Penitentiary in Latin America*, pp. 44–77 (quote p. 68); Anderson, *Convicts*, pp. 1–9.

Chapter 7 Model Prison No. 1, Beijing (China, 1912)

1 Michael Tsin, 'Overlapping histories: Writing prison and penal practices in late Imperial and early Republican China', *Journal of World History*, 20 (1), 2009, pp. 95–7.

2 Jan Kiely, *A Compelling Ideal: Thought Reform and the Prison in China, 1901–1956*, Yale University Press, 2014, pp. 6–14 and 29–34; Klaus Mühlhahn, *Criminal Justice in China: A History*, Harvard University Press, 2009, pp. 82 and 91. See also Weiqi Chu, 'Capital Model Prison: A political tool for government power', *WIT Transactions on the Built Environment*, 203, 2021, pp. 215–27; Johnston, *Forms of Constraint*, pp. 132–3.

3 This chapter draws on a historiographical update initiated by Frank Dikötter, *Crime, Punishment and the Prison in Modern China*, Columbia University Press, 2002. Essential elements (including the anecdote about Howard's portrait) are in these works by Frank Dikötter: 'Crime and punishment in early Republican China: Beijing's first model', *Late Imperial China*, 21 (2), 2000, pp. 140–62; 'The promise of repentance: Prison reform in modern China', *British Journal of Criminology*, 42, 2002, pp. 240–9; 'The promise of repentance: The prison in modern China', in Dikötter and Brown (eds), *Cultures of Confinement*, pp. 269–303.

4 Douglas Reynolds, *China, 1898–1912: The Xinzheng Revolution and Japan*, Harvard University Press, 1993, pp. 172–8; Finnane, 'Introduction: Crime and justice in the Age of Empire', p. 8; Anderson, *Convicts*, pp. 239–42 (quote p. 239); Daniel Botsman, *Punishment and Power in the Making of Modern Japan*, Princeton University Press, 2007, pp. 201–29: For contributions dating from the first decades of the Republic, see 'Prison reform in Japan', *Journal of the American Institute of Criminal Law and Criminology*, 2 (5), 1912, pp. 758–60; John L. Gillin, 'Japan's prison system', *Social Forces*, 7 (2), 1928, pp. 177–89.
5 Foucault, *Discipline and Punish*, p. 184.
6 Tsien-Tai, 'La réforme pénitentiaire en Chine', *Revue pénitentiaire*, 3, 1919, pp. 158–65 (quote p. 159).
7 Charles Richmond Henderson, *Report of the Proceedings of the Eighth International Prison Congress (1910)*, Washington, DC, House of Representatives, 63rd Congress, 1st Session, Document no. 52, 1913, p. 8; Dikötter, 'Crime and punishment in early Republican China, p. 161.
8 The *Public Ledger* is quoted in 'Prisoners in Peking', *The Prison Journal*, April 1926, p. 13. Mühlhahn, *Criminal Justice in China*, pp. 58–126.
9 Dikötter, 'Crime and punishment', p. 140, and 'The promise of repentance', 2002, p. 245; Børge Bakken, 'Introduction: Crime, control, and modernity in China', in Børge Bakken (ed.), *Crime, Punishment, and Policing in China*, Rowman & Littlefield, 2005, pp. 1–26.
10 Kiely, *A Compelling Ideal*, p. 57.
11 Ching-Yueh Yen, 'Penal reform and criminology in China', *Journal of Criminal Law and Criminology*, 22 (4), 1931, pp. 576–8 (quote p. 578).
12 Reuters, 'European tours Chinese "model" jail: EU Group skeptical of prisoners' rights', *The Washington Post*, 25 February 1998; Charles Hutzler, 'Prisoners sing, work, study: China shows off model prison', *Associated Press Newswires*, 21 April 1999; 'Prison modèle à la chinoise', *Le Soir*, 26 October 2012.

Chapter 8 Model Jail Lucknow (India, 1949 [1867])

1 Inspector General of Prisons, *Prison Statistics Uttar Pradesh 2007*, February 2009, especially tables 4 and 5, pp. 13–15.
2 Anand A. Yang, "Disciplining 'natives': Prisons and prisoners in early

nineteenth century India', *South Asia: Journal of South Asian Studies,* 10 (2), 1987, pp. 29–45; Watts, 'Imperial vision, colonial prisons', pp. 157 and 163.

3 Watts, 'Imperial vision, colonial prisons', pp. 146 and 161; David Arnold, 'India: The contested prison', in Dikötter and Brown (eds), *Cultures of Confinement,* pp. 147–84 (quote p. 148). See also David Arnold, 'The colonial Prison: Power, knowledge and penology in nineteenth-century India', in Ranajit Guha (ed.), *A Subaltern Studies Reader, 1986–1995,* University of Minnesota Press, 1997, pp. 148–87. On the architectural aspect: Johnston, *Forms of Constraint,* pp. 100–1.

4 B. K. Nagla, 'Prison administration in India', *Indian Journal of Public Administration,* 35 (4), 1989, pp. 1011–21.

5 Arnold, 'India: The contested prison'.

6 Jawaharlal Nehru, *Toward Freedom: The Autobiography of Jawaharlal Nehru,* The John Day Company, 1941, pp. 85–92.

7 Frederic A. Barker, *The Modern Prison System of India: A Report to the Department,* The Macmillan Company, 1944, p. 13. Not unsurprisingly in retrospect, this report was reviewed in several academic journals, such as the *American Sociological Review,* the *Journal of Criminal Law and Criminology,* and *Mental Health.* The role of indoor labour and production is emphasized in Anand A. Yang, 'The prison-handicraft complex: Convict labour in colonial India', *Modern Asian Studies,* 57, 2023, pp. 808–34. The author shows that an official account published in 1865 made two jails, Alipore and Hughli, 'models of financial management' (p. 824).

8 R. S. Rastogi, *The Selection, Training and Status of Correctional Personnel in Uttar Pradesh,* United Nations, 1955, pp. 14–16; Indra J. Singh, *Indian Prison: A Sociological Enquiry,* Concept Publishing, 1979, pp. 29–36.

9 Human Rights Watch, *Prison Conditions in India,* 1991. Lucknow's reputation as a 'model' institution continued to be showcased nonetheless: in the late 1990s, an Australian delegation is said to have been so taken with what they saw that they conceived a documentary film (Anupam Sheshank, 'Model jail fame goes down under', *The Times of India,* 23 January 1999).

10 Bureau of Police Research and Development (Ministry of Home Affairs), *Model Prison Manual for the Superintendence and Management of Prisons in India,* New Delhi, 2003.

11 Shipra Chauhan and Swati Upadhyay, 'Prison management: Recent

trends', *The Indian Police Journal*, 59 (3), 2012, pp. 4–21 (quote p. 6); Mahuya Bandyopadhyay, 'Reform and everyday practice: Some issues of prison governance', *Contributions to Indian Sociology*, 41 (3), 2007, pp. 387–416, and 'Carceral cultures in contemporary India', in Anna Aliverti et al. (eds), *Decolonizing the Criminal Question: Colonial Legacies, Contemporary Problems*, Oxford University Press, 2023, pp. 125–41 (quotes pp. 127 and 138).

12 Pervez Iqbal Siddiqui, 'Lucknow to have biggest jail in world', *Times of India*, 23 June 2008; 'Rajnath promises more funds for overhaul of India's "miserable" jails', *Times of India*, 15 November 2014; 'Home Minister Rajnath Singh emphasises on prison reforms, by using technology and improving infrastructure', *Business Standard*, 14 November 2014; 'Government promises more funds to states for prison reforms: Rajnath Singh', *The Economic Times*, 24 November 2014; Vinod Aggarwal, *Visit to Model Jail Lucknow, District Jail Dasna and Discussion with IG Prisons*', National Human Rights Commission, January 2018; Keshabananda Borah, 'Privatisation of prisons in India: Possibilities and challenges', *Indian Journal of Public Administration*, 69 (1), 2023, pp. 221–8; Vijay Raghavan, 'Guidelines for public–private partnership in prison management', *Economic & Political Weekly*, 46 (4), 2011, pp. 16–19. In writing this chapter, I also consulted: Amarendra Mohanty and Narayan Hazary, *Indian Prison System*, New Delhi, S. B. Nangia/Ashish Publishing House, 1990 (especially pp. 23–32 and 48); Sudipto Roy, 'Jail reforms in India: A review', *Kriminologija i socijalna integracija*, 2 (1), 2003, pp. 33–40; L. P. Raju, 'Historical evolution of prison system in India', *Indian Journal of Applied Research*, 4 (5), 2014, pp. 298–300; N. R. Madhava Menon (ed.), *Criminal Justice India Series*, III: *Uttar Pradesh, 2001*, Allied Publishers Private/NUJS, 2002, pp. 151f.; Vijay Hiremath, 'Draft policy on prison reforms', *Economic and Political Weekly*, 43 (26–7), 2008, pp. 29–32; Mudasir A. Bhat, 'Prison laws in India: A socio-legal study', *Uttarakhand Judicial & Legal Review*, 2 (1), 2011, pp. 93–108; Sohail Nazim and Kulsum Haider, 'Historical analysis of the development of prisons in India: Human rights in retrospect', *History and Sociology of South Asia*, 17 (2), 2023, pp. 190–205.

Counterpoint IV The 'Nordic/Scandinavian' model

1 See, for example, Rebecca Beyer, 'Model prisons', *American Bar Association Journal*, 103 (10), 2017, pp. 18–19. Strictly speaking, Scandinavia only comprises Denmark, Norway, and Sweden.

The term 'Nordic' countries is a way to include others, mainly Finland.

2 John D. Sutter, 'Welcome to the world's nicest prison', CNN, 24 May 2012; John Pratt, 'Scandinavian exceptionalism in an era of penal excess – Part I: The nature and roots of Scandinavian exceptionalism', *The British Journal of Criminology*, 48, 2008, pp. 119–37 (quote p. 123).

3 Amelia Gentleman, 'Inside Halden, the most humane prison in the world', *The Guardian*, 18 May 2012; Erwin James, 'The Norwegian prison where inmates are treated like people', *The Guardian*, 25 February 2013; Jessica Benko, 'The radical humaneness of Norway's Halden Prison', *The New York Times*, 26 March 2015.

4 Thomas Mathiesen, *The Defences of the Weak: A Sociological Study of a Norwegian Correctional Institution*, Routledge, 2013 [1965]. For an illustration of the progressive penal spirit in the United States during the 1960s, see Martin Weil, 'Model prison set here. Center to offer rehabilitative aid to inmates', *The Washington Post*, 24 November 1968.

5 John R. Snortum, 'Sweden's "special" prisons: Correctional trends and cultural traditions', *Criminal Justice and Behavior*, 3 (2), 1976, pp. 151–68 (quote p. 166); 'Profile: Denmark', *Corrections Magazine*, March 1977, pp. 23–46.

6 Claude Arrighi, 'La prison d'État mixte de Ringe ou l'apprentissage d'une vie normale', *Revue criminelle et de droit pénal comparé*, 4, 1977, pp. 936–9.

7 Doran Larson, 'Why Scandinavian prisons are superior', *The Atlantic*, 24 September 2013; David Skarbek, *The Puzzle of Prison Order*, Oxford University Press, 2020, especially pp. 44–61.

8 Pierre-Olivier Sur, Laurent Martinet, and Étienne Lesage, 'Quel modèle pour nos prisons: Scandinavie ou États-Unis?', *Libération*, 25 June 2014. On Scandinavia's prison architecture: Johnston, *Forms of Constraint*, pp. 110f.

9 John R. Snortum and Kåre Bødal, 'Conditions of confinement within security prisons: Scandinavia and California', *Crime and Delinquency*, 31 (4), 1985, pp. 573–600.

10 Christie, *Crime Control as Industry*, p. 49; Tapio Lappi-Seppälä, 'The fall of the Finnish prison population', *Journal of Scandinavian Studies in Criminology and Crime Prevention*, 1 (1), 2000, pp. 27–40.

11 Marcel Gilquin, 'Les prisons suédoises', *Revue pénitentiaire et de droit pénal*, 1960, pp. 401–30; Jean Sundin, 'Prisons préventives et

réformatrices en Suède', in Petit (ed.), *La prison, le bagne et l'histoire*, pp. 201–12; Camille Olsen, 'Origines et limites des prisons modèles danoises', *Le Monde*, 16 August 1974. 'In my opinion, the Swedish national and local institutions represent a model for a well-balanced prison system,' declared a high-ranking public official in 1987 (Vilhelm Karlström, 'Point de vue suédois sur la construction de prisons', *Bulletin d'information pénitentiaire*, Conseil de l'Europe, 10, 1987, p. 9).

12 Brendan O'Flaherty and Rajiv Sethi, 'On prison systems', *Politics, Philosophy & Economics*, 24 (3), 2025, pp. 231–41 (quote p. 238). We will return to Tommie Shelby's book in our conclusion.

13 Jennifer Couzin-Frankel, 'How will "Little Scandinavia" experiment play out in US prisons?', *Science*, 19 March 2025; Sam Levin, '"Ending San Quentin": Plan would turn prison into "Norwegian style" rehab center', *The Guardian*, 17 March 2023.

14 On the 'exceptionalism debate', see, for example, John Pratt and Anna Eriksson, '"Mr Larsson is walking out again": The origins and development of Scandinavian prison systems', *Australian & New Zealand Journal of Criminology*, 44 (1), 2011, pp. 7–23; Victor Lund Shammas, 'The pains of freedom: Assessing the ambiguity of Scandinavian penal exceptionalism on Norway's prison island', *Punishment & Society*, 16 (1), 2014, pp. 104–23; Vanessa Barker, 'Nordic exceptionalism revisited: Explaining the paradox of a Janus-faced penal regime', *Theoretical Criminology*, 17 (1), 2012, pp. 5–25; Ben Crewe et al., 'Nordic penal exceptionalism: A comparative, empirical analysis', *The British Journal of Criminology*, 63, 2023, pp. 424–43.

15 Michel Foucault, '"Alternatives" to the prison: Dissemination or decline of social control?', *Theory, Culture & Society*, 26 (6), 2009, pp. 12–24 (quotes p. 14; translation revised by Matthew Cunningham); Kristian Feigelson, 'Le charme discret des prisons suédoises', *Esprit*, 11, 1979, pp. 93–101.

Chapter 9 Stammheim, Stuttgart (Federal Republic of Germany, 1963)

1 *Info Rundbrief*, 19, July 1985. The document comes from Amsterdam's International Institute of Social History (RAF collection, file 204 at the time of consulting, mid-2000s).

2 Frédéric Audren and Dominique Linhardt, 'Un procès hors du commun? Le procès de la Fraction Armée Rouge à Stuttgart-Stammheim, 1975–1977', *Annales*, 63 (5), 2008, pp. 1003–34 (quote p. 1003). In

English, see Jacco Pekelder and Klaus Weinhauer, 'Germany confronts the Baader–Meinhof Group: The Stammheim trial (1975–1977) and its legacies', in Alex Schmid and Beatrice de Graaf (eds), *Terrorists on Trial: A Performative Perspective*, Leiden University Press, 2016, pp. 231–309. Despite local protest in the 1980s, a prison was eventually established in Weiterstadt in 1997. It was originally scheduled to open in 1993, but after several warning signs, the building was finally targeted by an explosive RAF attack. This was the group's last spectacular action five years before it officially dissolved. There are archives of this unprecedented event, which temporarily brought fame to a previously anonymous town. After the dust had settled, officials promised that it would be the country's most humane and modern remand prison. Although it met high security standards, it drew the ire of the conservative opposition, which accused it of being a 'luxury prison' and labelled it a '*Nobelknast*' (*nobel* meaning both noble/aristocratic and massive/imposing), particularly because of its swimming pool and 'natural' decorative elements. The fact is, the RAF decided to destroy it precisely because they had recognized it as a 'model prison'. The group saw the Weiterstadt Prison as a harmful yet revealing creation of an increasingly repressive state. Ironically, while German environmentalists were initially in favour of reducing the capacity and footprint of prisons, sometimes even advocating abolition, this prison opened under the aegis of a 'green', left-leaning regional justice minister. See Lars Zimmermann, 'Mit voller Kraft von Links. Über den Anschlag der RAF auf den Neubau der JVA Weiterstadt 1993', *Archivnachrichten aus Hessen*, 2 (14), 2014, p. 28; 'Moderner Vollzug oder "Nobelknast"?', *Rhein Zeitung*, 3 May 1997; RAF, 'Anschlag auf den Knast Weiterstadt', *RAF Info*, 30 March 1993.

3 Emsley, *Crime, Police, and Penal Policy*, p. 260; Johnston, *Forms of Constraint*, p. 152; Thomas Nutz, *Strafanstalt als Besserungsmaschine. Reformdiskurs und Gefängniswissenschaft 1775–1848*, Oldenbourg, 2001.

4 Friedrich Hoefer, 'Georg Michael von Obermaier: A pioneer in reformatory procedures', *Journal of Criminal Law and Criminology*, 28 (1), 1937, pp. 13–51 (quotes p. 50); Nutz, 'Global networks and local prison reforms', p. 448.

5 *German History for Dummies* refers to Christian von Ditfurth, *Deutsche Geschichte für Dummies*, Wiley, 2012 [2009].

6 Hanno Balz, *Von Terroristen, Sympathisanten und dem starken Staat*, Campus, 2008, pp. 120–77.

7 Bernard Brigouleix, 'La prison de Stammheim avait été conçue comme un établissement modèle', *Le Monde*, 26 October 1977; Jean-Marcel Bouguereau, 'Visite à la prison de Stammheim', *Libération*, 10 March 1978; Kurt Oesterle, 'Nur für Stammheim spreche ich', *Tazmag/ Tageszeitung*, 27–8 April 2002.

8 Sabine Bergstermann, *Stammheim. Eine moderne Haftanstalt als Ort der Auseinandersetzung zwischen Staat und RAF*, De Gruyter, 2016, especially pp. 29–31 and 73–82 (the author uses the word '*Idealbild*'); Werner Sonntag, 'Gefängnis mit Komfort', *Die Zeit*, 13 September 1963.

9 Bergstermann, *Stammheim*, p. 86. The documentary film is *Das Stammheimer Gefängnis* by Ingo Helm, ARD; series *Geschichte im Ersten: Geheimnisvolle Orte*, episode 4, 2014.

10 Kurt Oesterle, 'Der Knast aller Knäste. Eine Wanderung nach Stuttgart-Stammheim, zum berühmtesten Gefängnis der Bundesrepublik', n.p., n.d., 5 pp.; Justizministerium Baden-Württemberg, *Dokumentation über Haftvollzug der in Stammheim inhaftierten Mitglieder anarchistischer Gruppen*, Stuttgart, December 1974.

11 Michael Sontheimer, 'Fotorecherche im Todestrakt', *Der Spiegel*, 15 November 2012; Oliver Masche, 'Im Größere Zellen und trockene Räume', *Stuttgarter Zeitung*, 6 June 2013.

Chapter 10 Fleury-Mérogis (France, 1968)

1 Denis Demonpion, 'La prison qu'on ne visite plus', *Le Point*, 16 June 2000.

2 Augustin Rosenstiehl (interview with Luc Bronner), 'En 1968, "Paris-Match qualifiait Fleury-Mérogis de 5-étoiles"', *Le Monde*, 18 December 2008; Olivier Quéant, *Le Monde inconnu des prisons*, Plon, 1970 (quote p. 45); Nicolas Peskine, *Histoire de sortir*, L'Athanor, 1977; Léonore Le Caisne, *Avoir 16 ans à Fleury. Une ethnographie d'un centre de jeunes détenus*, Seuil, 2008, p. 33. See also Jean-Lucien Sanchez, 'La prise en charge pénitentiaire des mineurs. L'exemple du Centre des jeunes détenus de Fleury-Mérogis, 1963–2016', *Travaux & Documents*, 93, 2025, and his related virtual exhibition 'Le centre de jeunes détenus de Fleury-Mérogis', *Criminocorpus*, 21 March 2023.

3 Dominique Rouillard, 'Architecture', in Michèle Riot-Sarcey, Thomas Bouchet, and Antoine Picon (eds), *Dictionnaire des utopies*, Larousse, 2007, pp. 10–14 (quotes pp. 10 and 13).

4 Contrôleur général des lieux de privation de liberté, *Rapport de visite: maison d'arrêt de Fleury-Mérogis*, 2010, p. 3.

5 Pierre Tartakowsky, *La Prison. Enquête sur l'administration pénitentiaire*, Payot & Rivages, 1995 (quote p. 15); Jacques Floch and Louis Mermaz (eds), *Rapport fait au nom de la commission d'enquête sur la situation dans les prisons françaises*, II ('Auditions'), Assemblée Nationale, 2000 (quotes pp. 182 and 434); Jean-Louis Daumas (with Pierre Mezinski), *La Zonzon de Fleury*, Calmann-Lévy, 1995 (quote p. 33).

6 Philippe Alexandre, 'Prison modèle', *Le Bien Public*, 22 February 2010; Alain Salles, 'Rapport d'expertise accablant sur l'insalubrité du "mitard" de Fleury-Mérogis', *Le Monde*, 3 October 2007.

7 Accounts from the nurse and the former inmate: Martine Schachtel, *Femmes en prison. Dans les coulisses de Fleury-Mérogis*, Albin Michel, 2000, pp. 19–25; Élisabeth Cons, *La Boîte à oubli. Dix ans à Fleury-Mérogis*, J.-C. Lattès, 2000, pp. 21 and 258. On the protest: Benoît Hopquin, 'Les gardiens ont protesté deux jours devant ce qui fut une prison modèle', *Le Monde*, 8 May 2009. Similar protest movements have occurred since then: see, for example, Kim Willsher, 'French police clash with striking guards at Europe's largest prison', *The Guardian*, 19 January 2018.

8 Foucault, *Discipline and Punish*, p. 271; Petit et al., *Histoire des prisons en France*, p. 217; Bellanger, *Vivre en prison*, pp. 235f.

9 Daniel Vitoux, 'Une illustration architecturale du nouveau mode de vie du détenu: la maison d'arrêt de Fleury-Mérogis', *Vie collective*, 405, 1969, pp. 435–43 (quote p. 443); Compte-rendu de la réunion du 9 avril 1974, groupe de travail no. 13 ('Une nouvelle conception de l'établissement pénitentiaire'), Direction de l'administration pénitentiaire, section 'Programmes' (Archival collection of the Institut d'histoire du temps présent (IHTP), 'Étienne Bloch' series, ARC 3017-15 [IV-24]).

10 Jean Ferniot, 'Une prison différente', *France Soir*, 13 March 1971.

11 The archives of the Atelier de Montrouge are held at the Centre d'archives d'architecture contemporaine, part of France's Cité de l'architecture et du patrimoine. See Franck Delorme, 'Guillaume Gillet, architecte, acteur majeur du renouveau du parc pénitentiaire dans les années 1960', in Dieu and Mbanzoulou (eds), *L'Architecture carcérale*, pp. 45–9. The mentioned documents come from the archival collection of the Centre d'archives d'architecture contemporaine, 'Guillaume Gillet' series (especially 152 IFA and 162 IFA).

12 Groupe d'information sur les prisons, *Le GIP enquête dans une prison-modèle: Fleury-Mérogis* ('Intolérable n° 2'), Champ Libre, 1971,

republished in GIP, *Intolérable* (ed. Philippe Artières), Gallimard, 2014; Comité d'action des prisonniers, *Journal des prisonniers*, 20 September 1974; André Armazet (pseud.), *Les Prisons*, Paris, Filipacchi, 1973 (quote p. 72). Echoing such accounts, Foucault would write that prison revolts 'were revolts against an entire state of physical misery that is over a century old: against cold, suffocation and overcrowding, against decrepit walls, hunger, physical maltreatment. But they were also revolts against model prisons, tranquillizers, isolation, the medical or educational services' (*Discipline and Punish*, p. 30).

13 Marc Kunstlé, 'Voici pourquoi les choses vont mal dans les prisons de France', *Journal du dimanche*, 19 December 1977; Marc Kunstlé and Claude Vincent, *Le Crépuscule des prisons*, Julliard, 1972 (quote p. 97); Francis Cornu, 'Plutôt ce vieux clapier qu'une prison modèle', *Le Monde*, 2–3 December 1973; Francis Puyalte, 'Ces "prisons modèles" où éclatent les révoltes', *L'Aurore*, 8 July 1974; Bellanger, *Vivre en prison*, pp. 238 and 270–1. Similar expressions of this paradox can be found in other countries, including Switzerland: see Alix Heiniger, 'Contre la prison et l'isolement. Deux cycles de mobilisations en Suisse (1972–1990)', *SZG/RSH/RSS*, 74 (1), 2024, pp. 92–110 (especially p. 94 about the Champ-Dollon Prison).

14 Hélène Dorlhac de Borne, *Changer la prison*, Plon, 1984, pp. 34–7; Anon., *Une Succincte histoire des luttes anti-carcérales depuis l'intérieur des prisons*, Hobolo, March 2007.

15 Jean-Denis Espinas, 'Révolution pénitentiaire: les chemins de l'architecture', *Déviance et société*, 13 (4), 1989, pp. 367–77 (quote p. 369).

Counterpoint V 'Open prisons' (utopia/heterotopia)

1 Michel Foucault, 'Of other spaces', trans. Jay Miskowiec, *Diacritics*, 16 (1), 1986, pp. 22–7 (quote p. 27).

2 Jean-Jacques Yvorel, 'Les mineurs et la justice pénale ou pourquoi condamne-t-on plus sévèrement les enfants?', in Frédéric Chauvaud (ed.), *Le Droit de punir, du siècle des Lumières à nos jours*, Presses universitaires de Rennes, 2012, pp. 99–110 (pp. 101–2 on 'great confinement'); Robert Badinter, *La Prison républicaine*, Fayard, 1992, p. 26; Jean-Lucien Sanchez, book review of Stephen A. Toth's *Mettray: A History of France's Most Venerated Carceral Institution* (Cornell University Press, 2019), *International Review of Social History*, 65 (2), 2020, p. 363.

3 Matthew DelSesto, 'Norfolk's "model prison community": Howard Belding Gill and the social process of prison reform', *The Prison Journal*, 101 (2), 2021, pp. 127–46 (quotes pp. 135 and 143). On (the ambivalence of) participation and self-government, including the case of Norfolk (where Malcolm X spent some time), see Christopher D. Berk, *Democracy in Captivity: Prisoners, Patients, and the Limits of Self-Government*, University of California Press, 2023, especially fig. 1, p. 2.

4 Jacques-Bernard Herzog, 'La crise de la prison et les établissements ouverts', *Revue internationale de droit comparé*, 7 (2), 1955, pp. 309–405 (quotes pp. 400, 401, 404–5).

5 Howard Jones and Paul Cornes, *Open Prisons*, Routledge & Kegan Paul, 1977, chs 1 and 3; Charles E. Heilmann, 'Open prisons, British style', *The Prison Journal*, 58 (2), 1978, pp. 3–17; Helen Johnston, 'Punishment in Britain in the twentieth century', in Paul Lawrence (ed.), *A Global History of Crime and Punishment in the Modern Age*, Bloomsbury, 2023, pp. 145–64 (pp. 156–7 on Lowdham Grange). Although Heilmann identified Lowdham Grange as 'the first open penal establishment in the United Kingdom', he also acknowledged an earlier example: Borstal Institution in Rochester, Kent, which dates back to 1923 (its origin is in fact earlier), 'following the lead given by institutions in Italy' ('Open prisons, British style', pp. 4–5). He also noted subsequent experiments in other industrialized countries, such as Israel and Japan, alongside the well-documented Scandinavian model (counterpoint IV).

6 Paul-Roger Gontard, *Le Régime ouvert de détention peut-il être étendu dans le champ pénitentiaire français?*, Mission d'étude de faisabilité, Ministère de la Justice, March 2010. See also the documentary film by Bernard Nicolas, *Prisons ouvertes: un pas vers la reinsertion?*, ARTE, 2014.

7 Jacques Floch and Louis Mermaz (eds), *Rapport fait au nom de la commission d'enquête sur la situation dans les prisons françaises*, I ('Rapport'), Assemblée Nationale, 2000, p. 59.

8 Christian Carlier, 'Histoire des prisons et de l'administration pénitentiaire française de l'Ancien Régime à nos jours', *Criminocorpus*, 14 February 2009, § 44; Kunstlé and Vincent, *Le Crépuscule des prisons*, pp. 202–5; Frédéric Pottecher, 'Casabianda, prison ouverte', *Promovere*, 31, 1982, pp. 105–10; Jean-François Mongibeaux, 'Une prison pas comme les autres', *Le Figaro*, 15 July 2000; Erich Inciyan, 'La "prison sans les murs" de Casabianda, 60 ans et toujours pas

d'enfant', *Mediapart*, 26 August 2009; Bellanger, *Vivre en prison*, pp. 111f.; Pierre Lombard, 'Une prison sans barreaux!', *Gendarmerie*, 65, 1965, pp. 7–10.

9 Ian Brown, 'South East Asia: Reform and the colonial prison', in Dikötter and Brown (eds), *Cultures of Confinement*, pp. 221–68 (pp. 261 and 266 for 'self-governing republic'); Clive Parry, 'Imrali: Turkey's island Prison', *The Howard Journal of Crime and Justice*, 6 (4), 1945, pp. 201–2 (quote p. 201). For an overview: Eric Fougère, *Île-prison. Bagne et déportation*, L'Harmattan, 2003.

10 'Open prisons in India: A review', *Social Defense*, 17 (68), 1982, pp. 16–28; A. S. Raj, 'The Sampurnanand camp in Uttar Pradesh (India)', *Open Institutions*, United Nations, Geneva Conference, 1955; Anju Sinha, 'Open prisons: Their working and utility as institutions of reformation and rehabilitation', *International Journal of Humanities and Social Science Invention*, 2 (11), 2013, pp. 73–7; Khushal I. Vibhute, *Open Peno-Correctional Institutions in India: A Review of Fifty-Five Years – Experiences and Expectations*, Max Planck Institute for Foreign and International Criminal Law, 2006.

11 'Neuer Strafvollzug: Hinter Schloß, ohne Riegel', *Der Spiegel*, 14 February 1971.

Chapter 11 Mauzac (France, 1986)

1 Unless otherwise specified, quotes from Christian Demonchy in this chapter come from: 'L'institution mal dans ses murs', in Claude Veil and Dominique Lhuilier (eds), *La prison en changement*, Erès, 2000, pp. 159–84; 'L'architecture des prisons modèles françaises', in Artières and Lascoumes (eds), *Gouverner, enfermer*, pp. 269–93; 'Rapport entre les mots et les murs', in Dieu and Mbanzoulou (eds), *L'Architecture carcérale*, pp. 15–20. See also Barbara Liaras and Christian Demonchy, 'Architecture carcérale: interdire toute vie sociale', *Dedans/Dehors*, 77–8, 2012, pp. 28–30; Anne Chemin, 'Culture, une et double: archi prisons', *Le Monde*, 2 June 2014.

2 On prison privatization in France: Nathan Rivet, 'Privatization as bureaucratization: Contracts, accountability, and uses of law in the privatization of French prisons', *Oñati Socio-Legal Series*, 15 (4), 2025, pp. 1210–32. Overview of French prisons in the 1980s and 1990s: Jean-François Jodry and Michel Zulberty, 'Prisons in Europe: France', in Leslie Fairweather and Sean McConville (eds), *Prison Architecture: Policy, Design and Experience*, Routledge, 2000,

pp. 109–117; Philippe Combessie, 'France', in Dirk van Zijl-Smit and Frieder Dünkel (eds), *Imprisonment Today and Tomorrow*, Brill/Nijhof, 2001, pp. 253–87.

3 Christian Carlier, 'L'administration pénitentiaire et les prisons, 1969–1974', *Expressions pénitentiaires*, 28, 2008, pp. 11–12; Éric Malo, 'De Vichy à la Quatrième République: le camp de Noé (1943–1945)', *Annales du Midi*, 199–200, 1992, pp. 441–58; Jacky Tronel, 'Le repli de la prison militaire de Paris à Mauzac. Un exode pénitentiaire méconnu', *Criminocorpus*, 23 March 2012, § 75f.; Direction de l'administration pénitentiaire, *Rapport général sur l'exercice 1970*, Ministère de la Justice, 1970 (quote p. 45).

4 Specifications quoted in Paul-Roger Gontard, *L'utilisation européenne des prisons ouvertes: l'exemple de la France*, PhD thesis in law and criminal science, Université d'Avignon, 2013, p. 355.

5 Documents on 'Prisons of Tomorrow' come from the archival collection of the Institut d'histoire du temps présent (IHTP), 'Étienne Bloch' series, ARC 3017-15 (IV-24). Additional references to Simone Buffard, *Le froid pénitentiaire. L'impossible réforme des prisons*, Seuil, 1973; *Architecture et Justice. Deux siècles d'évolution*, Ministère de la Justice, 1988, p. 46; Philippe Artières, 'Les écrits de la révolte. La prise d'écriture des détenus (1970–1972)', *Drôle d'époque*, 8, 2001, pp. 37–47.

6 Descriptive elements are mainly based on Agathe Logeard, 'La prison aux champs', *Le Monde*, 29 January 1986; Nathalie Mazier, 'Mauzac, la prison village en pleine campagne', *France Soir*, 12 March 2010; Anne Chemin, 'Un horizon entre les barreaux', *Le Monde*, 7 June 2014; Delphine Payen-Fourment, 'Zoom sur Mauzac, la prison des champs', *Dedans-Dehors*, 90, 2015, pp. 38–41.

7 Brossat, *Pour en finir avec la prison*, p. 90.

8 Gontard, *L'utilisation européenne des prisons ouvertes*, pp. 355–6.

9 Contrôleur général des lieux de privation de liberté (CGLPL), *Rapport de visite: centre de détention de Mauzac*, August/September 2010; *Rapport de (contre-)visite: centre de détention de Mauzac*, September 2012; *Rapport de visite: centre de détention de Mauzac*, June 2022; Notre affaire à tous, *Double peine: les risques climatiques et environnementaux dans les prisons françaises*, July 2024, p. 83.

Chapter 12 Haren (Belgium, 2022)

1 Among many press reports on the process and protest, see, for example, Vanessa Lhuillier, 'Les opposants à la prison de Haren se mobilisent', *Le Soir*, 20 May 2015; Antonin Marsac, 'Des citoyens s'opposent à la "méga-prison" d'Haren', *L'Écho*, 20 May 2015; Vanessa Lhuillier, 'La future prison de Haren provoque une bataille juridique', *Le Soir*, 25 September 2015; 'La prison de Haren à l'arrêt', *Le Soir*, 2 October 2015; Nicolas Ghislain, 'Les zadistes du Keelbeek: "De toute façon, on reste!"', *La Libre Belgique*, 14 September 2015; Mathieu Colleyn, 'Le projet de mégaprison sous enquête judiciaire', *La Libre Belgique*, 20 January 2016; Arthur Sente, 'Le contrat de la prison de Haren, secret impénétrable', *Le Soir*, 6 May 2019; 'Les trois destins possibles de la prison de Haren', *Le Soir*, 24 June 2019.

2 On 'repertoires of contention', see Charles Tilly, 'Contentious repertoires in Great Britain, 1758–1834', *Social Science History*, 17 (2), 1993, pp. 253–80. On 'ZAD', see, for example, Joshua Armstrong, 'Against the airport and its world: The ZAD and frontiers', *Contemporary French and Francophone Studies*, 25 (1), 2021, pp. 95–105.

3 *Ni prison, ni béton. Contre la maxi-prison de Bruxelles et son monde*, Brussels, Collectif Vrije Keelbeek Libre/maelstrÖm reEvolution, 2019. Among many accounts from associations' spokespersons, see 'Contre la prison de Haren et toutes les prisons modernes', *Kairos*, April–May 2015, pp. 9–18; Florence Dufaux, 'Masterplan pour méga-prison', *Bruxelles en mouvements*, 264, 2021, pp. 3–5. An environmental justice perspective is elaborated in Jérôme Pelenc and Iker Etxano, 'Capabilities, ecosystem services, and strong sustainability through SMCE: The case of Haren (Belgium)', *Ecological Economics*, 182, 2021, art. 106876; Jérôme Pelenc, 'Free the Keelbeek from the prison! A deep analysis of the individual and collective empowerment within the resistance movement against the Brussels mega-prison project', in Iokiñe Rodríguez, Mariana Walter, and Leah Temper (eds), *Just Transformations: Grassroots Struggles for Alternatives Futures*, Pluto Press, 2024, pp. 153–72. In March 2026, the Haren Observatory website (https://www.harenobservatory.net) was still active, providing a large number of documents.

4 Kristel Beyens, Marie-Sophie Devresse, and Elli Gilbert, *Vivre et travailler en prison: à l'écoute des personnes concernées. Compte rendu de tables rondes identifiant les besoins en termes d'architecture et d'aménagement des nouveaux établissements pénitentiaires*, Fondation Roi Baudouin, 2011.

5 David Harvey, *The New Imperialism*, Oxford University Press, 2003, ch. 4, and 'Notes towards a theory of uneven geographical development', in *Spaces of Global Capitalism: A Theory of Uneven Geographical Development*, Verso, 2019 [2006], pp. 69–116.

6 Jay Merrick, 'Prisons of conscience: Storstrøm Prison in Gundslev, Denmark by CF Møller', *The Architectural Review*, 13 June 2018; Grégory Salle, 'How we got from prisons located in cities to city-like prisons: A relationship between metamorphoses and contradictions', *Politix*, English issue, 97, 2012, pp. 75–98; Valérie Icard, 'Qu'est-ce qu'une prison modèle? L'exemple des "centres-types" espagnols', *Métropolitiques*, 21 December 2017.

7 Michel Callon and Madeleine Akrich, 'L'intrusion des entreprises privées dans le monde carcéral français: le programme 13 000', in Lascoumes and Artières (eds), *Gouverner, enfermer*, pp. 295–317; Guillermo Kozlowski and David Scheer, 'Haren, le futur village pénitentiaire', *Revue nouvelle*, 6, 2015, pp. 39–46.

8 On professional splits (termed as cultural, generational and functional), see Delphine Pouppez, 'Des prisons panoptiques au village pénitentiaire. Entre humanisation de la peine et cultures professionnelles ancrées, la négociation des pratiques pénitentiaires', in Isabelle Fouchard et al. (eds), *Les populations de la privation de liberté*, Mare & Martin, 2025, pp. 117–33.

9 Conseil central de surveillance pénitentiaire, *Rapport annuel de la Commission de surveillance de Haren*, 2023. For news reports in English, see Lukas Taylor, 'Haren super-prison under-fire over "inhumane" conditions', *The Brussels Times*, 22 May 2023; '"Haren is a disaster": Belgian prisons go on 48-hour strike to protest inhumane conditions', *The Brussels Times*, 24 September 2023.

10 Olivia Nederlandt, 'Belgium: What is Haren?', *Prison Insider*, 29 March 2021.

Counterpoint VI Counter-models (utopia/dystopia)

1 Norbert Elias's texts on the theme of utopia are available in English in *The Collected Works of Norbert Elias*, vol. 14: *Essays I: On the Sociology of Knowledge and the Sciences*, ed. Richard Kilminster and Stephen Mennell, UCD Press, 2009).

2 Irwin, *The Warehouse Prison*, 2004; Ruth Wilson Gilmore, *Golden Gulag: Prisons, Surplus, Crisis, and Opposition in Globalizing California*, University of California Press, 2007.

3 Zygmunt Bauman, 'Social issues of law and order', *The British*

Journal of Criminology, 40 (2), 2000, pp. 205–21; Keramet Reiter, 'Parole, snitch, or die: California's supermax prisons and prisoners, 1997–2007', *Punishment & Society*, 14 (5), 2012, pp. 530–63, and *23/7. Pelican Bay Prison and the Rise of Long-Term Solitary Confinement*, Yale University Press, 2018; Christie, *Crime Control as Industry*, p. 101 (quoting *Corrections Digest*, 27 June 1990); Yasmine Bouagga, 'Qui sont les "pires des pires"? Des usages des classifications en Supermax aux États-Unis', *Déviance et société*, 34 (2), 2010, pp. 201–16, and 'Incarcération totale. L'enfermement solitaire aux États-Unis à l'ère de la prison de masse', *La Vie des idées*, 24 November 2015.

4 Loïc Wacquant, 'Probing the meta-prison', in Jeffrey Ian Ross (ed.), *The Globalization of Supermax Prisons*, Rutgers University Press, 2013, pp. ix–xiv.

5 Roy King, 'The rise and rise of supermax: An American solution in search of a problem?', *Punishment & Society*, 1 (2), 1999, pp. 163–86; Jeffrey Ian Ross, 'Supermax prisons', *Society*, 44 (3), 2007, pp. 60–4, and 'The invention of the American supermax prison', in Jeffrey Ian Ross (ed.), *The Globalization of Supermax Prisons*, pp. 10–24. The documentary film is David Dufresne and Philippe Brault (directors), *Prison Valley, l'industrie de la prison*, Upian/ARTE, 2010.

6 Malcolm M. Feeley and Jonathan Simon, 'The new penology: Notes on the emerging strategy of corrections and its implications', *Criminology*, 30, 1992, pp. 449–74; Petit, 'Aspects de l'espace carcéral', pp. 162–4.

7 Mike Davis, *Ecology of Fear: Los Angeles and the Imagination of Disaster*, Verso, 2022 [1998], p. 412.

8 Michael D. Gordin, Helen Tilley, and Gyan Prakash, 'Introduction: Utopia and dystopia beyond space and time', in Michael D. Gordin, Helen Tilley, and Gyan Prakash (eds), *Utopia/Dystopia: Conditions of Historical Possibility*, Princeton University Press, 2010, pp. 1–17 (quote p. 1).

9 Foucault, *Discipline and Punish*, p. 137; Max Weber, *Economy and Society: A New Translation*, ed. and trans. Keith Tribe, Harvard University Press, 2019, pp. 134–5. See also John O'Neill, 'The disciplinary society: From Weber to Foucault', *The British Journal of Sociology*, 37 (1), 1986, pp. 42–60.

10 Sara M. Benson, *The Prison of Democracy: Race, Leavenworth, and the Culture of Law*, University of California Press, 2019. Incidentally, she mentions that Kansas State Penitentiary – built in the 1870s before

Leavenworth became 'the nation's first prison and the beginning of a federal prison system that radiates from the center of the nation' (p. 1) – was presumed to be a model prison until inmates described it as a 'hell' or 'inferno' (p. 75).

11 Grégory Salle '"Escaping from hell is a right!": The case of France's "QHS" (1975–1982)', in Tomas Max Martin and Gilles Chantraine (eds), *Prison Breaks: Towards a Sociology of Escape*, Palgrave Macmillan, 2018, pp. 191–210; Lorna Rhodes, 'Questioning supermax', *Anthropology Now*, 2 (1), 2010, pp. 48–56.

12 Samuel Moyn, *The Last Utopia: Human Rights in History*, The Belknap Press of Harvard University Press, 2010.

Conclusion: The meaning of model prisons

1 Sandra Bucerius and Michael Tonry, 'Has the prison a future?', *Crime and Justice*, 51, 2022, pp. 1–5 (quotes pp. 1 and 2). The idea of a third historical stage of penal incarceration was advanced (in hypothetical terms) by Thomas Mathiesen, *Prison on Trial*, Waterside Press, 2006 [1990], pp. 18–22 and taken up by David Scott, 'Why prison? Posing the question', in David Scott (ed.), *Why Prison?*, Cambridge University Press, 2013, pp. 1–22.

2 See Wacquant, *Punishing the Poor*, and *Rethinking the Penal State*, Polity, 2026.

3 On the paradox of prison modernization: David Scheer, 'Le paradoxe de la modernisation carcérale. Ambivalence du bâti et de ses usages au sein de deux prisons belges', *Cultures & Conflits*, 90, 2013, pp. 95–116. Note that this differs from what Amy E. Lerman has termed the 'modern prison paradox' in *The Modern Prison Paradox: Politics, Punishment, and Social Community*, Cambridge University Press, 2014.

4 Philippe Combessie, *Sociologie de la prison*, La Découverte, 2001, p. 12. In some recent cases, the term 'model prison' has been used to praise sound leadership or efficient management rather than the prison infrastructure (e.g. Jorge Zaverucha, 'De Caruaru para o Brasil', *Jornal do Commercio*, 25 October 2009, about Caruaru Prison, in the Brazilian state of Pernambuco).

5 On CECOT: Samantha Schmidt et al., 'Welcome to hell: Inside the megaprison where the US deported migrants', *The Washington Post*, 4 August 2025; James C. Reynolds, 'Inside El Salvador's hellish supermax prison of torture', *The Independent*, 16 November 2025; 'Colombia's Medellin builds mega-prison inspired by El Salvador's

CECOT', *AFP*, 20 February 2026. On McKean: Robert F. Worth, 'A model prison', *The Atlantic Monthly*, November 1995.

6 On Norway's 'Model 2015': Hedda Giertsen, 'Prison ideas and architecture 1850–today: Relevance to Norwegian prisoners and prison policy', *Nordisk Tidsskrift for Kriminalvidenskab*, 1, 2021, pp. 163–4. Serge: *Men in Prison*, p. 56. He added: 'Modern prisons are imperfectible, since they are perfect. There is nothing left but to destroy them' (p. 57).

7 On French prison revolts in the 1970s, see Philippe Artières, Michelle Zancarini-Fournel, and Laurent Quéro (eds), *Le Groupe d'Information sur les Prisons: archives d'une lutte, 1970–1972*, IMEC, 2003; Guérin, *Prisonniers en révolte*, 2013; Nicolas Derasse, 'De l'ombre à la lumière: les révoltes pénitentiaires dans la France des années 1970', *Criminocorpus*, 9 September 2019. Guy Autran is quoted in Anne Chemin, 'Prisons nouvelles, prisons modèles?', *Le Monde*, 7 June 2014.

8 Baz Dreisinger and Alexus McNally, 'How the Global South got caught in the West's prison pipeline', *Time*, 2 December 2025. On the transfer of standards and procedures, see, for example, Laurent Quéro, 'Les standards pénitentiaires internationaux', in Artières and Lascoumes (eds), *Gouverner, enfermer*, pp. 319–39; Yasmine Bouagga, 'Une mondialisation du "bien punir"? La prison dans les programmes de développement', *Mouvements*, 88, 2016, pp. 50–8.

9 Yvonne Jewkes and Dominique Moran, 'The paradox of the "green" prison: Sustaining the environment or sustaining the penal complex?', *Theoretical Criminology*, 19 (4), 2015, pp. 451–69. This is *not* to say that all prisons are more or less the same, objectively (institutional operation) or subjectively (lived experiences). This is far from being the case. There can be considerable differences between prisons, even within the same region. Their occupants tend to be the first to say so, even if the distinctions and hierarchies they establish do not necessarily align with those of external observers. My argument is simply that in the medium or long term, nothing inherently distinguishes 'model prisons' per se. In some cases, prisons with a reputation for decent conditions are nevertheless not labelled as 'models'. In others, a mediocre prison may be deemed exemplary simply because it enjoys a 'relative advantage' compared with other prisons amid catastrophic prison conditions in a given country.

10 Foucault, *Discipline and Punish*, pp. 89 and 272. As noted in introduction n.5 above, Alan Sheridan's translation of '*illégalismes*' as 'illegalities' is somewhat misleading. In any case, it should be clear

that this is a relational concept, referring to social relations with legal rules, not with specific, countable acts or facts. In the same period (the mid-1970s), and from a parallel perspective, Mathiesen identified four (and more recently five) 'functions' that remain relevant today: see his foreword ('On stemming the tide') in Scott, *Why Prison?*, pp. xv–xxii (especially p. xvi). Other critical or radical perspectives distinct from, but compatible with, Foucault's views include Paddy Hillyard et al. (eds), *Beyond Criminology: Taking Harm Seriously*, Pluto Press, 2004; Michael Lynch, Paul Stretesky, and Michael Long, *Defining Crime: A Critique of the Concept and Its Implication*, Palgrave Macmillan, 2015.

11 Foucault, *Discipline and Punish*, p. 281. On 'the generalization of a balance of forces bound up with mobility' as central to 'the new spirit of capitalism' ('Great men do not stand still. Little people remain rooted to the spot'): Luc Boltanski and Ève Chiapello, *The New Spirit of Capitalism*, trans. Gregory Elliott, Verso, 2005, pp. 361–71 (quotes pp. 361 and 371).

12 A nod to John Hagan, *Who Are the Criminals? The Politics of Crime Policy from the Age of Roosevelt to the Age of Reagan*, Princeton University Press, 2010. This is not to imply that progressive activists are unaware of these issues: in the United States and elsewhere, their focus extends well beyond detention conditions to encompass the structural injustice of the legal-judicial system more broadly. My point is rather that a powerful mainstream media narrative still tends to frame the prison as a mere response to 'crime' and in predominantly 'internalist' terms, depicting it as a closed, self-contained world set apart from society, rather than as one component of a broader punitive system founded on questionable assumptions about what does or does not deserve to be criminalized and punished.

13 On the history of penal abolitionism starting from the late eighteenth century (though 'abolitionist notions existed long before this time', the preface suggests, pp. x–vx (quote p. x)), see David Gordon Scott and Emma Bell (eds), *Envisioning Abolition*, Bristol University Press, 2025. Mike Davis, 'Who will build the ark?', *New Left Review*, II (61), 2010, pp. 29–46 (quote p. 45). For a sympathetic yet critical engagement with the case for prison abolition, see Tommie Shelby, *The Idea of Prison Abolition*, Princeton University Press, 2022.

14 Frédéric Lordon, 'Violences néolibérales', *Mouvements*, 23, 2002, pp. 47–8.

15 Michel Foucault, 'Le grand enfermement', in *Dits et écrits I (1954–1975)*, pp. 1164–74 (quote p. 1174). English translation by

Perry Zurn and Erik Beranek in Kevin Thompson and Perry Zurn (eds), *Intolerable: Writings from Michel Foucault and the Prisons Information Group (1970–1980)*, University of Minnesota Press, 2021, pp. 266–78 (quote p. 277).

Index